The Play of Paradox

The Play of Paradox

Stage and Sermon
in Renaissance England

Bryan Crockett

University of Pennsylvania Press

Philadelphia

Library of Congress Cataloging-in-Publication Data

Crockett, Bryan.
    The play of paradox : stage and sermon in Renaissance England / Bryan Crockett.
       p.   cm.
    Includes bibliographical references and index.
    ISBN 0-8122-3316-6 (alk. paper)
       1. English drama—Early modern and Elizabethan, 1500–1600—History and criticism.
2. Christianity and literature—England—History—16th century.   3. Christianity and
literature—England—History—17th century.   4. English drama—17th century—History
and criticism.   5. Preaching—England—History—16th century.   6. Preaching—
England—History—17th century.   7. Paradox—Religious aspects—Christianity.
8. Sermons, English—History and criticism.   9. Theater—England—History—16th
century.   10. Theater—England—History—17th century.   I. Title.
PR658.R43C76   1995
822'.309382—dc20   95-36750
                                                                                                          CIP

Frontispiece: Bishop John King preaching at Saint Paul's Cross before King James I, the
Lord Mayor William Cockayne, and other Londoners (detail). Oil on wood, circa 1616.
Reproduced by permission of The Society of Antiquaries of London.

For Pam,
Joe, Becky, and Rosemary

Contents

Preface

A good bit of the most fruitful literary theory in early modern studies has for the last fifteen years or so implicitly (and sometimes explicitly) relied on the paradigm of *masking*: religious discourse for example is only superficially about contact between the human and the divine. In fact it is encoded language of political subjugation. One removes the mask to reveal the face of power. Despite the enormous appeal of this kind of analysis, I can't help thinking that it ascribes to early modern thought an anachronistic innocence of the mask's potential. For the Renaissance is the great age of the mask, the *persona*. If ever a culture understood what a mask can and can not disguise, it is that one.

The drama of Shakespeare and his contemporaries flaunts its theatricality. It delights in calling attention to its own artifice, to its layers upon layers of metatheatrical maskings. At times the literary-critical discussion has lost sight of the way this kind of drama actually functions. At its best, whether conceived by Webster or Brecht, metatheater leaves the audience not with the feeling that essential reality has been unmasked but that reality is complex, conflicted, implicated in the masks it wears. A case in point is a moment in Webster's *The Duchess of Malfi* that bears on the standard theme of appearance masking reality but that complicates that theme in an exchange entirely gratuitous in terms of the play's action. In typically graphic prose, Bosola compares an old woman wearing heavy make-up to

> a lady in France, that having had the smallpox, flayed the skin off her face, to make it more level; and whereas before she look'd like a nutmeg grater, after she resembled an abortive hedgehog. (2.1.28–31)

With sufficient ingenuity one could perhaps unmask the phallogocentric core to Bosola's tirade, but it seems safe to say that the *experience* of the scene in the early seventeenth century (or the twentieth) would not have been so neatly edifying. To behold this actor in make-up playing the part of an ambitious courtier disguised as a melancholic (or perhaps a malcontent) saying what he says to a boy actor made up to look like an old lady trying to look like a young lady is not to "discover" any solid reality at all, political/misogynous or otherwise. Working through the layers here is more like peeling an onion than removing a mask: the whole thing is peelings. But to say that the onion has no solid ideological core is not to say that it is therefore without any meaning whatever. It still tastes exactly like an onion.

All this is to suggest that contradiction (or contrariety or paradox) might provide a more useful paradigm than masking for understanding the period's performances—whether on the stage or in the pulpit. The following chapters will make that case by attending to the interplay between drama and theology in a few of the stage and pulpit performances of the late sixteenth and early seventeenth centuries: an age that continues to confront us with its odd combinations of strangeness and familiarity.

B.C., Baltimore, 1995

Acknowledgments

My debts of gratitude are many. The University of Iowa, the Center for the Humanities at Loyola College, and the Loyola College Faculty Development Committee generously supported much of my research, especially my use of the excellent resources at the Folger Shakespeare Library. At meetings of the Shakespeare Association of America and the Sixteenth Century Studies Conference I gave preliminary shape to several of the ideas developed in this study. An earlier version of Chapter 3 appeared in the *Sixteenth Century Journal* and some of the material in Chapter 4 in *Classical and Modern Literature*. I am indebted especially to Jerry Singerman, the anonymous readers, and the editorial staff at the University of Pennsylvania Press as well as to my friends and colleagues Jody Bottum, Stavros Deligiorgias, Huston Diehl, Lisa M. Flaherty, Miriam Gilbert, Bob Miola, Brennan O'Donnell, Debora Shuger, Alvin Snyder, and Jim Spalding. While the responsibility for any infelicities in this study's argument rests with me, its strengths owe a great deal to the generous counsel of others.

1. Introduction: Bucer's Round Church and Shakespeare's "Wooden O"—The Circulation of the Reformation Sermon and the Renaissance Play

I

In the middle of the sixteenth century, the influential Reformation theologian Martin Bucer made an unsuccessful plea for a sort of sermon-in-the-round. Bucer's idea was to replace the usual cruciform churches with round ones; the cross-shaped structures, it seems, were reminiscent not only of lingering notions of the sacrificial mass but also of the idolatrous adoration of crosses and crucifixes. Bucer claimed that according to the Holy Fathers the earliest churches had been round, and the preacher had occupied the exact center of the building.[1] The claim is historically dubious, but the idea behind it says a great deal about the way Reformation preachers thought of themselves.

While Bucer's plan was based in part on an iconoclastic impulse, his proposal didn't do away with representation altogether; it invested the preacher with a new kind of iconic significance. Bucer's vision was that of a little world, a microcosm of the invisible church, an enclosure within which the single, continuous wall would be without distinctive features. The right angles of the cruciform structures would be replaced with one smooth surface; there would be no sharp corners, no niches for statuary, no sacrificial altar, no crux—that is, no crossroads, with all its unsettling implications. Instead, the preacher would occupy the single architectural focal point. Without visual distractions, the concentric rings of auditors would be free to attend to the hour-long sermon.

English clerics did not embrace Bucer's proposal with much enthusiasm. One reason is no doubt that church polity seemed more pressing than new building projects, but there may have been another factor: to those sympathetic to architectural along with theological reform, circles seemed suspiciously pagan. The Elizabethan period was, after all, the heyday of the mage and the witch, whose charmed circles were thought to pose a threat to the faith. And the circular buildings that did begin to crop up along the Bankside were hardly houses of worship. Bear-baiting pits and theaters, they were embodiments of pagan excess. The sermons of the period are filled with polemics against such indulgence: against the mage and the witch, the pit and the playhouse. The "cunning men" who practiced magic throughout the country were thought to be in competition with the churches for the people's attention, as were the London theaters.[2]

But competition implies kinship. There is no doubt of the antitheatrical prejudice among some Puritans of the late sixteenth century,[3] but the evidence of this antitheatricalism works both ways: on the one hand the polemics amply demonstrate a perceived antipathy between stage and pulpit; on the other, the same polemics imply that the two modes were perceived as closely enough related to compete. Beneath all the polemics, all the bitter disagreements about godly and ungodly pastimes, lie closely related cultural forces. It would be a mistake to assume, for example, that playwrights responded to King James's 1606 act outlawing theatrical references to controversial religious topics by suddenly becoming "secular"; the term is an anachronism for most of the period's discourse.[4] Rather the playwrights, like the preachers, engaged in rhetorically subtle and forceful ways the period's peculiar synthesis of magic, drama, and religion: forces impossible to dissociate, as the general failure of attempts to do so before the Enlightenment attests.

Shakespeare is a case in point: the "wooden O" of the Globe Theatre, to which the Prologue in *Henry V* refers in asking the audience to imagine that the enclosure encompasses a vast space, often functions as an arena for something nearer to communal alchemy than to mere pastime.[5] There is a moment in *The Tempest*, for example, when the magician Prospero traces a magic circle with his staff.[6] Wearing his enchanted robe and employing the heightened, incantatory diction appropriate to the moment, he abjures the "rough magic" that has allowed him not only to raise tempests but also to eclipse the sun and awaken the dead (5.1.40–50). In renouncing in the service of a higher calling the very powers he invokes, Prospero casts a spell— the incantation is based on a speech that Ovid gives to the sorceress Medea —but it is a spell renouncing his own sorcery, his own spellbinding powers. In this moment he is magical, dramatic, and religious all at once, and the power of the moment depends on the audience's registering the synthesis.

My claim in this study is that this synthesis occurs not only on the stage but also in the pulpit performances of Shakespeare's day. Since the Renaissance stage play and the Reformation sermon perform the same work—helping audiences adjust to and control the peculiar ambiguities of the early modern period—the two modes can be evaluated in the same terms. The lines of analysis can be various: anthropological, rhetorical, epistemological, generic, thematic. I will range fairly freely among these approaches, focusing on plays and sermons that address one of the main obsessions of the age: the principle of contrariety, or paradox.[7] It seems to me that this obsession throws a good deal of light on those points of contact that literary historians have increasingly seen as characteristic of the Renaissance: the conflicts and contradictions that all the artistic modes of the period both reflect and attempt to resolve. All seven chapters, then, have to do with contrariety, the coincidence of opposites. After this introductory chapter, which examines the theatrics of preaching and the rhetoric of paradox, the remainder of the study is divided into three parts, each containing two chapters. The first chapter in each pair highlights performances that rhetorically contrast with those of the second. While every chapter examines the interplay between theology and drama, Chapters 2 and 3 focus especially on sermons, 4 and 5 on comedies, and 6 and 7 on tragedies. By this arrangement I hope to show that the cultural interplay between the Renaissance stage play and the Reformation sermon cuts across generic boundaries and apparent antipathies.

II

Back to Bucer and his round church. Where did he get his idea? He was in exile at Cambridge when he made his plea for circularity. There he no doubt would have been familiar with a twelfth-century structure in the heart of the town, one of the few round Norman churches left in England.[8] A second possibility is that Bucer was influenced not just by the local Norman architecture (the nave of the Church of the Holy Sepulchre in Cambridge, only twenty feet in diameter, can hardly be what he had in mind) and not just by the purportedly round churches of primitive Christianity, but by the very real centrally planned churches that flourished at the height of the Italian Renaissance. But one need only glance at the architectural use of the circle in these churches to get a sense of the difference between their design and what Bucer seems to have had in mind.

During the century before Bucer wrote *Scripta Anglicana*, which contains his argument for the round church, the Platonist architects of Renaissance Italy were designing churches in which the defining shapes were the circle and the sphere rather than the cross. These churches were based on the geometric principle of the circle's ideal simplicity. From Plato to Plotinus to Ficino to the architects of the quattrocento, the commonly held view was that the circle—or, better yet, the sphere—is the geometric form that most closely approximates divine perfection. In fact, in the first architectural treatise of the Renaissance, Alberti's *De re aedificatoria* (written about 1450), the section on ecclesiastical architecture begins with a eulogy on the circle.

It is doubtful that Bucer actually visited any of the centrally planned churches designed by Alberti, Filarete, Bramante, or Giorgio (although he no doubt would have been familiar with the numerous small, round churches of Northern Europe, some of which date from Carolingian times). In any case, the point here is that the similarities between his design and those of the Italian humanists are not as telling as the differences. It is true that Bucer shared with his Italian forebears a desire for simplicity, a freedom from the visual distractions of ornament. As Filarete's treatise on architecture has it, "In looking at a circle the glance sweeps round instantaneously without interruption or obstacle."[9] Alberti's plan was to paint the centralized choir of the SS. Annunziata white, leaving it absolutely without ornament.[10] One thinks of a similar impulse behind the whitewashed churches of Reformation Europe: the impulse to transcend the mediating effects of visual display, to remove the statues and paintings of the saints, to get beyond the icons that always carried the danger of idolatry. But again, there is a difference, and the difference has to do with what happens once the mediating object is removed.

In the Italian Platonist churches the move is away from ritual sacrifice, away from the suspiciously theatrical contingencies of enacted history, and toward a timeless, ideal perfection.[11] In these churches the dominant architectural feature is the dome. The hemisphere suspended above the worshipper draws the attention upward, inviting a sense of transcendence above the plane of human activity. As Filarete puts it, the design of a church should ensure "that those who enter feel themselves elevated and the soul can rise to the contemplation of God."[12]

If the medieval cruciform churches were designed to encourage contemplation of and participation in an *action* (the atoning, sacrificial martyrdom, re-enacted at every mass), the centrally planned churches were designed to foster contemplation of *perfection*, to lift the worshipper out of the conflicted world of history and into a state of serene transcendence. As

Rudolph Wittkower has said, in the architectural move from the medieval cross to the Renaissance circle, "Christ as the essence of perfection superseded Him who had suffered on the Cross for humanity; the Pantocrator replaced the Man of Sorrows" (30).

Bucer and the Platonists are alike in rejecting the theater, the spectacle, of enacted sacrifice. They agree that there is something suspect in all that seems "theatrical" about the Catholic mass—the visual display, the mediating role of the priest, the performance of a sacrifice, the processions, the elevation of the Host, the very shape of the building. But Bucer's design would accommodate theater of another sort. His round church would be an *auditorium*, an arena where the air would be filled with sound. The theatrical activity of the mass would be replaced not by the Platonists' serene transcendence but by the action of the *word*. In this sense it was closer to Shakespeare's "wooden O" than to the centrally planned Italian churches.

Bucer himself argued that he wanted round churches for a purely practical reason: so that everyone would be able to hear the preacher. In the medieval Roman-cross churches the priest not only kept his back to the congregation as he performed his sacred offices at the altar, which was often separated from the main body of the church by an elaborate rood screen, he was also at a great distance from most of the worshippers—the distance from the choir to the nave. According to Bucer,

> this is Antichristian. For the choir to be so far removed from the rest of the church serves this end: that the ministers, whatever their faith and life, are nevertheless by their very order and placement held to be nearer to God than lay people, and empowered to appease God by the force of external works, which they perform for themselves.[13]

The round church with the preacher in the center would solve the problem, Bucer claimed, both ensuring that the preacher would be visible and audible to everyone present, and emphasizing the priesthood of all believers; all would be enclosed in the fold of the same circle, no one by virtue of office any nearer than anyone else to God.

Clearly, mere practicality forms only a part of Bucer's vision; the reformer is also aware of the symbolic force of his design. If hearing the preacher's words were really the paramount concern, would the sermon-in-the-round be the most practical scheme? What would become of the numerous worshippers who would find themselves behind the preacher, no matter which way he turned? Wouldn't an amphitheater design—or even a round church with the pulpit against the wall—better serve the purely acoustic purpose? The center of the church could then be reserved for the communion table, the proper placement of which Bucer does not mention. In his view the preacher was to be at the center, making it iconically plain that the word had superseded all sacramental representations of the divine presence.

Or, rather, a *newly embodied* word superseded the traditional sacraments, refiguring in the physical presence of the speaker the Word that had been incarnate in bread and wine. The reformers' impulse to shift the mode of representation from the visual to the aural was checked by the preacher's bodily presence, just as the impulse to abolish the priest as mediator resulted in a different kind of mediation in the person of the preacher. Rather than beholding a profusion of visually alluring icons and then taking part in a communal act of sacrifice, all of which could be denounced as "theatrical," the worshipper in Bucer's church would watch and listen as the preacher performed. Paradoxically, then, the Reformation insistence on the centrality of the spoken word reintroduced an element of theater into the liturgy—albeit theater of a different order from the theatricality of which the medieval liturgy stood accused.

In addition to the physical presence of the speaker, the very nature of oral performance fosters an experiential sense of history, of action, of drama. The modulations of sound through the course of an auditory performance—whether a sermon or a symphony—immerse the audience in a sequential experience: one that works through time to present change, conflict, resolution. The preacher's reliance on the action of the word means that there is an element of drama inherent in the sermon-centered liturgy. This is particularly true of pre-Enlightenment sermons, whose audiences' habits of perception are still primarily aural rather than visual. These habits of aural synthesis conceive of a world in flux: a dynamic, dramatic, threatening world compared with the relatively static world a visually-centered synthesis constructs.[14]

III

Before the great watershed of the middle of the seventeenth century, stage plays and sermons performed complementary roles in what has been called the "social drama" of the Protestant Reformation.[15] In Elizabethan England one finds not only the mutual influence of drama and theology that would be present in any age in which both modes flourished, but also the cultural interdependence that results from the readiness on the part of both Renaissance playwrights and Reformation preachers to experiment, to create new genres out of old forms, to use whatever cultural materials were at hand in the service of successful performance.[16]

There is little doubt that Reformation preaching styles influenced dramatists, just as there is little doubt that Renaissance stage plays influenced preachers. The substantial audience overlap between the two modes meant that preachers could assume a high degree of receptivity to oral performance, as the playwrights could assume their audiences' tendency to cast their experiences in religious terms.[17] Henry Smith, dubbed by Thomas Nashe the "silver-tongued" preacher of Elizabethan England, demonstrates the ease with which the language of the pulpit could mix with that of the stage:

> How many years of pleasure thou hast taken, so many years of pain: how many drams of delight, so many pounds of dolor: when iniquity hath played her part, vengeance leaps upon the stage: the comedy is short but the tragedy is longer.[18]

One of the problems in appreciating the cross-fertilization of Reformation sermons and Renaissance plays is the assumption that Protestantism implies antitheatricalism. Martin Butler points out that Protestantism, even Puritanism, was inextricably entwined with Tudor/Stuart drama right up until the closing of the theaters in 1642.[19] Protestant moral interludes were frequently performed in the middle of the sixteenth century, and some of the leading English reformers, including John Foxe, were also playwrights.[20] These preacher/playwrights objected not so much to the theater as an institution as to the theatricality of Roman Catholicism. Foxe, for example, refers to the typical medieval pope as a "remarkable actor,"

> that wholly theatrical contriver, [who] descended into the orchestra for the purpose of dancing his drama. While the other actors were driven off the stage little by little, he wished to keep the stage alone and to keep up all of the roles of everyone.[21]

Yet Foxe himself wrote the plays *Titus et Gesippus* (1544) and *Christus Triumphans* (1556). Politically influential Englishmen who were both Puritan sympathizers and lovers of the theater include Leicester, Walsingham, the third and fourth earls of Pembroke, Cromwell's chaplain Peter Sterry, and

Milton.[22] Calvin's English translator, Thomas Norton, coauthored the first English tragedy in blank verse. Nor was Calvin himself antitheatrical; he allowed the production of a play in Geneva, and in his *Institutes* he repeatedly refers to the world as a glorious theater in which angels behold human actions.[23]

A second problem in appreciating the affinity between Reformation sermons and Renaissance plays is that we are heir to the style of preaching that emerged in the eighteenth century, a style that valued analytics over theatrics.[24] But both in their manner of delivery and in their effects on audiences, Tudor/Stuart sermons were performances. Preachers repeatedly made the point that they were neither mere instructors nor orators. In a mid-century preaching manual that John Ludham translated into English in 1577, the Marburg theologian Andreas Hyperius says,

> They that teach no otherwise in the temple than professors are accustomed in the schools, it cannot be that they should be the authors of any great spiritual fruits, and very few or none are seen to be induced with such sermons to repentance and amendment of life.[25]

In a remark to his congregation, John Donne is more concise: "We are not upon a lecture but a sermon."[26]

Just as preaching involved more than instruction, it demanded more than mere oratory. The popular Puritan Samuel Hieron says, "I am come hither to discharge the duty of a Preacher, not of an Orator."[27] And Hyperius: "the action of a Preacher in the Church of God is much discrepant from the action of a Rhetorician in the guild hall" (17ᵛ). Even if it is clear why a preacher would be called on to be more animated than a lecturer, precisely what is the difference between the preacher and the orator? (One of the standard studies of seventeenth-century preaching, after all, is called *English Pulpit Oratory*.)[28] It seems to me not only that there is a clear distinction between preaching and oratory in the Tudor/Stuart period but that the distinction goes beyond even the import of the subject matter: the difference is essentially theatrical. What distinguishes the Reformation preacher from the instructor or the orator is his *role*.[29] The preacher self-consciously takes on the mantle of the divinely inspired prophet. Like Shakespeare's Prospero, the preacher quite literally dons a robe and heightens his language for the prophetic performance.

Reformation preachers explicitly think of themselves as prophets. As Stephen Gosson says, "Believe we cannot but by preaching, whereby it grows that the object of this act in this place is the Prophet."[30] Hieron points out that whereas in the Old Testament "prophesying" meant predicting the future, in the New Testament "It is even the very same which we term *Preaching*."[31] In Hieron's view the Reformation preacher is to be a prophet in the New Testament sense. His inspired utterances do not merely explain or interpret the divine Word, nor do they simply predict God's actions; they *precipitate* those actions during the course of the performance. The role of the preacher/prophet is to work a kind of sacred magic, transforming the very souls of the listeners.

Theologians throughout the period echo Gosson's claim that a prophetic style of preaching is necessary for the salvation of the soul; without it all other measures, including the sacraments, are useless. Both Luther and Calvin hold that the sacraments of the Eucharist and baptism require preaching in order to beget faith, and Thomas Cartwright insists that the sacraments should be administered only *after* preaching.[32] As William Sclater puts the matter in a 1609 sermon,

> I cannot yet see what that great and important business of the ministry should be to which it may beseem Preaching to give place. I am sure not Sacraments. Christ sent me not to baptize (saith the Holy Apostle) but to preach the Gospel.[33]

Protestant reformers frequently support their position by quoting Paul's statement, "Then faith is by hearing, and hearing by the word of God" (Rom. 10:17).[34] When Henry Smith says, "without the word never any was converted to God," he refers explicitly to the word preached.[35] Hieron is more blunt: "he who thinks to be saved without preaching shall be damned."[36] Nor does John Marbecke mince words: "no priest, no more than a dead man is a man, which doth not preach."[37] If the ministers were to work the sacred magic of imparting divine life to their audiences—if in fact they were to be spiritually alive themselves—they must assume the role of the prophet.

Gosson makes a clear distinction between the minister in his ordinary human capacity and in his divinely inspired role in the pulpit, calling it the devil's work to confuse the two offices.[38] In his manual for preachers *The Art of Prophecying*, the popular theologian William Perkins also distinguishes two offices, both proper to the prophet: "And every Prophet is partly the voice of God, to wit, in preaching: and partly the voice of the people, in the act of praying."[39] In both offices the preacher mediates between the people and God, and in both cases the preacher is essentially an actor; he speaks with a voice other than his own. But the two roles are quite different. If it is relatively easy to stand in for the people in prayer, it is daunting to assume the role of God's spokesman, to realize the full implications of Gifford's statement, "The Preacher is the mouth of God unto the people, not the mouth of men," or Donne's that the preacher has "come from God" and "speaks in the person of God himself."[40] As the prolific seventeenth-century preacher Richard Baxter says, "It is no small matter to stand up in the face of a congregation, and deliver a message of salvation or damnation, as from the living God, in the name of our Redeemer."[41]

In fact the Reformation preacher is asked to stand in for each person of the Trinity. Hieron insists that in addition to serving as the prophet of God the Father, the preacher must assume the voice of the Son: "where is Christ's voice now, but in those, who by their calling are in Christ's *stead*? and of whom he hath said plainly, 'He that heareth you, heareth me'?" (*Dignity*, 16). And Perkins says,

> the Minister of the word doth in the time of preaching so behave himself that all, even ignorant persons and unbelievers, may judge that it is not so much he that speaketh as the Spirit of God in him and by him. (*Art of Prophecying* 2:759)

Under the expectation that he would deliver a message "as from the living God," speaking "in Christ's stead" with "the Spirit of God in him," the preacher labored under tremendous psychological pressure. In such circumstances questions were bound to arise: just how was the preacher to put the principle of inspiration into practice? What if he felt uninspired? What if he thought himself incapable of playing the role? The advisors to the prophets were armed with answers, but the answers themselves present problems.

Perkins, for example, explains what the preacher's "demonstration of the holy Spirit" entails: "This demonstration is either in speech or in gesture. The speech must be spiritual and gracious. That speech is spiritual which the holy Spirit doth teach" (759). If the circularity of this explanation provides little help to the preacher, the same is true of the requirements for the appropriately "spiritual" style: "it is a speech both simple and perspicuous, fit both for the people's understanding and to express the majesty of the spirit" (759). No small task: the sermon must be both perspicuous and majestic, appealing to the people's simplicity while simultaneously doing justice to divine grandeur.

Moreover, the preacher must not only *understand* the workings of the Holy Spirit but *feel* them. In a passage that looks back to Cicero, Horace, and Quintilian and forward to the "Method" school of acting, Perkins tells the preacher to stir up his own emotions if his performance is to be successful:

> Wood, that is capable of fire, doth not burn, unless fire be put to it: and he must first be godly affected himself who would stir up godly affections in other men. Therefore what motions a sermon doth require, such the Preacher shall stir up privately in his own mind, that he may kindle up the same in his hearers. (760)

Hyperius echoes the sentiment:

> Before all things it is very necessary that he which speaketh do conceive such like affections in his mind, and raise them up in himself, yea, and (after a sort) shew them forth to be seen unto others, as he coveteth to be translated into the minds of his auditors. For he that in words, voice, countenance, and apt gesture, declareth himself to lament and be sorry either for the peril of some, or for the common misery of all men, he alone seemeth forthwith to provoke the residue to pity and compassion. (*Practise of Preaching*, 43ʳ)

While Hyperius apparently believes that the preacher's affections should be sincere, a few of his expressions mark the difficulty of drawing the line (as it is difficult to draw in acting) between being sincere and seeming so: having conceived and raised up his own affections, the preacher is to display them "after a sort"; he "declareth himself" to lament; he alone "seemeth" to arouse pity in the audience.

Hyperius lists three ways of the preacher's kindling his own "godly affections": "by the diligent consideration of the things that are before his eyes . . . , by a vehement imagination or fantasy," and by reading emotional passages from Scripture (43ʳ⁻ᵛ). If these methods fail, the minister is to do his best to conceal the failure from his audience. Perkins:

> It is an ecclesiastical secret: That the Minister ought to cover his infirmities, that they be not seen. For simple people behold not the ministry, but the person of the Minister. (760)

The preacher is supposed to be able not only to distinguish between the workings of the Holy Spirit and the merely human ingenuity that would produce an artful performance, but also to conceal the human element. Like the actor, the preacher is to disguise his own identity in the service of a convincing impersonation. Perkins says,

> In the Promulgation two things are required: the hiding of human wisdom, and the demonstration (or shewing) of the spirit. Human wisdom must be concealed, whether it be in the matter of the sermon, or in the setting forth of the words: because the preaching of the word is the Testimony of God, and the profession of the knowledge of Christ, and not of human skill: and again, because the hearers ought not to ascribe their faith to the gifts of men, but to the power of God's word. (759)

Perkins goes on to defend both the use of human ingenuity in composing the sermon and the concealing of that ingenuity in the sermon's actual performance:

> If any man think that by this means barbarism should be brought into the pulpits, he must understand that the Minister may, yea and must privately use at his liberty the arts, philosophy, and variety of reading, whilst he is in framing his sermon: but he ought in public to conceal all these from the people. (759)

The paradox is that while the impulse behind concealing eloquence is to avoid deceptive ostentation, the deliberate concealment amounts to an artful, dramatic deception.

In the twentieth century such instructions might appear disingenuous—the combination of moral earnestness and deliberate deception impossible to maintain—but sixteenth- and seventeenth-century pulpit performances depend on this earnest theatricality. Advice similar to Perkins's comes from as fervently religious a poet and priest as George Herbert. In *The Country Parson* Herbert advises preachers to compose themselves properly in order to make their performances effective:

> When [the country parson] preacheth, he procures attention by all possible art, both by earnestness of speech, it being natural to men to think, that where is much earnestness, there is somewhat worth hearing; and by a diligent, and busy cast of his eye on his auditors, with letting them know, that he observes who marks, and who not.[42]

The preacher is to employ not only "earnestness of speech" and "a busy cast of his eye" but also appropriate gestures (or as Perkins calls them, "holy motions of affections") (758). The number of complaints about overdone gestures indicates that preachers frequently got carried away with their theatrics. Hyperius says, "By reason of their undiscreet and unseemly gesture, some are made the common talking stock and public pastime of the people" (177ᵛ). Two mid-seventeenth-century preachers object to the extravagance of "holy performance." John Eachard says,

> How often have you seen a preacher heat himself, beyond the need of any vestments? Throwing off his cloak, nay and his gloves too, as great impediments to the holy performance, squeaking and roaring beyond the example of any lunatic? [43]

Robert South asks,

> can any tolerable reason be given for those strange new postures used by some in the delivery of the word? Such as shutting the eyes, distorting the face, and speaking through the nose, which I think cannot so properly be called preaching, as toning of a sermon. . . . For none surely will imagine, that these men's speaking as never man spoke before, can pass for any imitation of him.[44]

One is reminded of Hamlet's instructions to the players at Elsinore:

> do not saw the air too much with your hand, thus, but use all gently. . . .
> O, there be players that I have seen play—and heard others [praise], and that highly—not to speak it profanely, that, neither having th' accent of Christians nor the gait of Christian, pagan, nor man, have so strutted and bellow'd that I have thought some of Nature's journeymen had made men, and not made them well, they imitated humanity so abominably. (3.2.4–5, 28–35)

Just as Hamlet would replace bad acting with good acting rather than no acting at all, those who complained of the excesses of Tudor/Stuart pulpit performances were not necessarily arguing that there should be no performances in the pulpit; like Hamlet, they simply wanted the performers to "suit the action to the word, the word to the action" (3.2.17–18).

Hamlet also pleads with the players not to allow any ad-libbing: "And let those that play your clowns speak no more than is set down for them . . ." (3.2.38–40). As Hieron points out, the same objection is often raised against preachers. Hieron's *The Preachers Plea* is a religious dialogue, a popular sub-genre of Tudor/Stuart theological discourse that by its very format as an exchange between two characters shades toward the drama. In all these dialogues there is an ignorant character who is put in his place by the godly protagonist. In Hieron's exchange Nymphas, the ignorant character, voices a common objection to the practice of delivering sermons extemporaneously rather than reading from a carefully prepared text:

> Nymphas: men that write, write with great deliberation and advice; as for you when you preach, you speak many times at adventure, and nothing so judicially as do those who commit things to writing.
> Epaphras: compare like with like, . . . sound writers with sound preachers. (*Preacher's Plea*, 102)

In Epaphras's view "sound preachers" should not only be allowed but should be encouraged to speak extemporaneously, to move from merely reading a prepared text to using the text as only a set of notes for a live performance. Epaphras goes on to vilify those who "go about to equal bare and naked reading unto preaching" (117). He finds "the word being urged and pressed by preaching to be far more powerful, more piercing, more majestical, more awaking to the conscience" than mere reading (123).

The dedicatory epistles to printed editions of sermons often bear witness to what is lost in reducing the spoken word to print. John King, for example, complains of the "prodigal and intemperate age of the world, wherein every man writeth more than need is."[45] King claims that even to read the titles of all books recently published "were the sufficient labor of our unsufficient lives" and then laments,

> [I] have changed my tongue into a pen, and whereas I spake before with the gesture and countenance of a living man, have now buried my self in a dead letter of less effectual persuasion. (3–4)

Thomas Playfere complains that while the readers of his sermon *The sickmans Couch* will be able to discern the preacher's meaning, unfortunately they must remain "unacquainted with his affection."[46] Henry Smith, constrained by illness late in his life to refrain from preaching, says that he is "ashamed" to resort to the dead letter of the written word, for "the bane of printing" is the absence of the "pains" with which the preacher performs.[47]

Even a theologian like Richard Hooker, who is troubled by the one-time "speech event" of the extemporaneous sermon, is unsatisfied with sermons that are merely read. In *Of the Laws of Ecclesiastical Polity*, Hooker objects on the one hand to those who insist that original sermons are the only means of salvation:

> whatsoever is spoken concerning the efficacy or necessity of God's word, the same they tie and restrain only unto sermons, howbeit not sermons read neither (for such they also abhor in the Church), but Sermons without book, Sermons which spend their life in their birth, and may have public audience but once.[48]

On the other hand, it is not the preacher's animated style of delivery that bothers Hooker; he notes universal recognition of the lively sermon's rhetorical effectiveness. It was difficult for the preacher who merely read his sermons from the official *Book of Homilies* to match the performative force of the preacher who composed a sermon for the occasion, a sermon responsive to the needs of the audience, one with the power "to put life into words by countenance, voice, and gesture, to prevail mightily in the sudden affections of men" (5.22.12).

The issue of preaching versus reading from the *Homilies* was very much a live one in Renaissance England.[49] Just as Tudor/Stuart plays were subject to censorship, Elizabeth and James attempted to exercise control over the pulpits. In 1559 Elizabeth revised and reissued the first *Book of Homilies* (1547), of which Cranmer had been one of the principal authors, and in 1563 she issued an expanded version. A few preachers were licensed to compose their own sermons, but the vast majority were required to read theirs from the *Homilies*. As Elizabeth attempted to control the well-attended sermons at Paul's Cross in London, she tried to use the *Homilies* to control the parish clergy throughout England.[50] It is noteworthy that the one sermon added to the *Second Book of Homilies* during Elizabeth's reign was the 1570 *Homily against Disobedience and Wilful Rebellion*. James similarly attempted to keep wayward clergy in check with both the *Homilies* and his own *Instructions regarding Preaching* (1622).[51] The magistrates' relentless efforts to control the preaching clergy, as well as the numbers of preachers brought before the ecclesiastical courts (where playwrights also made occasional appearances), testify to the rhetorical power of the pulpit.

The political elite's suspicions of the preaching clergy were very like the fear that Jonas Barish has identified with the antitheatrical prejudice in Western culture: the fear of Proteus. Barish argues that one reason players have often seemed suspect is their resistance to a single, stable identity.[52]

Their very profession as role players carries the threat of instability, the threat of Proteus. Writing in 1630, the theologian and poet Richard James makes a similar argument about preachers:

> 'tis almost impossible to hinder schisms, malignancies and heresies, where there is and hath been still permitted that liberty and luxury of preaching. If we be senseless not to feel the mischief, our neighbors smart in the Netherlands. And where hath not the lavish tongue of our preaching infected? so that it seemed long since good wisdom in the Greek Church to cut off and root out the voluntary use and abuse of it. . . . For 'tis not for us saith Jeremie the Patriarch of Constantinople in an answer to the Ministers of Wittenburg, in trust of our own wisdom to understand and expound the Scriptures, lest we should be carried up and down, as changeable as Proteus in variety of opinions.[53]

James is here arguing against both the theologically (and therefore socially) schismatic force of preaching and its unsettling effect on the individual: if preaching causes theological and social "schisms, malignancies, and heresies," it also leaves the individual dangerously untrustworthy, "as changeable as Proteus." There is no small irony in the fact that James delivered his tirade against preaching from the pulpit. It seems that the threatening flexibility of pulpit performances allows for a protean variety of stances: even an anti-protean one.

Certainly Elizabeth registered the threat. Throughout the country during the 1570s "prophesyings"—weekday preaching workshops in which several ministers would participate while a lay audience observed—gained such widespread popularity that Elizabeth feared that they would shift the balance of power away from the central authorities. She instructed the Archbishop of Canterbury, Edmund Grindal, both to reduce the number of licensed preachers and to suppress the prophesyings. Grindal refused. In 1576 he wrote a letter to the Queen, arguing that reading from the official *Homilies* was a poor substitute for pulpit performance:

> The godly preacher . . . can apply his speech according to the diversity of times, places, and hearers, which cannot be done in homilies: exhortations, reprehensions, and persuasions, are uttered with more affection, to the moving of the hearers, in sermons than in homilies. Besides, homilies were devised by the godly bishops in your brother's time, only to supply necessity, for want of preachers; and are by the statute not to be preferred, but to give place to sermons, whensoever they may be had. (*Grindal*, 382)

Other passages in the letter attest to the extent of Grindal's willingness to play the prophet. He not only says, "I cannot marvel enough how this strange opinion should once enter into your mind, that it should be good for the church to have few preachers"; he goes on to say, "Remember, Madam, that you are a mortal creature" (378, 389). The letter effectively ended Grindal's career.

Despite the risk involved in preaching one's own sermons rather than simply reading from the *Book of Homilies*, the number of original sermons increased dramatically during the last half of the sixteenth century. Martha Tuck Rozett reports that the number of regular parish clergy who preached rose from 27 percent in 1561 to 88 percent in 1601, and the number of published volumes of sermons increased from nine during the 1560s to 113 during the 1580s (Rozett, 19–20). Still, change was not proceeding fast enough for the more zealous reformers. They continually petitioned Parliament with their demands for a learned, preaching clergy, and in 1584 and 1585 some of them conducted a survey of more than two thousand English parishes in order to convince Parliament that the clergy of England were still in a sorry state. The surveyors' report to Parliament includes descriptions of individual ministers. One was "an alehouse haunter, a companion with drunkards and a gross abuser of the scriptures"; another was "consumed by carding, dicing, and gaming"; a third was "a drunkard and a whoremaster [who] continually weareth a pocket dag"; and one was described as "a common gamester, the best wrastler in Cornwall." Given the surveyors' aim of demonstrating the generally unimpressive character of the English clergy, it is all the more noteworthy, and intriguing, that the rector at Stratford-upon-Avon—the man who may well have preached before the young Shakespeare—was described as "learned, zealous and godly, and fit for the ministry; a happy age if our Church were fraught with many such."[54]

Like the playwrights, the preachers found ways of using irony, sometimes to endorse the dominant ideology and sometimes to frustrate the authorities' attempts to appropriate the pulpits for official propaganda. On the one hand is a performance like Richard Bancroft's famous 1589 Paul's Cross sermon denouncing Puritanism. Bancroft uses language that must have had enormous appeal in a time of widespread economic oppression:

> You can not but groan under the heavy burden which is laid upon you. Your landlords do wring and grind your faces for the maintenance of their pride in apparel, their excess in diet, their unnecessary pleasures, as gaming, keeping of hawks and dogs, and such like vanities.[55]

The rhetoric seems genuinely subversive until Bancroft reveals that the whole argument against oppression is "Anabaptistical" (26). Bancroft's irony would seem a dangerous tactic, even for one (or especially for one) in a position of authority.

On the other hand is John Donne, who employs irony of a different sort. In 1622 Donne was called on to defend at Paul's Cross both the King's attempt to regulate preaching and, as John Chamberlain reported at the time, to defend the King's "constancy in the true reformed religion, which the people (as should seem) began to suspect."[56] In a tactic reminiscent of Marc Antony's funeral oration in *Julius Caesar*, Donne let it be known through the manner of his delivery that he himself had doubts. Chamberlain goes on to say,

> his text was the 20th verse of the 5th chapter of the book of Judges ["They fought from heaven, even the stars in their courses fought against Sisera"], somewhat a strange text for such a business, and how he made it hold together I know not, but he gave no great satisfaction, or as some say spake as if himself were not so well satisfied. (2:451)

The preachers, like the playwrights, found ways of circumventing the censors. The "strategies of indirection" that Annabel Patterson finds in Renaissance plays appear in sermons as well (*Censorship and Interpretation*, 45). A persistent rhetorical slipperiness informs both modes. Like the playwrights, the preachers employ a whole arsenal of rhetorical devices in the service of effective performance. As I hope to show in the following pages of this chapter, one rhetorical figure—the paradox—throws light on the process of cross-fertilization peculiar to the period: a process that results in the extraordinary flowering of Renaissance sermons as well as stage plays.

IV

Debora Shuger has argued that the general shift from premodern to modern thought involves a "thickening" of boundaries, an increasing tendency to think in rigidly exclusive categories:

> Generally speaking, the sacramental/analogical character of premodern thought tends to deny rigid boundaries; nothing is simply itself, but things are signs of other things and one thing may be inside another, as Christ is *in* the heart, or turn into something else, as the substance of the eucharistic bread turns into the body of Christ. With the advent of modernity the bor-

ders between both conceptual and national territories were redrawn as solid rather than dotted lines.[57]

While the redrawing of boundaries heralding the advent of modernism undeniably took place, the process was anything but smooth. Shuger points out that for a period in intellectual history—roughly the period of the Renaissance and Reformation—the sacramental/analogical and the empirical/skeptical mentalities coexisted in "a persistent and unsettling pluralism within the high official culture" (22). To some degree this pluralism may be evident in all cultures, but "the Renaissance was probably the last era in the West where mystical and demystifying habits of thought obtained relative parity within the central discourse" (24). Applying to intellectual history a term from cultural anthropology, we might say that the period is "liminal" and therefore inherently unstable; human beings are in an uneasy moment of transition from a medieval to a modern way of perceiving the world. Of course, it is only in hindsight that a culturally liminal moment appears to be composed of an interplay between two well-defined epistemological systems. At the time, the *limen*, or threshold, marks off the ordered world from a chaotic, unknowable, and therefore potentially fearsome alternative.

It seems to me that in such circumstances Shuger's two "habits of thought" jostling within and between individuals as well as institutions are played out just beneath the surface of what Rosalie Colie calls a characteristic Renaissance "figure of thought": the paradox.[58] Such a dynamic helps to explain not only the heightened concern for a whole constellation of Christian paradoxes in Renaissance discourse (not the least of these concerns being the renewed interest in the exact nature of the Eucharist) but also the literary prevalence of paradoxical motifs not explicitly Christian.

Certainly the early modern period witnesses an unflagging fascination with what Stephen Greenblatt calls "the occult relation between opposites."[59] The lament of Donne's Holy Sonnet XIX, "Oh, to vex me, contraries meet in one," is not only a personal cry of anguish but also an epitome of a pervasive cultural contrariety.[60] The prevalence of paradox in various genres of Tudor and Stuart literature is symptomatic of a widespread concern—one might even say obsession—with the simultaneous experience of contrary states.

In Renaissance usage the word "paradox" sometimes refers to an idea that we would now call "heterodox," but more often it denotes the kind of holding together of experiential opposites with which this study is concerned. And there are other Renaissance terms for the same idea: George Puttenham calls paradoxes "wondrers"; to Lyly they are "contrarieties"; to Bishop Joseph Hall "sacred riddles"; and to Thomas Playfere, perhaps the most habitually paradoxical of Elizabethan preachers, the "intermingling of extremities."[61]

Of course, examples of Renaissance paradox could easily be multiplied. Stephen Gosson's riddling inquiry in his sermon *The Trumpet of Warre* is fairly typical:

> what is that, that is the highest the lowest, the fairest the foulest, the strongest the weakest, the richest the poorest, the happiest the unhappiest, the safest and the most in danger of any thing in the world? (F6)

The answer: the good Christian. Or take the imprisoned Richard's thoughts about thoughts in his soliloquy near the end of *Richard II*:

> The better sort,
> As thoughts of things divine, are intermix'd
> With scruples and do set the word itself
> Against the word,
> As thus: "Come, little ones," and then again,
> "It is as hard to come as for a camel
> To thread the postern of a small needle's eye." (5.5.11–17)

The fascination with Christian paradox runs through the Reformation/ Renaissance period; by the middle of the seventeenth century, whole collections of paradoxes become extremely popular. The following two are typical entries in Ralph Venning's *Orthodox Paradoxes*.[62] The first of his 107 theoretical paradoxes is that the Christian "believes that which he cannot comprehend, yet there is reason enough why he should believe it" (1). The first of Venning's 127 practical paradoxes is that the believer "cries out, 'What must I do to be saved?' and yet he never expects to be saved by doing" (17). Another popular edition of paradoxes was Herbert Palmer's *The Character of a Christian in Paradoxes and Seeming Contradictions*.[63] By the time the Venning and Palmer collections came out the taste for theological and literary paradox was anything but new; for more than a hundred years paradoxes had been prevalent enough in England to be cited in grammar school texts.[64] In 1593 Anthony Munday translated into English Ortensio Lando's *The Defence of Contraries: Paradoxes Against Com-*

mon Opinion—a collection that may have inspired the young John Donne's *Paradoxes and Problems*.[65] In the late sixteenth and early seventeenth centuries paradoxes were a common feature at the Inns of Court revels. A character named Paradox had the lead role in the 1618 revels at Gray's Inn.[66]

Of course, these examples are anything but exhaustive. As Colie has amply demonstrated, one finds paradox operating pervasively in the intellectual life of early modern England. On the level of rhetorical practice, there is such a proliferation of the oxymoron in Renaissance love poetry that its use is in danger of becoming cliché by the late sixteenth century.[67] But paradoxical discourse in Renaissance England is more than a passing fad; the abuse of the oxymoron in love poetry is a symptom of a pervasive epistemological contrariety, a way of knowing that has rightly been called "one of the primary intellectual modalities of the period."[68] Whether in the Petrarchan sonneteer's combinations of opposing emotional states or in the Calvinist preacher's assertions that human beings are utterly vile and at the same time unutterably glorious, an insistent assertion throughout the early modern period is that one can simultaneously experience contradictory extremes. The period's peculiar intermingling of Classical and Christian influences engenders and nurtures this kind of thinking, so that paradox becomes pervasive in various modes of Renaissance discourse. The meanings that arise from paradox are richly varied, but similar rhetorical principles are at work in plays and sermons informed by contrariety.

Part of the appeal of paradox in a time of considerable political and ecclesiastical censorship may have been its ideological slipperiness. Paradox has the power to be simultaneously subversive and conservative; even as it undermines established ideas, it reinforces some fundamental orthodoxy.[69] Because of this inherent ambiguity, it is difficult to pin down in ideologically exclusive terms an author whose language is paradoxical. Whether employed by the philosopher, the politician, the preacher, or the playwright, the paradox becomes an extremely versatile and effective rhetorical tool.

Renaissance paradoxes achieve their force in part through their restatement of central Christian mysteries. The language of Christian thought is insistently paradoxical, from the sayings of Jesus to the epistles of Paul to the creeds developed in the ecumenical councils of the early church to the meditations of the medieval mystics to the *coincidentia oppositorum* of Renaissance Platonists like Nicholas of Cusa, Pico della Mirandola, and Giordano Bruno to the language of the Protestant reformers. Paradox is as central to Browne's *Religio Medici* as to Pascal's *Pensées*. Throughout the history of Western (and Eastern) Christian theology, the paradoxical high mysteries of the *creatio ex nihilo*, the *felix culpa*, the eternal, spiritual God's birth into time and flesh in the Incarnation, the death of God in the Crucifixion, the death of death in the Resurrection, and the believer's attaining freedom through servitude are repeatedly affirmed.[70]

Not surprisingly, the history of Christianity has seen repeated attempts to slacken the tension of doctrinal paradox, to make sense of what appears nonsensical. In fact it can be argued that the history of Christian theology has been the history of resistance to such attempted slackenings.[71] The first of Venning's practical paradoxes will serve as an example. In asserting that the believer must cry out, "What must I do to be saved?" even while "he never expects to be saved by doing," Venning calls for the believer to maintain a state of psychological tension that resists an exclusive emphasis on either faith or works. Nor is the answer some Aristotelian (or Catholic) golden mean: one is not to suppose the faith composes half of the spiritual life and works the other half. Venning's claim is that *each* of the apparently antithetical impulses must be kept *wholly* in force. The Christian must embrace both principles at once, resisting any attempt to lessen the tension.

Venning's emphasis on paradox follows very much in the tradition of Martin Luther, who saw himself as a leader in the resistance movement— a champion of paradoxical mystery in an age that threatened to reduce the faith to a mere series of pious works. Luther's was a mind congenial to paradox. He preached the inefficacy of human effort even as he stridently urged his followers to exert themselves; he held that the believer is *simul justus et peccator*: simultaneously a saint and a sinner, not a sinner gradually becoming a saint; he remained relatively unconcerned about an omnipotent God's desiring universal salvation but not accomplishing it; he reveled in the idea that a God simultaneously human and divine was a puzzle to the intellect.[72] The following passage is fairly typical of Luther's paradoxical rhetoric:

> God's faithfulness and truth always must first become a great lie before it becomes truth. The world calls this truth heresy. And we, too, are constantly tempted to believe that God would abandon us and not keep His Word; and in our hearts he begins to become a liar. In short, God cannot be God unless He first becomes a devil. We cannot go to heaven unless we first go to hell. We cannot become God's children until we first become children of the devil. All that God speaks and does the devil has to speak and do first. . . . By the same token the lies of this world cannot become lies without first having become truth. The godless do not go to hell without first having gone to

heaven. They do not become the devil's children until they have first been the children of God.[73]

Luther was fond of such dizzying assaults on ordinary reason, insisting that true faith embraces all paradoxes. He intended to relieve his followers of a tremendous burden—the burden of having to make human sense of divine actions—but how many of those followers could share his ability to find comfort in paradox, could simultaneously strive and believe that striving was useless, could find their own sinfulness a hallmark of salvation? [74]

Calvin was less willing than Luther to welcome paradox as an expression of divine transcendence over reason, less willing to countenance what he called "promiscuous mixtures," more systematic in his handling of the logic of predestination.[75] Calvin intensified the position that Augustine had been forced to take against Pelagius: if an omnipotent God had predestined certain souls to election and others to reprobation, then there was absolutely no room for any degree of free will among fallen humankind. Luther had said the same, but his language regarding the bondage of the human will had not been so insistent, except perhaps in his polemic exchange with Erasmus.[76] In Calvin's view, the predestinarian thesis had to be urged relentlessly in order to guard against the heresy of righteousness attained by pious works. Like Luther, Calvin saw the doctrine of a predestined, limited atonement as a means of both protecting God's omnipotence and offering comfort to the elect.[77]

But this comfort came to those certain of their election; those who had doubts were advised to persevere in their spiritual struggles despite the fact that no human effort could be of any consequence. In Calvin's formulation of the paradox,

> man being informed that there remaineth in him no goodness, and being compassed about with most miserable necessity, may yet be taught to aspire to the goodness whereof he is void. (2.2.1)

As Henry Smith puts it, "thine own heart can tell that it is wicked, but it cannot amend: therefore it is high time to amend" (*Trumpet*, B4ʳ). Unless one maintained an unswerving certainty of salvation, the psychological pressure of this situation was enormous. If one had doubts, did not such doubts call into question one's very status as a member of the elect? Then what was one to do? There was nothing that could be done to affect one's election, and so it seems fairly natural that believers should seek greater *as-*

surance of election. As I will argue more fully in Chapter 4, late sixteenth-
and early seventeenth-century English Calvinism reflects a shift in emphasis from moral activity to knowledge—from ethics to epistemology. If
one can not become a member of the elect, one wants assurance that one
already is such a member. And the case for certainty is compelling; Arthur
Dent speaks for a great many of his contemporaries when he says, "he that
knoweth not in this life that he shall be saved, shall never be saved after
this life."[78]

The resulting development, an obsessive desire to find signs of election, is one that Calvin foresees—and one that he takes considerable pains
to forestall:

> And of Election what revelation hast thou? which thought, if it have once
> taken place in any man, either perpetually beareth the miserable man with ter-
> rible torments, or bitterly dismayeth him. . . . For the mind can be infected
> with no error more pestilent, than that which plucketh down the conscience
> from her peace and quietness toward God. (3.24.4)

But "peace and quietness toward God" depends upon assurance of salvation, which in turn depends upon the very sort of proof Calvin wants to
dismiss. Or so it seems, at least, to the one who has doubts.

The pressure generated by this paradox, a pressure that arguably
boosted the European suicide rate by a considerable margin, takes shape
as a fervent quest for certainty of salvation.[79] The one who has any shade
of doubt about the matter is placed in an extremely uneasy position.[80] As
Arthur Dent's treatise makes clear, the one who has doubts, who questions the efficacy of human action in a wholly predetermined universe, is
displaying clear evidence of reprobation: "This is a very wicked and carnal
objection, and sheweth a vile and dissolute mind in them that use it" (288).
It seems that one must begin with certainty of election before one can attain such certainty, and the pressure of this paradox is intensified by the
doctrine of limited atonement—the belief that only a few shall be saved.[81]
Even where the New Testament seems to offer hope of universal salvation
(in Jesus' ambiguous response to an unnamed questioner in Luke 13:24),
Dent is quick to close the loophole:

> albeit our Savior doth not answer directly to his question, either negatively
> or affirmatively; yet doth he plainly insinuate by his speeches, that few shall
> be saved. (256)

English Calvinism thus generates a radical, paradoxical dualism even more pronounced than the dualistic division of grace and nature, saved and damned, in Calvin himself.

Of course, it was not only Calvin who foresaw this problem but Roman Catholic theologians as well. Erasmus, for example, despite all his sympathy for church reform, disagreed strongly with the Protestant reformers' willingness to engage in public disputes about matters of theological paradox; he doubted that ordinary churchgoers needed to concern themselves with thorny theological problems. And according to Erasmus, of all the difficult matters implicit in the Scriptures, the biggest "labyrinth" is the doctrine of predestination:[82]

> Let us assume the truth of what Wycliffe has taught and Luther has asserted, namely, that everything we do happens not on account of our free will, but out of sheer necessity. What could be more useless than to publish this paradox to the world? (11)

Luther responded that he was not the author of Christian paradox; God was:

> My dear Erasmus, let me too say in turn: If you think these paradoxes are inventions of men, what are you contending about? Against whom are you speaking? Is there anyone in the world today who has more vigorously attacked the dogmas of men than Luther? Therefore, your admonition has nothing to do with me. But if you think these paradoxes are words of God, how can you keep your countenance, where is your shame? . . . Naturally, your Creator must learn from you his creature what is useful or useless to preach![83]

Needless to say, Luther felt constrained to publish the paradox to the world.

In fact the rapid growth of the Protestant movement was due in large part to the the reformers' readiness to publish their ideas. The printing press saw widespread polemical use; for the first time laymen had access not only to contemporary theological disputes but also to vernacular versions of the Bible, the ground of those disputes. More than at any previous time in Western culture, it seemed possible for ordinary people to make their own decisions about weighty theological matters.[84] And the heat of the controversy waged by theologians made decisiveness seem imperative. Hieron, for example, insists that ordinary people *must* judge sound doctrine, that it is only the Papists who say otherwise (*Preachers Plea*, 234). In Gifford's dialogue *The Countrie Divinitie*, the author's spokesman responds to his opponent's objection that while the Bible is utterly reliable, it contains mysteries that the ordinary believer cannot fathom:

> Ye say the word is certain and sure: but the interpretation thereof ye make doubtful: but what are we the better that the word of God is sure and certain, unless it be sure and certain unto us, which cannot be except the interpretation be so? It is as good for ye to say the word is doubtful, as for to say the sense is doubtful. (53ᵛ)

The pressure was enormous for definitive resolutions of theological paradoxes, for certainty in a time of cultural upheaval. But of course paradoxes resist definitive resolution. And so the same theological controversies that demanded unwavering certainty served to highlight the inherent undecidability of Christian mystery, further developing the receptivity to paradox characteristic of the age.

Even the sixteenth-century Church of England reflects the polarization of experience informing various Renaissance discursive modes. The church was not a settled structure with broad popular support for a centrist orthodoxy but an inherently unstable blend of opposing elements. Despite her rhetoric to the contrary, Elizabeth exploited the via media not as a stable place, an ideal mean, but as a practical strategy for negotiating the dangerous extremes of radical Protestantism and Roman Catholicism.[85] The Church of England was able to survive in a state of tension for a few generations, at least, fending off the ever-present threat of civil war, largely because of Elizabeth's political finesse and her personal ability to inspire some degree of national and ecclesiastical solidarity. Of course, the same can hardly be said of James I, much less Charles I.

The conflicting impulses that were held together uneasily in the Church of England came to a head in the middle of the seventeenth century, but for a while the precarious balancing act of the Elizabethan Settlement worked. During that time the urge toward definitve structure often took the form of theological polemics that seem startling today in their vituperative energy. The fliting rhetoric of these polemics becomes understandable, though, when one grasps what was at stake: the delineation of a whole new way of perceiving the world.

As I have already mentioned in passing, more than one scholar has located the period's incessant polemics in the shift from the aural/oral "sensorium" of the ancient and medieval worlds to the visually-centered print culture of the modern age.[86] The next two chapters will examine some of the roles of the ear and the eye in pulpit performances, both polemic and irenic. Here it is enough to point out that during the Renaissance the habit of embracing antithetical terms shifted into polemical use. The antitheses that had expressed the deepest mysteries of God and self became imagined enemies, "others" in contrast to whom the self was defined.[87]

When William Symonds, for example, preached a sermon in 1609 to a group of adventurers and planters about to embark for Virginia, he justified the new enterprise by defining its value in the face of some imagined "objectors." He describes one set of objectors as influenced by

> the devil himself, with all his distinctions that ever he made, which are recorded in scripture or which he left in hell, in his cabinet of *Abstruse Studies* (locked safe, till he found out the Jesuits his trusty secretaries to keep them).[88]

The other set, says Symonds, are "objectors that come dropping out of some Anabaptist's spicery" (13). The characterization of these two enemies, the Jesuit and the Anabaptist, is typical of the polemics that tend to arise from within the Church of England when the urge toward definition rather than suspension of antitheses informs the speaker's rhetoric. Symonds is defining a position, making distinctions, even as he denigrates the abstruse distinctions of the Jesuits and the objections of the Anabaptists. Even if the depiction of his enemies is a mere caricature of real Jesuits and Anabaptists, Symonds's perception of the extremes against which he must define his views is indicative of the mentality that tends toward a definitive rhetoric in a time of cultural crisis.

Hieron registers a similar uneasiness in his dialogue *The Preachers Plea*, which he writes to answer two objections:

> The one is, What need all this preaching? The other is, Who knoweth whom to believe among these Preachers? These two demands were first hatched in hell, but since being cherished by Anabaptistical and Popish spirits, and by them buzzed into the heads of unlearned, unstable, and irreligious people, they are brought unto a devilish perfection. (sig. A3ᵛ)

Hieron's defensiveness about sermons, as reflected in his anxiety about the source and character of objections to preaching, provides an index of the sermon's performative potential.

Especially those Renaissance performances that center on paradox both reflect and negotiate the widespread anxiety that characterizes any moment of epistemic crisis. As a number of commentators have suggested, perhaps one reason the connections between the late twentieth century and the late sixteenth seem so compelling is that the two ages are similar in their epistemological liminality.[89] In any case it is clear (in hindsight, at least) that cultural performances centering on paradox in the early modern period invite two radically distinct forms of communal response as a way of negotiating the passage from a medieval to a modern sensibility. Either response can be called a resolution of the contradiction, as long as it is remembered that paradoxes can be resolved experientially but not logically, and that the term "resolution" does not imply final closure, as though the energies of paradox were used up once one experienced an artistic presentation of those energies. A paradox is not like a riddle, in which the tension is forever slackened once the solution has been realized. Paradoxes remain open-ended, problematic, challenging. But performative presentations of such contradictions hold out the possibility of an experiential resolution, however partial or fleeting. As the following chapters will demonstrate, the Renaissance stage play and the Reformation sermon offer themselves as particularly effective ways of resolving—or at least promising to resolve— the contradictions endemic to the culture.

PART I

Polemics and Irenics at Paul's Cross

2. The Pulpit Performance and the Two-Edged Sword

I

Three years before Shakespeare was born, a dramatic incident sparked a polemic exchange between the Protestant bishop James Pilkington and the staunch Catholic John Morwen. Polemic exchanges, of course, were hardly rare in those days, but this one arose out of a rare event: it seemed that God had raised his hand against his own house, causing lightning to strike and burn the steeple of St. Paul's Cathedral. On June 8, 1561, shortly after the incident, Pilkington devoted his Paul's Cross sermon to an explanation of why God had chosen to reveal his wrath so emphatically: the cause was the people's superstition and ignorance. By their refusal to give up their popish ways, Pilkington said, they profaned God's sanctuary to such a degree that the wrath of the Almighty was kindled. Nor could the people expect a return to the days of God's mercy until the whole realm had repented, showing "humble obedience of the laws and superior powers" of Protestant England.[1] This was too much for Morwen. He replied with *An Addicioun, with an Appologie to the Causes of the Brinninge of Paules Church*, explaining the real reason for the visitation of God's disfavor: the fire was both a call for all of England to return to the old faith and a warning that a greater plague awaited an unrepentant nation (647–48). Pilkington responded with *A Confutation*, but the exchange ended there.[2]

The question, it seems, was not *whether* God was involved in the destruction, but *whose* God. A single event was given two interpretations that must have seemed to their adherents radically different, each with its own implications for defining the body of true believers. Yet Pilkington and Morwen are alike in reflecting a pervasive cultural anxiety about interpretation in general. Both are on the attack, but only because both are on the defensive. The imagined enemy—Papist or Protestant—represents a threat to what both sides see as a centuries-old epistemic privilege: the ability to read the book of the world. The relentless polemics in the early modern period's numerous calls to arms arise out of a general crisis of signification. Even in their militant insistence on staking out ideological ground in the emerging world, theologians like Pilkington and Morwen still participate in medieval sacramental patterns of thought: something like a bolt of lightning is not an isolated meteorological event but a bearer of a divine message. Yet the relation between the divine and the social seems radically threatened. It is by no means clear who is empowered to interpret signs of the divine will, and so all who have a stake in the matter take up public defensive postures. In performative terms, the participants take on roles in the social drama that negotiates the crisis.

II

The rhetorical relations between Renaissance sermons and plays can be described in anthropological terms. The two modes are related in their complementary responses to the widespread demand for ritualistic performances that provided a sense of orientation in a world of dizzying change.[3] Whether the "cultural performance" is that of a sermon or a play, in each case the performance allows the spectator to respond to a social crisis that might otherwise seem impossible to resolve.[4] If, as Steven Mullaney, Louis Montrose, and others have argued, Shakespeare's theater performs a vital social function in helping the audience adjust to and control the ambiguities arising out of the epistemological crisis of early modern England, the same can be said of the Reformation sermon.[5] At a time when whole areas of the medieval epistemic system were being replaced by new ways of knowing, the sermon—like the stage play—performed a vital cultural task. In fact the two modes often performed the same kind of task, and they often performed it similarly.

It is difficult in the twentieth century to appreciate the cultural shock that accompanied the suspension of ritual in the early days of the Church of England. Because the Protestant reformers were successful in purging the English liturgy of the "theatrical" ceremony of enacted sacrifice, a sort of liturgical vacuum resulted.[6] People in a culture still very much sacramental in mentality suddenly had to do without some of the ritualistic forms that had been central to their very orientation as human beings. In his analysis of the results of this process, Michael O'Connell makes an intriguing observation:

To an articulate part of [the religious] elite [the theater] appeared religiously atavistic, dangerously so, and able to appeal to sensibilities that should properly have atrophied in the reform of religion. The popularity of the London theaters testifies to the survival of those sensibilities, even as the reform was successful in eliminating them from worship. Theater was not worship, but as a cultural institution, its roots lay deep in the centuries in which it had performed a religious function. Its status was ambiguous in the late sixteenth and early seventeenth centuries—not religious in the same sense it had been, and yet, in the terms by which the culture defined it, not secular either.[7]

O'Connell is quite right that the theater as aesthetic and secular is a post-Renaissance phenomenon, and he argues compellingly that some of the theatricality of Roman Catholicism was displaced onto the Renaissance stage. What is missing from O'Connell's analysis, though, is an account of the ways in which the Protestant movement itself incorporated and transformed Roman Catholic ritual.[8] As I have suggested, the preachers of Reformation England took on an authoritative role as mediators of sacred mystery—the role that the priests of the old order had performed not as much by preaching as by celebrating the sacrificial mass and administering the other sacraments. The Protestant insistence on a commemorative rather than a sacrificial liturgy, together with the elimination of all the other sacraments except baptism, vastly reduced the ritualistic, performative dimensions of Protestant religious life. One result was that the Protestant sermon naturally took on some of the ritual force, some of the theatricality, that it was meant to replace.

The Reformation sermon, like the Renaissance play, is not merely a static reflection of ideology, nor is it merely a manipulative didactic device. While both modes of course have ideological import and didactic elements, the ritualistic dimension of both goes beyond the reflection and inculcation of established dogma. As Clifford Geertz observes, ritualistic social structures are neither purely aesthetic nor purely functional but something in between.[9] Such is certainly the case with cultural performances like sermons and stage plays, which involve a cognitive and affective response from the audience. Typically this response takes one of two forms: it yields either the reinforcement of a polemic position or the effacement of such positions.

The process can be described in terms of Victor Turner's cultural anthropology. Turner argues that cultural performances, whether in the ritual enactments of tribal cultures or the ludic pastimes of industrialized societies, develop in the redressive phase of social dramas. That is, a period of widespread social disruption like the Reformation generates performances that evoke some sort of resolution to the anxiety brought on by the disruptive breach in social relations. This resolution typically takes one of two forms: social experiences involving the reception of ritual performances tend toward either "structure" or "communitas." Turner explains the difference:

> the bonds of communitas are anti-structural in that they are undifferentiated, equalitarian, direct, nonrational (though not *ir*rational), I-Thou or Essential We relationships, in Martin Buber's sense. Structure is all that holds people apart, defines their differences, and constrains their actions.[10]

Communitas is most evident in the "liminal" phase of the ritual process (one thinks of Homi Bhabha's "inbetween"), the period of transition between separation from and reintegration into structured society.[11] Insofar as drama participates in the liminality of ritual,[12] one can speak of the prevailing rhetoric of a play as stressing either the structured definitions of reëntry into the ordinary world or the protean instability that marks the transitional world of communitas. The same is true of sermons.

Another of Turner's insights is helpful in understanding how sermons and plays generate their rhetorical force. According to Turner, one aspect of social dramas is their tendency to bring a culture's "root paradigms" to the surface. Root paradigms are "cultural models in the heads of the main actors" in social dramas (*Dramas, Fields, and Metaphors*, 64). It is a culture's root paradigms, Turner says, that inform and interpret the relations between these actors, inclining the relationships to either divisiveness or alliance. A single root paradigm has the rhetorical potential to divide or unite, to bring war or peace. Although root paradigms emerge for examination and reaffirmation during the crises of social dramas, they ordinarily stay beneath the surface of social discourse, finding articulation only indirectly:

> These root paradigms are not systems of univocal concepts, logically arrayed; they are not, so to speak, precision tools of thought. Nor are they stereotyped guidelines for ethical, esthetic, or conventional action. Indeed, they go beyond the cognitive and even the moral to the existential domain, and in so doing become clothed with allusiveness, implicitness, and metaphor. (64)

According to Turner the central root paradigm in European culture is essentially sacrificial, involving the individual's death to "selfhood" as a response to Christ's martyrdom. Turner argues that social dramas in the

Western tradition tend to evoke the sacrificial paradigm, even if obliquely, drawing on its energies to resolve crises.

One of the most striking aspects of a culture's root paradigms is that any focal symbol growing out of a paradigm is "numinous" because it is paradoxical, "a coincidence of opposites, a semantic structure in tension between opposite poles of meaning."[13] The Eucharist, for example, embodies both death and life for the believer, who vicariously participates in Christ's death and resurrection every time the elements are received. In periods of crisis the paradoxical status of root paradigms is reinforced and heightened. As a result, performative negotiations of the crisis tend toward either a conscious embracing of the paradox in all its contradictoriness or a resolution of the paradox into one of its contrary principles. That is, these performances either maintain or slacken the paradoxical tension. It seems that this tension must be maintained if a root paradigm is to retain its power to shape the responses to social dramas. If not, a new paradigm, a new *episteme*, eventually replaces the old.

Such a dynamic helps to explain the relentlessly militant tenor of so much Renaissance discourse, not to mention historical events. Certain plays and sermons are figuratively (and sometimes literally) calls to arms: they define the enemy and inspire the audience to take up arms—that is, adopt an ideologically exclusive posture. Other plays and sermons respond to this rhetoric by calling for its opposite: a disarming recognition of human solidarity, a posture that effaces the distinctions of the more militant ideologies.

III

For the audiences of the time, performances on the stage as well as in the pulpit take on a good deal of their rhetorical force from their resonance with the Christian story. This is the case with the so-called "secular" drama of the age as well as the sacred. A culture's central myths inform its art even in times (perhaps especially in times) of cultural upheaval—times when a social drama like the Reformation calls into question the traditional ways of orienting the self in relation to those myths. In such times a polemical rhetoric develops in response to disoriented groups' demand for definition and order; and in dialectic with this process, an irenic rhetoric emerges to efface the rigid boundaries between ideological categories.[14]

The theater provides a particularly effective forum for this cultural dialectic. A sort of microcosm of the larger social drama, the Renaissance play presents characters in dialogic response to a crisis that opens the possibilities of both kinds of rhetoric. The audience's experience of the play is controlled by the characters' reactions to the crisis. Of course individual members of the audience can and do respond in different ways, but one can still speak of a play's prevailing rhetoric as ideologically polemic or irenic. Since both principles perform a vital social function—ideological definition on the one hand and human solidarity on the other—it makes sense to speak of both drama and theology as engaging the audience's basic existential needs.

Both principles can be found in Shakespeare. While most of his plays tend toward irenic rhetoric (think of the way, say, *King Lear* or *The Winter's Tale* resists any sort of ideologically definitive response), a play like *Henry V* is notorious for its divisive effect on audiences; commentators on the play are divided into two well-defined camps. It seems that Henry is either an ideal monarch or a ruthless hypocrite, and it is nearly impossible to reconcile these two views in a single vision.[15]

On the theological side, a good example of the split between irenic and polemic rhetoric is the exchange between Erasmus and Luther on free will. While Erasmus entitles his treatise *De libero arbitrio, diatribe sive collatio*, his half of the exchange is hardly the heated invective that the word "diatribe" connotes today; Erasmus draws on the classical tradition of diatribe as reasoned investigation, playing the role of the peace-seeking inquirer rather than the dogmatist.[16] He approaches the exchange with Luther very much in the spirit of the *sermo*, or conversation. But for Luther the conversation must have a polemic edge: "the divine *sermo* descends only to convict and change the world."[17] Luther's side of the exchange is a diatribe in the modern sense.

Luther's divisive style found a readier audience in the early sixteenth century than did Erasmus's conciliatory approach. This preference for polemics is reflected not only in the period's theology but also in its drama. In fact, the stage and the pulpit are mutually influential forces both in nurturing a receptivity polemic discourse and in providing performative resolutions to deep-seated ambiguities of early modern culture. If Shakespeare's *Henry V* and Luther's *De servo arbitrio* dare the individual to choose between two opposing camps, the dare is an endemic cultural principle.

IV

As I argued in the introductory chapter, Renaissance sermons and plays are closely related, especially in their facility for providing performative resolutions to paradox. The readiness on the part of both preachers and playwrights to address paradoxical issues is particularly acute in late sixteenth-century England in part because the age is simultaneously informed by two impulses: the insistence on maintaining the tension of Christian paradox and the slackening of that tension by reducing Christian paradox to one of its constituent contraries. The failure of attempts to reconcile these two opposing impulses eventually signals the abandonment of the whole enterprise and the development of a new human orientation to the world: the secular self-assertion characteristic of the modern age.[18]

In the sixteenth and seventeenth centuries, however, the preachers took the lead in negotiating the period's protracted crisis of self-definition. When Reformation preachers define their own roles, they frequently do so in militaristic terms. As John Donne puts it, "Preaching is God's ordinance; with that ordinance he fights from heaven, and batters down all errors."[19] Stephen Gosson complicates the traditional image of the Church as a ship weathering the world's storms by adding a second vessel, the devil's pirate ship in hot pursuit of the elect. But the ship of the faithful, like the pirate vessel, is a man-of-war. If Christ is the Captain, his cross the mast, his sanctimony the sails, his patience and perseverance the tackle, he depends on his preachers for gunfire: they are his "cast pieces" whose "sound hath been hard [sic] over all the world."[20] Or, as Gosson says in the same sermon, "preaching is hail-shot; we send it among the thickest of you, desirous to hit you all" (G6ʳ). As Sampson Price claims in a 1613 sermon, the "holy violence" of pulpit performances dates from the early days of the Reformation; Price praises Luther, who "knew that the kingdom of God was to be got with *violence*. He remembered that of Christ, He that is not with me, is against me: He that gathereth not with me, scattereth."[21]

The urge to gather the elect into a readily identifiable community fuels a good deal of the controversy over church polity throughout the Elizabethan period. The ecclesiastical authorities' continual thwarting of the widespread movement for presbyterian reform left many believers convinced that there were no broad social structures to support their beliefs. In the absence of such supports, English reformers used what weapons they had at hand—the stage, the printing press, and the sermon—both to define their own social roles and to move their audiences toward similar self-definition. It was John Foxe, the English Protestant martyrologist, who said of an obstinate bishop,

> He thwarteth and wrangleth much against players, printers, preachers. And no marvel why; for he seeth these three things to be set up of God, as a triple bulwark against the triple crown of the Pope to bring him down; as, God be praised, they have done meetly well already.[22]

Players, printers, preachers: the Word in all its available forms was marshaled against the enemy—here embodied in the Pope. Foxe's statement is instructive both in its easy acceptance of the cultural continuities between sermons and stage plays and in its polemic force. Rhetoric such as Foxe's typically encourages an audience to form an identity in contrast to that of some opposing group—real or imagined. Thus sixteenth-century English sermons are filled with militant invectives against Roman Catholics; against such radical Protestant groups as Anabaptists, Brownists, and the Family of Love; against atheists.[23]

Such polemic rhetoric is nowhere more apparent than in the open-air sermons at Paul's Cross, where the most famous preachers in England were invited to perform before audiences of as many as six thousand.[24] As the sermons at Paul's Cross typically lasted for two hours, twice the usual length of Elizabethan sermons, the preacher had to do everything in his power to hold the attention of an audience that tended to be unruly—so much so that the royally appointed authors of the 1552 *Reformatio Legum Ecclesiasticarum* were obliged to include the following proviso not just for the Paul's Cross sermons but also for ordinary church services:

> If there are any people of such rudeness that, while the preacher is still speaking from the pulpit, they wish to raise an outcry, or interrupt him or rail at him in some manner, they are to be separated from the Church and separated from communion with it until they openly acknowledge the crime and have returned to their senses. In the same way, whoever either by aimlessly walking about, or by inopportunely chattering, or by walking out of the sacred assemblage in such a way that contempt of the sermon or of the preacher can be detected or who knowingly and willingly turns the people's attention away from the sermon in any way whatsoever or disturbs them, will pay the merited penalties for this kind of wicked frivolity.[25]

Francis Marbury also complains of this "wicked frivolity":

> And it were to be wished that some even of those which resort to Paul's Cross
> and will not come at their own church, and when they are here delude the law
> with walking and talking, were better ordered.[26]

The audiences at sermons, it seems, were sometimes as disruptive as the crowds at the playhouses.

Even the physical setting of Paul's Cross is remarkably similar to that of the Elizabethan public theaters: ordinary Londoners milled about in the churchyard of St. Paul's, while the gallery seats in the main structure of the Cathedral itself were reserved for members of the Court. Well-to-do citizens got seats on or near the wooden stage where the preacher stood when he descended from the pulpit for the ritualistic drama of public penance. In these services the preacher shared the stage with a public penitent who wore a white sheet and carried a taper and faggots representing the death by fire that sinners deserved. Offenses ranged from disapproval of Henry VIII's divorce from Catherine of Aragon (for which Elizabeth Barton and some companions were hanged after having done penance), to a priest's consecrating ale rather than wine at a mass (1536), to another priest's counterfeiting the blood of Christ (he had cut his own finger, making it bleed on the Host at a 1545 mass, and so was made to wear a red-spotted gown during his penance), to one Putto's denial in 1549 of Christ's descent into hell (Putto had to do penance twice since the first time he had neglected to remove his cap), to conjuring (1549), to counterfeiting "a voice in a wall" that spoke during Queen Mary's reign against the mass and the king of Spain (1554), to bigamy (1560), to a minister's consorting with women of ill repute, including one Green Apron (1570).[27] Even if the penitent was to be pardoned, he had to endure the jeers of the crowd and, sometimes, the blows of the preacher wielding the "rod of correction."[28] The audience was thus encouraged to identify with the godly preacher and to reinforce this identification by vilifying the sinner.[29] As Millar MacLure says of the whole scene's theatricality, "A sermon at Paul's Cross, accompanied by the speech and act of the penitent, was a morality play, or rather life exhibited as a morality" (16). The Paul's Cross sermons served a function simultaneously religious and theatrical: expounding Christian doctrine and practice by engaging the audience in an individual's dramatic predicament.

Even a summary reading of the extant texts of these sermons reveals a pervasive tendency in the late Tudor/ early Stuart period to use the Paul's Cross stage to launch verbal attacks. Thus, Rozett notes, even when the focus was not on an act of public penance, the sermons served the polemic, dramatic function of denouncing an enemy—an "other"—albeit an enemy absent from the stage (41). And frequently even the enemies got a chance to defend themselves; since preachers of virtually every theological persuasion were invited by the ecclesiastical authorities (who were themselves a varied group) to speak at Paul's Cross, a good many of the sermons were counterattacks on previous ones. As MacLure says of the long series of accusations, replies, and confutations, "No summary of arguments, no collection of excerpts, can convey the insistence, the overwhelmingly tedious energy of these tirades from the Paul's Cross pulpit" (65). The Elizabethans' truly remarkable appetite for sermons might seem all the more striking in light of this "tedious energy," but in fact the sermons' polemical rhetoric helps to explain their popularity. In an age that confronts a new epistemology, a whole new human orientation in the world, one should expect a ready appetite for polemic performances; the need for order, for ideological definition, is insistent in a time of epistemic change.

In such circumstances it is not surprising that occasional fights broke out in the congregation at Paul's Cross.[30] The preachers themselves were hardly safe. Not long after August 6, 1553, when John Rogers vehemently attacked popery from the Paul's Cross pulpit, he became the first of the Marian martyrs. The Sunday after Rogers's sermon, the crowd attacked Gilbert Bourne for praising Edmund Bonner, Queen Mary's ruthless right-hand man. The next week Thomas Watson preached a sermon demanding order and obedience to the Queen. Watson emerged unscathed, no doubt due to the 200-member Queen's Guard who surrounded him. A few months later someone in the crowd shot at Bonner's chaplain Henry Pendleton as he preached. The bullet narrowly missed not only Pendleton but also the Lord Mayor.[31]

The danger of preaching at Paul's Cross did not end with the accession of Elizabeth. When Edmund Grindal prevailed on the very popular John Foxe to preach in 1570, Foxe attempted in a letter to the Archbishop to beg off: "I shall be received with derision, and driven away by the hisses of the auditory."[32] The same year Edwin Sandys preached at Paul's Cross upon his appointment as Bishop of London. He complained of the danger attendant on the office, a danger directly related to the bishop's central function as a preacher:

[The bishopric] is an office full of peril and danger. For if we preach things pleasant unto men, we discharge not the duty of the servants of God: if we preach his truth, we are hated as their deadly enemies to whom we preach.[33]

Situating himself in the prophetic tradition is perhaps a preëmptive rhetorical move on Sandys's part, an attempt to disarm his opponents from the start. But it is not *mere* rhetoric; the opposition was very real.

The danger of preaching persisted into the early decades of the seventeenth century. A 1633 letter from Archbishop William Laud to Richard Sterne illustrates the degree of official control (including a reduction of the allotted time for the sermon) that had come to seem necessary:

> You shall understand that you are appointed to preach at St. Paul's Cross on Sunday, the seventeenth day of November next ensuing, by discreet performance whereof you shall do good service to God, the King's Majesty, and the Church. These are therefore to require and charge you, not to fail of your day appointed, and to send notice of your acceptance in writing . . ., to bring a copy of your sermon with you, and not to exceed an hour and a half in both sermon and prayer . . . . And hereof fail not, as you will answer to the contrary at your peril.[34]

Despite Laud's efforts at control, ten years later zealous reformers physically dismantled the Paul's Cross pulpit. In the year before the demolition, and for similar reasons, the theaters had been closed. Because the performances at Paul's Cross and the secular theaters carried the potential to incite anti-Puritan sentiment, both institutions seemed a threat to the emergent regime. Yet to no small degree the emerging mentality had been shaped by the pulpit performances of the day. An examination of one frequently employed tactic sheds light on the process.

V

In the service of ideological definition, preachers at Paul's Cross and elsewhere frequently employed the *topos* of the two-edged sword. According to this idea, one function of the word of God is to drive a wedge between the elect and the reprobate, making the former better and the latter worse. The principle derives in part from Hebrews 4:12, which reads,

> For the word of God is lively, and mighty in operation, and sharper than any two-edged sword, and entereth through, even unto the dividing asunder of the soul and the spirit, and of the joints and the marrow, and is a discerner of the thoughts and intents of the heart.[35]

Commenting on this passage, George Gifford's spokesman in his dialogue *The Countrie Divinitie* says,

> by whomsoever this sword of the spirit be drawn forth, if it be rightly handled, it will pierce through, and through both the bodies and souls of the hearers, and will move every vein in the heart, even of the wicked.[36]

The two-edged sword leads the wicked not to repent their wickedness but simply to know that they are wicked. As Luther says in his *Lectures on Romans*, God "gives commands that the elect might fulfill them and the reprobate be enmeshed in them."[37] Henry Smith expands on the idea:

> Christ saith that men hear the word to their salvation or their damnation, "The word which I have spoken shall judge you in the latter day," John xii. It is called "the savour of life," because it saveth; and it is called "the savour of death," because it condemneth, 2. Cor. ii.16.[38]

Richard Bancroft also warns of the "giddy spirits" who "do wrest the Scriptures unto their own destruction."[39] The principle is the same whether the word of God is recorded in Scripture or expounded from the pulpit. George Abbot, for example, compares the preacher's utterance of the word of God to the sun, which "being one, doth give light to many, and doth harden the clay and yet soften the wax, and maketh the flowers to smell better, and dead carrion to savour worse."[40] No doubt very few in Abbot's congregation were quick to identify themselves as carrion, but imagining others who fit the description might not have been so difficult. In this way the rhetoric of the two-edged sword works to reinforce social distinctions based upon the identification of the elect.

William Perkins expands on the idea, explaining that preaching has "a two-fold use: one, in that it serveth to collect the church, and to accomplish the number of the Elect; the other, for that it driveth away the Wolves from the fold of the Lord."[41] This public discrimination of sheep and wolves is made possible by "binding the conscience," one of the primary offices of preaching: "To bind the conscience is to constrain it either to accuse us or to excuse us of sin before God" (732).

The power to ease or convict the conscience through performance is remarkably similar to one traditional defense of poetry in general and drama in particular. As John Taylor says in the prefatory verses to Heywood's *An Apology for Actors*, "A play's a true transparent crystal mirror, / To shew good minds their mirth, the bad their terror."[42] Heywood himself confirms the claim that the guiltless need not fear the rhetorical power of the drama while the guilty have every reason to fear. He cites actual examples of audience members who have confessed their guilt upon witnessing staged presentations of similar crimes. Those innocent of such crimes, however, will respond with reason rather than emotion.[43] Heywood's opponent, I. G., is much less sanguine about the prospect of anyone's remaining virtuous in the presence of staged villainy. He cites counterexamples of the theater's corrupting influence.[44] Interestingly, where Heywood assumes a stable identity for each member of the audience, an identity that is *revealed* by the fictive action, I. G. takes seriously the drama's power to *shape* identity. It is the opponent of the theater, not its defender, who acknowledges its transformative rhetorical power.

Shakespeare of course complicates the issue by staging the performative "binding of the conscience" in a play within a play: Hamlet's *Mousetrap* indeed reveals the conscience of the King, but just what effect the revelation has on the action is uncertain. Not only does *The Mousetrap* tip Hamlet's hand to his enemy; it also leads to Claudius's abortive attempt at repentance and Hamlet's mistaking of outward sign for inner conviction.[45] Meanwhile, the audience knows that Claudius is guilty but doesn't know what to make of Hamlet's insistence on sending his uncle to hell rather than heaven. Where does the insistence leave the hero's conscience? Or the audience's?

The prospect of such interpretive ambiguity is extremely disconcerting for a good many of Shakespeare's contemporaries, who want to see allegiances clearly declared. Sampson Price, for example, urges his congregation, "Be either a whole Protestant or a Papist" (36). Price is suspicious of middle ground, of mixtures of virtue and vice: "The open sinner revealeth himself that we may avoid him, but the Neuter walketh so secretly that we know not how to judge him; therefore they are more odious than the other" (24). The central issue is discrimination, and the real danger is the disturbingly ungendered one who walks in secret. Price's use of the term "Neuter" for his imagined enemy registers his uneasiness with synthesis, his desire to render unstable the conjunction of opposites. For Price, the ungendered center cannot—or ought not—hold. The role of the preacher is to bring this subversive secret into the open, to expose its workings as unnatural, to resolve the social world into binary forces:

> How shall we escape if we neglect so great salvation? [God] will spew us out of his mouth if we dissemble before him. Let us then now at the last *separate*

> light from darkness, God from an *Idol*, the Israelites from the Canaanites, the
> precious from the vile, the believers from Infidels, Protestants from Papists.
> (49–50)

The separation to take place "now at the last" is apocalyptic, bringing full circle the divine plan for earthly history: the separation of light from darkness at the dawn of time finds its culmination in the separation of light from darkness in the human community. Price's rhetoric serves both to embrace and to efface history, moving from the first act of creation through the biblical period (Israelites and Canaanites) even as it implies that separation is somehow inherent in the eternal nature of things. Here the rhetoric of the two-edged sword brings cosmic focus to a social problem.

In effect, the call to arms implicit in the use of this *topos* functions to transfer a matter of private devotion (the two-edged sword is "a discerner of the thoughts and intents of the heart") into the public realm. The Word does not simply appeal to the hearer's conscience, convicting the believer of unspiritual intentions, but encourages ideological armament in the service of social discrimination. This function of the pulpit performance helps to account for the rapid development in the late Elizabethan period of the desire to find outward, socially recognizable *signs* of election.

Protestant thinkers in the late sixteenth century become increasingly concerned not with justification—the atoning bond between God and the believer brought about by faith—but with the process of sanctification—steady improvement in one's outward conduct. While all sixteenth-century Protestants agree in theory that sanctification is always a result, and never a cause, of justification, in practice the concern for sanctification leads to a new pietism. The works-oriented theology so abhorrent to Luther reëmerges in full force within two generations of his death. It seems to have been all but impossible for most believers to adhere to Luther's vision of works as *mere* signs of election. The twelfth of the Prayer Book's Thirty-Nine Articles of Religion registers the tension that these believers found impossible to sustain:

> Albeit that good works, which are the fruits of faith, and follow after justification, cannot put away our sins, and endure the severity of God's judgment; yet are they pleasing and acceptable to God in Christ, and do spring out necessarily of a true and lively faith; insomuch that by them a lively faith may be as evidently known as a tree discerned by the fruit.[46]

Good works both "endure the severity of God's judgment" and are "pleasing and acceptable to God." These paradoxical signs of a lively faith are described variously by various preachers, often in both public and private terms.

Since the private signs are on the whole more difficult to sustain than the public, a tendency shared (perhaps unconsciously) by preachers and congregations is to look to the public signs as normative. While Protestantism unquestionably issues in a tendency toward introspection, toward the individual's internalized processing of the mysteries of the faith, the difficulty of maintaining interior equanimity opens on a countermovement: the preacher's rhetoric invites public resolution of internal anxieties. Jean Taffin, for example, lists among the inward signs of election the Holy Ghost's testimony in one's heart, a feeling of justification, and peace of conscience.[47] But what of the one who at one time or another perceives nothing of the Holy Ghost's presence, who has no feeling of justification, who has no peace of conscience? Taffin reminds such believers that public works of charity remain as signs of election. Among the signs of reprobation Arthur Dent lists not only swearing, whoring, and idleness, but also "cold prayers."[48] Reformation theologians develop such lists of signs in order to offer assurance to the elect, but these very signs can produce the opposite effect, troubling the believers they are supposed to comfort.[49] Can anyone be truly confident, for example, of maintaining at all times a feeling of inner peace, never finding prayer "cold"? Has anyone truly attained the inner spiritual perfection that should inevitably follow upon justification? In short, can anyone claim to be truly sanctified? Yet as Francis Marbury makes plain in a Paul's Cross sermon, the stakes of such a question are high, nothing less than the individual's eternal fate: "We may be well assured that the Spirit of God worketh not effectually in us if our affections be cold in turning unto him" (C1r). The rhetorical pressure applied in sermons employing the two-edged sword *topos* would be unbearable if resolution were confined to the private realm. The public arena, though, offers hope for definitive resolution: pious acts clearly distinguish the saved from the damned.

The preacher's role as mediator in this process is crucial. In the public utterance of the sermon, the two-edged force of the preacher's rhetoric marks off for the hearer what Richard Helgerson (following Benedict Anderson) calls an "imagined community" of believers.[50] This imagined community clearly overlaps but is not congruent with the political community of the English nation—a fact that the Prayer Book itself reinforces even as the liturgical uniformity it fosters functions as a nation-building tool. For example, the Thirty-Nine Articles employ the two-edged sword *topos* in the longest of the articles, the one concerning predestination:

> As the godly consideration of predestination, and of our election in Christ, is
> full of sweet, pleasant, and unspeakable comfort to godly persons, and such
> as feel in themselves the working of the Spirit of Christ . . ., so, for curious
> and carnal persons, lacking the Spirit of Christ, to have continually before
> their eyes the sentence of God's predestination, is a most dangerous downfall,
> whereby the Devil doth thrust them either into desperation, or into wretched-
> ness of most unclean living, no less perilous than desperation. (Article 17)

God's single decree works two ways, producing opposite effects on the
elect and the reprobate. Not surprisingly, the elect are those who find
the doctrine of election sweet and comforting: that is, the elect are the
thoroughgoing Calvinists. As George Gifford's spokesman says in *The
Countrie Divinitie*, "If the scripture speak any thing to the comfort of
the sorrowful heart, the devil doth teach the impenitent for to abuse it to
their hardening" (67^r).

If godly doctrine has a double-edged force, so does heresy. According
to John Knewstub, frequent polemicist against the Family of Love as well
as the Church of Rome,

> "There must be heresies" (sayeth Saint Paul) "even amnong you, that they
> which are proved among you may be known." The causes why it must be thus
> with the Church, do I find in the scripture to be these: that the good may be
> tried and known: and the wicked found out and punished.[51]

It is not only the word—whether godly or heretical—that has a
double-edged force, but also the Eucharist. As John Denison, chaplain to
both Buckingham and King James, says in a 1619 sermon,

> the blessed Sacrament is the bread of life, and as a sanctuary of comfort to a
> sanctified heart, but to the wicked and profane, it is the bane of their souls,
> and a gulf of eternal perdition.[52]

Once again we find a tremendous pressure to define oneself as possessing
a "sanctified heart." The hearer is encouraged not only to be introspective,
to search diligently for a feeling of assurance, but also to look for outward
signs of sanctification. Richard Rogers speaks for a whole generation when
he says, "I say, give no rest to your selves, till you can prove that you be
in the estate of salvation."[53] One sign of such proof, of course, is vigorous
participation in the community of the godly; association with the visible
body of believers implies membership in the invisible, eternal church. But
the overwhelmingly militant tenor of the theological disputes calls into

question the qualifications for membership in even the visible church.

In fact, during the course of the sixteenth century an increasing proportion of English Protestants set out to solve the problem by equating the visible church with the invisible, developing a narrower and narrower set of criteria for membership.[54] Among the second and third generations of Calvinists, hair-splitting distinctions frequently inform definitions of proper Christian doctrine as well as practice. Examples of this mentality could easily be multiplied, but here it will perhaps be enough to cite a theologian enormously influential in Elizabethan England: Theodore Beza, Calvin's successor at Geneva. Beza defends the doctrine of predestination against what he calls a "slander of the papists"—that is, the slanderous accusation that Calvinists make the following claim: "God in the bare and alone determination of his will hath created the greatest part of the world to perdition."[55] According to Beza, the accusation is slanderous not because it claims that God predestined most souls to damnation—an idea Beza readily accepts—but because it uses the phrase "bare and alone determination" rather than "just and alone determination" (10). And yet, even as he asserts God's justice, Beza denies that God is bound by any categories, including justice, external to his own will. The difference between a "bare" determination and a "just" one, then, becomes exceedingly difficult to comprehend. Beza is making a distinction that can have meant little to most theologians, let alone ordinary believers, and yet he is using the distinction to judge between true and false believers, insisting that the truly faithful will adhere to the proper doctrine. And nothing less than one's eternal salvation depends upon adherence to such narrowly defined ideas. It is easy for those who think otherwise to be seen as the enemy. Here, as in much of the polemic religious literature of the day, a militant divisiveness is in full force.

The period's insistence on social definition through theological definition inevitably highlights those articles of the faith that resist definition: the Christian paradoxes. An example is Luther's insistence on the believer's simultaneous saintliness and sinfulness:

> Thus a Christian man is righteous and a sinner at the same time, holy and profane, an enemy of God and a child of God. None of the sophists will admit this paradox, because they do not understand the true meaning of justification. (*Works*, 26:232–33)

As Stephen Ozment argues, many found the psychological strain of self-consciously attempting to embrace such a paradox unbearable.[56] As a result, within fifty years of Luther's death Protestant Europe saw a wave of attempts to lessen the paradoxical tension implicit in the faith. In England this broad cultural tendency can be discerned not only among Puritan theologians but also among the very playwrights who had declared themselves enemies of Puritanism.

When a paradox like that of the believer as simultaneous saint and sinner breaks down, the result is an either/or mentality, a vision of a world clearly divided into sheep and goats, believers and infidels, insiders and outsiders: Sampson Price's mutually exclusive communities that leave no quarter for the "neuter." The tendency toward exclusiveness among the Puritans is well known from contemporary satiric portraits of them. But as I will argue in Chapter 4, it is not only the Puritans, so effectively satirized by playwrights like Ben Jonson, who participate in this mentality; the satiric playwrights themselves contribute to the exclusivist rhetoric that is so characteristic a feature of Reformation England.

Another divisive question was whether one should pray that all might be saved. Luther held that since God himself desires universal salvation, one should pray for all souls even though universal salvation is impossible.[57] Despite a clear biblical injunction to pray for all souls, though, it seemed to some late sixteenth-century Calvinists that such prayer challenged the divinely ordained categories of election and reprobation.[58] The paradox that the body of believers is both exclusive and inclusive—that an omnipotent God is unable to accomplish his will—caused a great deal of uneasiness among sixteenth-century theologians, so that by the end of the century one finds a strong tendency to resolve the problem into either universalism or hard-line predestinarianism. Thus, one finds Oxford's John Dove declaring from Paul's Cross in 1597 that it is not God's will that all should be saved, that it is only Lutherans, papists, and atheists (and, one might add, Dove's own Church of England) that say so.[59]

Needless to say, an exclusive emphasis on the doctrine of predestination has implications for polemic sermons. The strength of this rhetoric's force is evident in the career of John Bolton, who was an elder in a separatist congregation in the 1560s. In a 1570 Paul's Cross sermon, Bolton recanted his heresies, condemning the separatist movement. The sermon's anti-separatist rhetoric supplanted his earlier attempt at ideological definition—that is, his attempt at identification and isolation of the body of true believers. Afterwards, it seems, Bolton became convinced that the true body of Christ was broad enough to include both separatists and conformists, but he was unable to include himself in the community, unable to forgive his own divisiveness. He hanged himself, it was said, in remorse for "judging and condemning a part of Christ's church."[60] Bolton's realization of the limits of ideological definition paradoxically ended in the ultimate act of violent self-isolation.

The Puritans' increasing tendency toward exclusive self-definition resulted in a turning of the tables; by the early seventeenth century, the godly were finding themselves ridiculed, excluded from the company of ordinary English people. One finds evidence of this tendency not only in the plays of the likes of Ben Jonson, but also in the sermons of the day. William Holbrooke, for example, asks his audience at Paul's Cross in 1609,

> Is it not a common and known trick amongst you, to vaunt what you have done in vexing the godly, saying . . ., "O, Sirrah, wot you will what and where I have been? I was where a Puritan one of those precise fellows was, that cannot endure an oath, but I so swore, stared, and swaggered that I rid him out of the house and company where I was?" O miserable and wretched![61]

Thomas Adams, called by Robert Southey the "prose Shakespeare of Puritan theologians," uses a 1612 Paul's Cross sermon to extend Holbrooke's observation to the clergy: "No jest ends in such laughter as that which is broken on a priest; the proof is plain in every tavern and theatre."[62] This sort of divisiveness was to play its part in the next generation, as the English chose their sides in the Civil War.

As I have suggested, the epistemological crisis of early modern England engendered a cultural dialectic involving the interplay between two kinds of rhetoric. The confusion generated by the impending collapse of medieval epistemology gave rise to a widespread demand for ideological definition and, as I will argue in the next chapter, a simultaneous call for conciliation. The terms of the order that would emerge in the eighteenth century involved the rejection of the paradoxical root paradigms on which the previous order had been based. One of the most eloquent prophets of the emergent order is Thomas Hobbes, who says in his *Leviathan*, "That which taketh away the reputation of wisdom in him that formeth a religion, or addeth to it when it is already formed, is the enjoining of a belief of contradictories."[63] Interestingly, Hobbes's statement is both an accurate index of the new epistemology's passion for a neat, non-paradoxical, taxonomical order, and an inaccurate statement about the origin and history of Christianity. As the Protestant Reformation dramatized, the "enjoining of a belief of contradictories"—that is, paradox—had been at the very heart of Western religious culture for fifteen centuries.

3. "Holy Cozenage" and the Renaissance Cult of the Ear

Thou wert a poet, but thy sermons do
Shew thee to be the best of preachers, too; . . .
What holy craft did in thy pulpit move?
How was the serpent mingled with the dove?
How have I seen thee cast thy net, and then,
With holy cozenage catch'd the souls of men?
—Jasper Mayne, to William Cartwright[1]

I

Thomas Playfere's 1595 sermon *The Meane in Mourning* brought his audience to tears.[2] So moving was the performance that two pirated editions of the sermon appeared before Playfere could issue a carefully edited version.[3] Among the most popular of the "metaphysical" preachers of Shakespeare's day (at which time their style was called "witty" or, interestingly, "spiritual"), Playfere shows a particular fondness for verbal pyrotechnics, especially for rhetorical figures that frustrate the categories of rational thought.[4] The paradox is among his favorites. In expounding on Luke 23:28, for example, Playfere confronts his audience with a dizzying set of paradoxes:

> Weep not too much, saith [Christ], for my death, which is the death of death. Not too much for my death, which is the death of the devil. Not too little for your own life, which is the life of the devil. Not too much for my death, which is my life. Not too little for your own life, which is your death. Not too much for my death, which is the life of man. Not too little for your own life, which is the death of Christ. (67)

This sort of language runs through the whole sermon, which is only ostensibly about a "mean," or middle way between dangerous extremes. In fact it is about embracing two extremes simultaneously, and so Playfere's task is to bring about a state of receptivity in which such a thing seems possible. The sermon's popularity suggests that in its original performance, at least, Playfere's rhetoric was successful.

Not surprisingly, the metaphysical preachers were sometimes accused of vain showmanship.[5] As "plain" style advocate John Stockwood puts it, "as for painted, labored, and of purpose sought for eloquence, I leave it unto them that seek rather the praise of men than the glory of God."[6] On the other side, in defense of the use of rhetorical figures in sermons, George Abbot points out that in an effort to reach as many people as possible Christ himself used such figures as well as plain teaching. Likewise, Abbot says, the preacher should minister to those "who must be enticed and allured with a bait of industry and eloquence, of pretty and witty sentences."[7] The idea is similar to the "heavenly fraud" Richard Hooker endorses in his defense of petitioning God for earthly benefits:

> These multiplied petitions of worldly things in prayer have therefore, besides their direct use a service whereby the Church under hand, through a kind of heavenly fraud, taketh therewith the souls of men as with certain baits.[8]

Interestingly, Andreas Hyperius defends both simplicity and the use of rhetorical conceits. He says that while Scripture, especially difficult passages, must "in deed be opened but soberly and in few words: then simply and plainly," and while "we have seen them that have mingled (even to the loathsomeness of the hearers) tropes or figures," the preacher must have all "requisite and necessary furniture. Therefore, let him know . . . argumentations tripartite, quinquepartite enthymemata: also schemes and tropes: further, the craft of amplifying and moving of affections."[9] Just as for Abbot and Hooker the audience must be enticed, allured, baited, for Hyperius the moving of affections is a "craft" (in both senses, it would seem: careful workmanship and benign deceit). The defenders of metaphysical preaching as well as the detractors use the language of trickery and seduction—of cozenage, enticement, and allurement. The question seems to be not whether cozenage takes place, but whether there can be such a thing as "holy cozenage."[10]

If the question was not resolved in the sixteenth century, neither has it been settled in the twentieth. On the one hand are almost wholly sympathetic studies of metaphysical preaching such as Horton Davies's *Like Angels from a Cloud*; on the other hand are judgments like the one in W. Fraser Mitchell's *English Pulpit Oratory*:

> [It is] the verdict of contemporaries and posterity alike, that the components of "metaphysical" preaching were not such as were in themselves intrinsically valuable, that the use to which they were put by the "witty" preachers was not consonant with the great ends of Christian oratory, and, that both the material and methods employed rendered impossible the cultivation of a prose style suited either to delivery in the pulpit or to give to religious discourses in their printed form the dignity of literature. On two counts, therefore, both for what it was, and for what it could not become, "witty" preaching stands condemned.[11]

Alexander Whyte echoes Mitchell's sentiment, commenting that he is "bewildered and confused" by Lancelot Andrewes' metaphysical sermons: "What a pity it is . . . that anything of Andrewes's has been preserved besides his *Devotions*."[12]

Some of Andrewes's contemporaries register a similar uneasiness about extravagant pulpit performance. Samuel Hieron, for example, warns of eloquence that functions merely as "a mist before a man's speeches, to cause him to be the more hardly understood."[13] And in a sermon on the Parable of the Sower, George Gifford calls those hearers "doltish" in whom the preacher's words do not take root:

> There needeth no more when a man preacheth unto them, but a glorious shew of learning, a sweet ringing voice, and matters so strange and strangely handled, that they may be brought into a wonderment of what they know not. And Satan hath many chaplains fit for this turn, to serve the vain humor of such people, and to set forth themselves after a pompous sort: more seeking their own vain glory, than the glory of the Gospel, in the conversion of the people.[14]

According to critics like Stockwood, Mitchell, Whyte, Hieron, and Gifford, the metaphysical preachers' rhetoric is merely epideictic, merely self-serving. As Gifford recognizes, the strangeness of the style is calculated to bring the hearer into a state of "wonderment." Gifford sees this condition as mere bafflement, a stultifying dead end. Clearly the metaphysical preachers themselves see it as a desideratum. Why? One could argue that what is at stake in the preachers' deliberate mystification of the faith is power. But there are other possibilities, including one suggested by an advocate of "plain" preaching. Stephen Gosson points out that the unprecedented exposure to the simple message of the gospel during the Elizabethan period paradoxically made the people deaf to it. There may be more than mere nostalgia in Gosson's 1598 sermon *The Trumpet of Warre*:

In the beginning of her Majesty's reign every man began to tremble at the word of God and to give heed to the preaching of the same: but the happy continuance thereof hath made it so familiar unto you that you care not for it.[15]

The metaphysical preachers, then, could have been doing what poets always do: finding fresh ways to combine words to reinvigorate language that has become deadened from overuse.

It is instructive that, in the same sermon in which Stockwood denounces the showiness of the metaphysical style of preaching, he inveighs against the theater. It would seem that an aversion for one mode implies an aversion for the other, that the denigration of metaphysical preaching is perhaps one component in the antitheatrical prejudice that Jonas Barish sees operating widely in Western culture.[16] Conversely, the tremendous popularity of metaphysical preaching in the late sixteenth and early seventeenth centuries, like the tremendous popularity of the theater, suggests that the rhetorical aim of such discourse is to be anything but self-serving. If certain sermons and stage plays of the period are rhetorically designed to serve not the author but the audience, what is the nature of this service? As Jasper Mayne wondered of the preacher/playwright William Cartwright's "holy craft," "How was the serpent mingled with the dove?"[17]

II

Renaissance Protestants are in general agreement that in matters of religious devotion the ear is to be trusted more than the eye.[18] Certainly this is true of the metaphysical preachers, whose sermons exploit a wide range of verbal devices. As one of the most prolific of these preachers, Ralph Brownrig, says, "Popery is a religion for the eye; ours for the ear."[19] Henry Smith plays on the paradox that "The eyes oftentimes draw the soul out of light into darkness."[20] William Rankins registers his distrust for spectacle in explicitly antitheatrical terms in the subtitle of his *A mirrour of monsters: Wherein is plainely described the manifold vices, & spotted enormities, that are caused by the infectious sight of playes, with the description of the subtile sights of Sathan, making them his instruments*.[21] Even those Protestants who do not wholly impugn the power of sight tend to subordinate the eye to the ear. John Donne, for example, says,

> Man hath a natural way to come to God, by the eye, by the creature; so visible things shew the invisible God: But then, God hath super-induced a supernatural way, by the ear. For, though hearing be natural, yet that faith in God should come by hearing a man preach, is supernatural. God shut up the natural way in Saul: seeing; he struck him blind; but he opened the supernatural way: he enabled him to hear, and to hear him. God would have us beholden to grace, and not to nature, and to come for our salvation to his ordinances, to the preaching of his word, and not to any other means.[22]

This displacement of the visual signs of God's presence with the aural reception of the preacher's words is typical of Reformation thought; to a large extent the ear displaces the eye as the primary organ of devotion.

But, as Huston Diehl has recently argued, the Protestant repudiation of the visual is not total:

> Although literary scholars often assume that when Protestants condemn the theatricality and spectacle of the Mass, they condemn theater and image, *per se*, early Protestants use these words pejoratively almost exclusively to refer to the silent actions, gestures, and visual display of the Mass, that is, to images and ceremonies that are *divorced from words*.[23]

Or, to put an even finer point on Diehl's argument, one might say that the Protestants object either to images and ceremonies *divorced from words* or to images and ceremonies accompanied by *misinterpreted* words. Thomas Becon, for example, attacks his imagined Catholic opponent's misunderstanding of Christ's "this is my body" as a matter of transubstantiation:

> After ye have once spoken these five words, *Hoc est enim corpus meum*, over the bread, and have blasted, breathed, and blowed upon it, ye kneel down to it and worship it like abominable idolaters, and afterward ye hold it up above your pestilent, piled, shaven, shameless heads, that the people by looking upon it, may be partakers of your abominable idolatry.[24]

Becon's objection is not only to the Catholic priest's misunderstanding of the word but also to the popular belief that the mere *sight* of the elevated Host is salvific:

> For the people believe it [the Host] to be their god. They believe that bread, which the Priest heaveth above his head, to be Christ, perfect God, and perfect man. Therefore kneel they down unto it, knock their breasts, lift up their heads, worship and honor it. When the bell once rings (if they cannot conveniently see) they forsake their seats, and run from altar to altar, from sacring

to sacring, peeping here, and tooting there, and gazing at that thing, which piled-pate Priest holdeth up in his hands.[25]

Becon continues his project of demystification by telling the story of a Jew invited by a Catholic friend to attend a Mass. The guest saw

> a fellow with a shaven crown going up and down in the church, and casting water in the people's teeth, and afterward having a jolly coat upon his back he saw him go about the church-yard, after an image, all the people following him. After all these things he saw that shaveling cast off the gay coat again, and put on other game player's garments, and so to address himself unto an altar. (283–84)

The Protestant project of demystifying Catholic spectacle is broad enough and successful enough that one can, bearing in mind the qualification that Protestants do not wholly impugn the power of sight, accept the argument that in the sixteenth century a Protestant "logolatry" supplants the idolatry of which the reformers accuse Catholicism.

Michael O'Connell has made this argument in terms that are on the whole compelling, but he focuses almost exclusively on the Protestants' reliance on the *written* word. His account of "Scripture as the sole connecting link between man and God" needs to be qualified ("Idolatrous Eye," 287). The usual Protestant claim is that biblical ideas are imparted not primarily by reading but by the spoken word. Similar qualification is in order for O'Connell's statement that for the reformers "religious truth was perceived to reside in exact texts" (287). Sixteeth-century Protestants are not twentieth-century fundamentalists; Calvin, for example, calls attention to the New Testament writers' habit of quoting the Hebrew Scriptures imprecisely: "They never made conscience in changing the words, so as they hit upon the effect of the matter."[26]

All this is not to deny that the Bible is central to the Reformation, but only to point out that preaching needs to be included in any account of logolatry. O'Connell is quite right, then, that early Protestantism tended toward logocentricity, but it should be remembered that there was still considerable resistance in sixteenth-century England to a merely textual understanding of the faith. To be sure, print culture was playing its part in ushering in a new epistemology, but Elizabethan England was also the great age of the performance: it is arguable that along with the song and the stage play, the sermon reached the height of its rhetorical effectiveness toward the end of the sixteenth century. An index of the power of the sermon in Renaissance England is the complaint of John Howson, no mean preacher himself, that the houses of prayer, the *oratoria*, have become *auditoria*.[27] Royalist Henry Hammond expresses a similar uneasiness, explicitly relating the liturgy to the theater as he inveighs against

> those seduced ones, who place so great a part of piety in hearing, and think so much the more comfortably of themselves from the number of hours spent in that exercise, which hath of late been the only business of the Church (which was by God enstil'd the House of Prayer) and the liturgy at most used but as music to entertain the auditors till the actors be attired, and the seats be full, and it be time for the scene to enter.[28]

If Protestants writing a century earlier spent their efforts attacking Roman Catholicism's idolatrous cult of the eye, Hammond is worried about a similarly dangerous cult of the ear.

The confluence of several factors makes the engendering of such a cult possible: the late sixteenth century's enhanced receptivity to the nuances of oral performance is in part indebted to the Protestant reverence for the spoken word, combined with the Reformation's rejection of visual allure and the humanists' revival of classical rhetoric. Some of the implications of this new receptivity for the Elizabethan theater will be considered in the chapters that follow. Here it is enough to note that the metaphysical preachers, like the dramatists, vigorously develop a wide range of verbal devices that exploit every opportunity for aural enticement.[29] If, as Izaak Walton reports, Donne preached "like an angel from a cloud," such preaching was made possible by cultural forces that had their impact on the pulpit as well as the stage.[30]

III

In the last chapter I argued that the combination of a number of factors in Renaissance England gave rise to a broad cultural demand for a polemical rhetoric valuing a static, definitive self-understanding. The urge toward stasis is reflected, for example, in the newly reformed churches' tendency to declare their systems infallible. In fact it is precisely this tendency that occasions Richard Hooker's *Of the Laws of Ecclesiastical Polity*, a sustained endorsement of flexibility rather than ecclesiastical infallibility.

Hooker's treatise has of course come to be known as a classic statement of theological tolerance, but the work is not entirely latitudinarian; it is in part an argument for consensus against the radical Puritans. This fact is obscured by the work's generally irenic tone, which may account for its poor sales in the late sixteenth and early seventeenth centuries.[31] On the whole, the theological climate of the age favored rhetoric with a harder edge. As Hieron says, "a man that indendeth to do any good in this frozen generation . . . had need to be rather Boanerges, one of the sons of thunder, than Bar-Jonah the son of a dove" (*Preachers Plea*, 203). Hooker ruefully admits the fact in the preface to his work, prophesying that "There will come a time when three words uttered with charity and meekness shall receive a far more blessed reward than three thousand volumes written with disdainful sharpness of wit" (2.10.12–15). There were no doubt many who shared Hooker's sentiments, but in most forms of theological discourse "disdainful sharpness of wit" remained the order of the day until Hooker's death and for more than a generation after.[32]

This rhetorical tendency is evident even in pulpit performances that apparently call for unity. Richard Bancroft's famous 1589 Paul's Cross sermon, for example, ostensibly appeals to a unified faith but actually does so by denouncing a broad section of believers: all those disagreeing with Archbishop Whitgift's resistance to church reform:

> Beware (saith the Apostle) of dogs, beware of evil workers, beware of concision, that is, of such as cut asunder the church of God. If any man preach unto you any other Gospel than that which you have received, let him be accursed.[33]

Even a seventeenth-century treatise called *Irenicum* turns out in fact to be a polemic:

> The Mohammedans who worship a cursed impostor; the pagans, who worship the sun, moon, and stars; the Egyptians, who worship onions, leeks, cats, and dogs, never had such divisions amongst them as the worshippers of Jesus Christ have had, and have at this day amongst ourselves.[34]

There were, of course, genuinely irenic thinkers, but these advocates of tolerance had to find oblique ways of asserting an alternative to polemics. Since doctrinal differences tended to encourage polemic rhetoric, one option was to lessen the emphasis on doctrine and increase the emphasis on liturgical worship. Hooker often takes this approach, repeatedly stressing the need for communal piety, the need for the congregation to weary their knees and hands rather than their ears and tongues.[35]

After Hooker's death the English Arminian party developed a system emphasizing worship rather than doctrinal explication. The Arminians endorsed the anti-Calvinist ideas of the potential universality of salvation and of communion as a higher ordinance than preaching.[36] Such doctrines appeal to a sense of human solidarity rather than social or ideological separateness. In anthropological terms, the very emergence of the English Arminians—or at least the universalizing aspect of their doctrines—can be seen as filling the cultural need for such solidarity at a time when divisiveness held sway. The Arminian party, though, did not gain prominence in England until after James's death in 1625. Until that time Calvinism remained orthodox. This meant that religious writers with Arminian leanings, especially those who wanted to avoid the denunciatory style of so many of their contemporaries, needed to exploit those resources of Calvinist doctrine that would best further their ideals. One way they did this was by invoking in the performances of their sermons the "root paradigm" of Christ's martyrdom.

I noted in the last chapter that Victor Turner defines root paradigms as "cultural models in the heads of the main actors" in social dramas.[37] Such a cultural model ordinarily remains the unexamined framework that orients the self in the world. According to Turner, to bring a root paradigm to the surface during the crisis of a social drama inevitably highlights the paradigm's paradoxical status (88–89). Thus, in terms of the Christian paradigm, death means life; weakness means strength; judgment means mercy. The invocation of such paradoxes, drawing attention as they do to the unfathomable paradox of the death of the eternal God in human form, has the potential to arrest thought, checking the impulse toward polemical definition.

A number of late sixteenth- and early seventeenth-century preachers exploit paradox to precisely this end. Moreover, the cultural tendency to evoke Christian paradox involves more than the explicitly theological discursive mode of the sermon; certain dramas of the period encourage community by drawing on the energies of paradox.[38] The sermons themselves, in fact, function dramatically—that is, as public performances. Unlike metaphysical poetry, which has been described as an essentially private mode,[39] the metaphysical sermon, like the drama, depends on an audience. Sermons and stage plays are very much public, communal occasions for the reception of the spoken word. Both modes achieve their effect in part by evoking a sense of wonder. As George Puttenham realized, paradoxes are uniquely suited to this end; he calls them "wondrers" in his *Arte of English Poesie*.[40]

The metaphysical preacher's task, then, is not so much to describe the contraries of Christian paradox as to evoke an existential sense of the tension between them—to resolve paradoxes not in logic, a task that is by definition impossible, but in communal experience. On the surface the paradox may appear to be nothing more than a gratuitous display of the speaker's wit. Its rhetorical task, though, is not simply to provoke admiration for the speaker's artistry but to evoke an existential posture of admiration—an experiential resonance with the culture's central paradigms.[41] Since at the very heart of the Christian story is the mystery of divine immolation, the paradox invites on the hearer's part a similar relinquishment of possessive power. This self-dispossession is one of the functions of wonder traced by Stephen Greenblatt in *Marvelous Possessions*, his study of the role of wonder in European encounters with the New World.[42] The paradox generates this sense of marvel by circumventing the categories of rigid definition—by challenging the absolute validity of rational constructs. Bassanio in *The Merchant of Venice* calls the appropriate response to this kind of rhetoric a "wild of nothing":

> there is such confusion in my powers,
> As after some oration fairly spoke
> By a beloved prince, there doth appear
> Among the buzzing pleased multitude,
> Where every something, being blent together,
> Turns to a wild of nothing, save of joy
> Express'd and not express'd. (3.2.177–83)

Or in Keatsian terms, the paradox serves to "tease us out of thought."

It would seem, then, that the metaphysical preacher performs an important cultural task: the evocation of a de-politicized solidarity in an age of fierce polemics. It is also, of course, an age in which audiences are particularly receptive to the nuances of oral performance. While no analysis of the surviving scripts of these performances can hope to capture all their original affective force, the metaphysical sermons that survive in print illustrate something of the historical importance of paradox in performance.

IV

The prevalence of paradox in Renaissance discourse both informs and is informed by Calvinism's dual perception of the human condition: even the elect are in their own nature so vile, so corrupted by sin, that they are utterly undeserving of any degree of divine favor; and yet the elect are exalted, redeemed, imputed in God's eyes to be as sinless as Christ himself. The biblical passage that perhaps best expresses the tension of this condition is Psalms 8:3–5:

> When I behold thine heavens, even the works of thy fingers, the moon and the stars which thou hast ordained, What is man, say I, that thou art mindful of him? and the son of man, that thou visitest him? For thou hast made him a little lower than God, and crowned him with glory and worship.

The glosses in the Geneva Bible attempt to ease the tension of this paradoxical condition, insisting that the concept of man's "crowning" refers to "his first creation" only. Calvin himself, though, recognizes the force of the paradox, calling attention to the wonder of "this matching of contraries" and insisting on a simultaneous recognition of human worthlessness and human glory. It is a marvel, says Calvin,

> that so great a workmaster whose majesty shineth in heaven will vouchsafe to deck this miserable and vile creature with singular glory, and to enrich it with innumerable riches. . . . Whosoever is not amazed at this miracle, he is more than unthankful and blockish. (*Psalmes*, p. 23ᵛ)

Calvin's emphasis on human depravity is well known, but less attention is paid to his insistence on the other half of the paradox: that human beings are simultaneously glorious. Calvin even suggests that the *Elohim* of Psalms 8:5 be translated "God" rather than "angels," so that human beings are not only "a little lower than the angels" (King James Version) but "a little lower than God" (Geneva Bible) (24ʳ).

Thomas Playfere explores this paradox of the human condition, insisting that the believer must embrace both contraries simultaneously in order to avoid presumption on the one hand and despair on the other:

> If a Christian always think of his own misery and never of Christ's mercy, he will despair; if he always think of Christ's mercy and never of his own misery,

he will presume. But he is the best Christian, so high that he cannot despair, so low that he cannot presume, which inclines as well to the one as to the other. (*Meane in Mourning*, 69)

It is important to note that Playfere is not suggesting mere compromise, as though it would be acceptable to find a middle ground that combined moderate portions of presumption and despair. The believer is not to forge a *via media* that avoids extremes but to adopt an existential posture that embraces both contraries at once—a tensional stance that "inclines as well to the one as to the other."

In the same sermon Playfere develops the idea that human beings are able to strike such a paradoxical posture only because Christ has already done it for us: "For he was not counted so good as a live worm, but was buried in the earth a dead lion to be meat for the worms."[43] Christ was made lower than God, angels, human beings, and worms so that we, "being now no better than worms," might be made higher than worms, higher than human beings, higher than angels, "partakers of the same life and kingdom with Christ" (49). Paradoxically, the freedom of this participation in the life of Christ can be obtained only by servitude. As John Cosin puts the paradox,

the only way to be great is to be little, lowly before God; the only way to be accounted kings, to be servants to come and worship God; which we acknowledge every day in our church service, *Cui servire regnare est*, as the old collect goes, "Whose service is perfect freedom," that is a Kingdom right.[44]

Or, as Hooker says in *A Learned Sermon of the Nature of Pride*, speaking as from "the very soul of Peter,"

My eager protestations made in the glory of my ghostly strength I am ashamed of, but those crystal tears wherewith my sin and weakness was bewailed have procured me endless joy; my strength hath been my ruin, and my fall my stay. (*Works*, 5:324)

The metaphysical preachers often play on such Christian paradoxes. To the charge that their frequent use of paradox amounts to no more than verbal showmanship, the preachers can reply that there is scriptural precedent in plenty for such usage: in the parables and sayings of Jesus as well as in the historical facts of the Incarnation, Crucifixion, and Resurrection, and in the writings of Paul. For example, in a Lenten sermon preached before Charles I in 1628, Bishop Joseph Hall expounds on Galatians 2:20 ("I am crucified with Christ: nevertheless I live; yet not I, but Christ liveth in me"):

> [This text is] full of wonders, full of sacred riddles: 1. The living God is dead upon the cross, Christ crucified. 2. St. Paul, who died by the sword, dies on the cross. 3. St. Paul, who was not Paul till after Christ's death, is yet crucified with Christ. 4. St. Paul, thus crucified, yet lives. 5. St. Paul lives not himself while he lives. 6. Christ, who is crucified, lives in Paul, who was crucified with him.[45]

These "sacred riddles," in encouraging contemplative wonder, function in contrast to the definitive, polemical rhetoric of so much of the period's theological discourse. Even when he refers to the church's liturgical calendar, a matter of some dissension between Puritans and Conformists, Hall uses the scriptural basis of his sermon not to add fuel to the fire of the controversy, but to subsume the liturgical elements into a larger paradoxical whole: "See then here both a Lent and an Easter; a Lent of mortification: 'I am crucified with Christ'; an Easter of resurrection and life: 'I live, yet not I, but Christ lives in me'" (380).

Some metaphysical preachers carry to an extreme the principle of basing their rhetoric on the language of the Bible, engaging in the practice of "text-crumbling": dividing a biblical passage into phrases, words, or even syllables, and expounding on the meaning of each.[46] Playfere, preaching on the eight-word text "Weep not for me, but weep for yourselves" (Luke 23:28b), divides his sermon *The Meane in Mourning* into no fewer than eight parts, according to the following scheme: "1. 'Weep not.' 2. 'But weep.' 3. 'Weep not, but weep.' 4. 'For me.' 5. 'For yourselves.' 6. 'For me, for yourselves.' 7. 'Weep not for me.' 8. 'But weep for yourselves'" (3–4). The principle of paradox is built into the very structure of the sermon. The contrary principles of parts 1 and 2 are resolved in part 3, which embraces both extremes simultaneously; the believer is to maintain "an equal intermingling of these two extremities, 'weep not but weep' both together" (21). Likewise, the contraries of parts 4 and 5 are resolved by their combination in part 6. And the whole sermon serves as the resolution of the opposing clauses of parts 7 and 8.

Playfere's rhetorical principle of the "intermingling of extremities" serves to circumvent categorical precision, inviting instead an affective response to the root paradigms on which his paradoxes are based. Playfere says that it is because of Christ's intermingling of joy and sorrow that "our sorrow must be joyful, and our joy must be sorrowful" (22). The paradigm of Christ's martyrdom shows that descent is really ascent.

In true metaphysical style, John Donne relates the paradox of rising by falling to statements by the Church Fathers Lactantius and Augustine that "those men that hang upon the other cheek of the earth must fall off":

> But whither should they fall? If they fall, they must fall upwards, for heaven is above them too, as it is to us. So if the spiritual Antipodes of this world, the Sons of God, that walk with feet opposed in ways contrary to the sons of men, shall be said to fall when they fall to repentance, to mortification, to a religious negligence, and contempt of the pleasures of this life, truly their fall is upwards; they fall towards heaven. (*Sermons*, 4:1.512–19)

Playfere makes the same point with a conceit drawn from the story of Noah's ark: the believer sees that "as the more the waters did rise the higher the ark was lifted up; after the same sort the more his sorrows increase, the higher his heart is lifted up to God" (98–99). Even the colors of Noah's rainbow, says Playfere, are emblematic of the paradox. Drawing on Gregory's idea that the red in the rainbow represents the fire of Christ's final judgment and the blue the waters of the Flood, Playfere says, "Therefore as there be two colors, red and blue, in one rainbow, so there must be two affections, joy and sorrow, in one heart" (23). The extravagance of such metaphysical conceits, like the yoking together of opposing paradoxical terms, has an anti-rational or supra-rational rhetorical force. As Davies points out, preachers like Playfere, Andrewes, and Donne believe that such devices are "the only fitting ways of trying to express mysteries of divine revelation which transcend human reason, and therefore can only be apprehended by faith."[47]

One of the central Christian articles of faith is the paradox of the Incarnation, the infinite God's localization in a human body. Daniel Featley, for example, offers the following meditation in one of his sermons:

> O king of glory, who hadst no palace in this world but an inn; no chamber of presence but a stable; no tapestry but straw; no chair of estate but a cratch; no scepter but a reed; and no crown but a wreath of thorns; work in me an holy high-mindedness to despise this world which so despised thee. Make the worldly greatness seem small, honor base, estimation vile, and pomp vain unto me.[48]

It is the paradox of the Incarnation, the king of glory's physical embodiment in the poorest of human conditions, that allows the Christian to adopt a similar combination of "holy high-mindedness" and lowliness.

Thomas Adams uses the paradox of the Incarnation to stress the limits of reason: "If your understandings can reach the depth of this bottom, take it at one view. The Son of God calls himself the Son of man. The omnipotent Creator becomes an impotent creature."[49] Adams calls on his listeners to strain their intellectual faculties, their "understandings," knowing full well that the paradox of the Incarnation frustrates the categorization of rational thought. Hooker, like Adams, uses paradox to assert the transcendence of divine over human categories. In sermons as well as the *Laws*, Hooker habitually dismantles his own magnificent verbal edifices:

> What good the sun doth by heat and light, the moon and stars by their secret influence, the air and wind and water by every their several qualities; what commodity the earth receiving their services yieldeth again unto her inhabitants; how beneficial by nature the operations of all things are, how far the use and profit of them is extended, somewhat the greatness of God but much more our own inadvertency and carelessness doth disable us to conceive. (*Sermon on Pride, Works*, 5:333–34)

In suspending image after image of the glorious works of God, and then in resolving the periodic sentence in humankind's inability to perceive such glory, Hooker leaves his audience in a state of wonder. In Stanley Fish's terminology, this is "self-consuming" language.[50] One could also point to Lancelot Andrewes, who underscores the wonder of the Incarnation by using language to call attention to Christ's abandonment of linguistic power:

> The Word, by whom all things were made, to come to be made it self . . . what flesh? The flesh of an infant. What, *Verbum Infans*, the Word an infant? The Word and unable to speak a word? (47–48)

Andrewes's word play, like so much in metaphysical preaching, simultaneously calls attention to the preacher's verbal artistry and undercuts the validity of its own verbal constructions.

If it is a paradox that God could take on human life, so it is that God could die. John Donne runs through a series of paradoxes in order to underscore the strangeness of divine immolation:

That God, this Lord, the Lord of life, could die, is a strange contemplation; that the Red Sea could be dry, that the sun could stand still, that an oven could be seven times heat and not burn, that lions could be hungry and not bite, is strange, miraculously strange, but supermiraculous that God could die; but that God would die is an exaltation of that. But even of that also it is a superexaltation, that God should die, must die, and *non exitus* (saith S. Augustine); God the Lord had no issue but by death, and *oportuit pati* (says Christ himself): All this "Christ ought to suffer," was bound to suffer. (*Sermons*, 10:11.486–95)

The paradox of God's death in the Crucifixion leads to another paradox in the Resurrection: the death of Death. Preacher and playwright Thomas Goffe plays on one formulation of the idea:

"*Uteri nova forma*," saith a Father, for the tomb to become a womb to take in a dead man, and bring him forth alive; for the grave to swallow up, not a dead corpse, but Death itself."[51]

Playfere spells out the implication of the death of Death for human beings: "the death of Christ is the death of Death: the death of the devil: the life of Himself: the life of man" (25). Or in Andrewes's formulation, the Christian says not, "'*dum spiro spero*' but '*dum expiro spiro*': his hope fails him not when his breath fails him."[52]

In another sermon Andrewes asks, "*Quis audivit talia?* The Physician slain; and, of his flesh and blood, a receipt made, that the patient might recover!"[53] The metaphysical preachers often play similarly on the illogic of vicarious salvation. William Cartwright says that as a consequence of the Crucifixion, the believer receives "a bundle of new miracles as far beyond the former as they are opposite to them; a condemnation that absolves us; a sickness that recovers us; a death it self that quickens us."[54]

This paradox is one of the metaphysical preachers' favorites. Often the idea is formulated in terms of the believer's simultaneous experience of God's judgment and God's mercy. Playfere, for example, referring to the Psalmist's "hide me under the shadow of thy wings" (Psalms 17:8b), says,

What are God's wings? His mercy and his justice. What is the shadow of his wings? Our love and our fear. Our love is the shadow of his mercy, which is his right wing. Our fear is the shadow of his justice, which is his left wing. (70)

Thomas Jackson expresses the judgment/mercy paradox in terms of the believer's faith:

faith, if it be not defective, hath two hands: as well a left hand to apprehend the truth of God's judgments threatened, whilst we swarve from the ways of life, as a right hand, to lay hold of the truth of his promises.[55]

In calling attention to God's judgments and mercies, Jackson reflects the Protestant idea that the Bible is a book of threats and promises: not that the Old Testament contains only judgment and the New Testament only mercy, but that both embrace both extremes—judgment and mercy—simultaneously. In a 1591 sermon, William Fisher explains that there is judgment in the New Testament and mercy in the Old:

> And as the book of the law shall shew what we ought to have done, so the book of the Gospel shall shew what we ought to have believed: and both to one end (Christ knoweth) that so much more just and dreadful may be our judgment. . . . What shall we do then? We are now called to repentance, both by the voice of God's vengeance, saying, "I will come now to you in judgment, and I will be a just witness against you," and also by the voice of his mercy, saying, "Return to me, and I will return to you." (Malachi 3:5, 7)[56]

According to Fisher, both judgment and mercy should lead to repentance. Given the public forum in which the sermon is heard, this repentance takes on a communal character, one that effaces any doctrinal distinctions that might divide the audience. Instead the sermon's rhetoric brings about an awareness of a shared human condition: a baffling, paradoxical subjection to both judgment and mercy.

If a sermon like Fisher's is intentionally puzzling, an example of "holy cozenage to catch the souls of men," John Donne goes even farther, developing a conceit that both explicitly develops the fishing motif and evokes the paradox of judgment and mercy:

> The Gospel of Christ Jesus is a net; it hath leads and corks. It hath leads: that is, the denouncing of God's judgments, and a power to sink down and lay flat any stubborn and rebellious heart, and it hath corks: that is, the power of absolution and application of the mercies of God. (*Sermons*, 2:14.757–62)

Donne warns that the tension of the believer's subjection to both judgment and mercy must be maintained; the one who ignores God's mercy, for example, is in grave spiritual danger: "Wilt thou force God to second thy irreligious melancholy, and to condemn thee at last, because thou hadst precondemned thy self, and renounced his mercy?" (*Sermons*, 10:4.524–

27). Using a typically extravagant comparison, Donne assures his audience that no depth of religious melancholy is beyond redemption:

> If some king of the earth have so large an extent of dominion, in north and south, as that he hath winter and summer together in his dominions, so large an extent east and west, as that he hath day and night together in his dominions, much more hath God mercy and judgment together: He brought light out of darkness, not out of a lesser light; he can bring summer out of winter, though thou have no spring. (*Sermons*, 6:8.140–46)

Donne sees the preacher's rhetoric as participating in the divine activity of bringing light out of darkness, summer out of spring, mercy out of judgment:

> The preacher doth so infuse the fear of God into his auditory, that first, they shall fear nothing but God, and then they shall fear God, but so, as he is God; and God is mercy; God is love. (*Sermons*, 8:1.252–54)

According to Donne, the preacher's task is to evoke in the audience a peculiar state of psychological tension involving both fear and comfort.

For Ralph Brownrig, such a paradoxical receptivity is the only way of apprehending a savior who is both lion and lamb. Commenting on John 3:19 ("And this is the condemnation, that light is come into the world, and men loved darkness rather than light because their deeds were evil"), Brownrig combines the doctrines of Incarnation and Last Judgment in the paradox of the *ira agni*, the wrath of the lamb:

> Here is the mercy of his Incarnation, if we have grace to make use of it; and here is the vengeance for his rejection at the day of retribution. Here is the sound of the harp, and the song of the angels at the day of his birth; and then there is the sound of the trumpet, the voice of the arch-angel at the day of judgment. Here is the shining of a star pointing out his first appearing and then there is a dismal comet in the text fore-running his second: both *vagitus infantis* and *rugitus leonis*: or, as St. John puts them together, *ira agni*, the fiercest wrath from the meekest lamb.[57]

In calling attention to a figure like the *ira agni*, Brownrig is evoking an image that is ludicrous on the literal level but that draws tremendous affective force from the root paradigm on which it is based. All the paradoxes of the metaphysical preachers, in fact, refer obliquely to the root paradigm of Christ's martyrdom. In each case the illogic of paradox serves to frustrate the categories of structured thought, evoking an experiential resolution of contraries.

V

If the metaphysical sermon engages the need for disarmament through a sort of "holy cozenage," the theater holds the principle of cozenage at its very center. Through their suspension of disbelief, the members of the audience willingly engage in the trickery of drama—the actors' impersonations of people they are not, the bare stage's representation of other places, and the action's pretense to actuality. In the theater, visual spectacle complements the aural seductiveness of heightened language to cozen the audience into the vicarious experience of living for a while in another world.

Some Renaissance playwrights, most notably Shakespeare, seem to have been comfortable with the theater's complementarity of visual and aural enticement. That the combination was alluring is unquestionable. As Stephen Gosson complains in *The Schoole of Abuse*,

> Cooks did never shew more craft in their junkets to vanquish the taste, nor painters in shadows to allure the eye, than poets in theaters to wound the conscience. There they set abroach strange consorts of melody, to tickle the ear; costly apparel, to flatter the sight; effeminate gesture, to ravish the sense; and wanton speech, to whet desire to inordinate lust.[58]

Gosson goes on to point out that of all the organs of sense, the ear is the most vulnerable to a truly debilitating seduction:

> Therefore of both barrels, I judge cooks and painters the better hearing, for the one extendeth his art no farther than the tongue, palate, and nose, the other to the eye; and both are ended in outward sense, which is common to us with brute beasts. But these by the privy entries of the ear, slip down into the heart, and with gunshot of affection gall the mind, where reason and virtue should rule the roost. (32)

As we have seen, even as reformers like Gosson were warning of the seductive power of the spoken word, Reformation preachers were responding to Protestantism's rejection of visual allure in favor of the word. One result of this widespread emphasis on the word, combined with humanism's attention to classical rhetoric, was the development of the new style of the metaphysical sermon, with its rhetoric of "holy cozenage." Paradoxically, then, the Reformation both censored and fostered verbal artistry.

This complex situation helps to explain certain paradoxical tendencies in a playwright like Ben Jonson. As O'Connell points out, Jonson's denunciation of the puritanical sensibility has its counterpart in a puritanical distrust of visual display (301). Jonson begins the prologue to *The Staple of News*, for example, with an apology on behalf of the playwright for the play's gratuitous spectacle:

> For your own sakes, not his, he bade me say,
> Would you were come to hear, not see, a play.
> Though we his actors must provide for those,
> Who are our guests, here, in the way of shows,
> The maker hath not so; he'ld have you wise
> Much rather by your ears, than by your eyes.[59]

O'Connell says of this passage,

> This comes but as an extreme version of what Jonson in one way or another always wanted: near exclusive attention to the verbal element of the mixed art that theater is. . . . For all the vigor of his satire of the Puritans, a part of him remained as convinced as they that sight distracted the mind from the truth of the word. (301)

If a driving force for a playwright like Jonson as well as for the Protestant reformers was a distrust of the Catholic cult of the eye, one recourse of both playwrights and preachers was what I have called the cult of the ear. Such a situation, in fact, helps to explain the explosive development of verbal art forms during the last quarter of the sixteenth century. The period is unquestionably informed by a pervasive desire to exploit the artistic potential of the spoken word.

The following chapters will examine certain Reformation sermons and Renaissance plays as cultural performances that draw in varying ways on the energies of paradox. Just as the *topos* of the two-edged sword has its counterpart in the period's comedies as well as tragedies, the rhetoric of the metaphysical preachers examined in this chapter is complemented by that of a playwright like Shakespeare. Just as Shakespeare's comedies, especially his late romances, employ paradoxical strategies similar to those of the

metaphysical sermons to achieve their disarming effects, so are the tragedies informed by an insistent contrariety. *King Lear*, for example, while
hardly "Christian" in the same sense as, say, the mystery cycles, nonetheless
achieves a great deal of its force from its incorporation of paradoxes that
grow out of Christian paradigms. Such thematic paradoxes as the wisdom
of the Fool and the sanity of Edgar's madness play their parts, but even
more basic to the power of the play is the massive theme of gain through
loss. Gloucester's finding sight in blindness figures Lear's appropriation
of humanity through the loss of everything dear to him. The excruciating
final scene brings all these paradoxes to a focus as Lear, having descended
in his spiritual blindness into madness and folly, enters with the body of
Cordelia in his arms. Because vision, sanity, and wisdom have come too
late for Lear, the play's paradoxes can be resolved only in the communal
experience of the audience.

Shakespeare, who apparently did not share Jonson's antipathy for the
visual aspect of theater, successfully capitalized on not only the the theater's alluring spectacle but also its linguistic potential for spellbinding
the audience. Such artistic "cozenage" was possible because the disruptive
social drama of the Reformation gave rise to an enhanced reliance on the
ear as well as to a renewed desire for an alternative to polemics. Preachers
and playwrights responded to the situation by cultivating a profusion of
aural devices. The rhetorical figure of the paradox in particular, intimating
as it did the root paradigm of Christ's martyrdom, offered the possibility
of cozening the audience into communal wonder.

PART II

Comic Edification and Inclusion

4. Satire and Social Structure

I know of no disease of the soul but ignorance.
—Ben Jonson[1]

Where ignorance reigneth, there reigns sin.
—William Perkins[2]

I

On February 9, 1612, the Roaring Girl did penance for her dissolute ways before an appreciative audience at Paul's Cross. The penitent was Mary Frith, known throughout London as Moll Cutpurse, the woman who not only led a band of thieves and prostitutes but who boldly mocked authority by wearing men's clothing wherever she went. Now the authorities called her to task. Three days after the service of penance John Chamberlain reported in letter to a friend that

> she had the daintiest preacher or ghostly father that ever I saw in pulpit, one Ratcliffe of Brazen Nose in Oxford, a likelier man to have led the revels in some Inn of Court than to be where he was, but the best is he did extreme badly, and so wearied the audience that the best part went away, and the rest tarried rather to hear Moll Cutpurse than him.[3]

According to Chamberlain, Frith "wept bitterly and seemed very penitent, but it is since doubted she was maudlin drunk, being discovered to have tippled three quarts of sack before she came to her penance" (1:334). One scholar reports that "her confederates picked pockets during the service, and the whole affair was anything but edifying."[4] It would seem, then, that Moll Cutpurse had once again flouted the hegemonic forces, using against itself a stage designed in large part for social control: the penitent's platform at Paul's Cross.

But is the subversive force of Frith's penance so clear? Were her friends really picking pockets during the service, as it somehow seems appealing to believe?[5] If, as it was "discovered," she was in fact drunk, was her drunkenness an act of defiance? Habitual behavior? A calculated ploy to make the requisite tears flow? A desperate attempt to bolster herself for the public ordeal? Some combination of such factors? The "real" Mary Frith, needless to say, remains elusive. It is difficult to discern with much precision even Chamberlain's view of her. He calls Frith a "notorious baggage" and seems dismissive of her penance as a mere sham (1:334). Yet presumably he, like others in the crowd, "tarried rather to hear Moll Cutpurse" than the preacher. Like a good many other Renaissance performances, Mary Frith's penance raises more questions than it answers. Did the people in the audience know precisely what to make of the spectacle? How much of the maudlin contrition was sincere and how much feigned? What forces are in play when a central cultural paradigm like the need for repentance is called into question?

II

Mary Frith's Paul's Cross performance was not her only appearance on the public stage. Less than a year earlier she had been at the Fortune Theatre, where according to later court records she offered some "immodest and lascivious speeches . . . and also sat upon the stage in the public view of all the people there present in man's apparel and played upon her lute and sang a song."[6] The performance caused quite a stir, leading two playwrights to capitalize on the incident's currency by writing a play with Moll Cutpurse as heroine. P. A. Mulholland plausibly dates the composition of Middleton and Dekker's *The Roaring Girl* in April or May of 1611, shortly after Frith's performance on the stage of the Fortune. The play's epilogue, in fact, includes the promise of a return engagement: "The Roaring Girl herself, some few days hence, / Shall on this stage give larger recompense" (Epilogue, 35–36).

But the Moll Cutpurse of *The Roaring Girl* is not the Mary Frith of 1611 London; even Middleton and Dekker are at pains to make the point: "'tis the excellency of a writer to leave things better than he finds 'em."[7] The heroine of this play is an idealized Moll Cutpurse, one who knows the ways of London's criminal underside but who is herself entirely upright, who is "loose in nothing but in mirth" (2.2.185). Whereas Mary Frith was widely reputed to be a prostitute and bawd, the play's Moll Cutpurse eloquently denounces the oppressive economic system that forces "poor shifting sisters" to become "lecher's food" (3.1.87–98). Although Middleton and Dekker's Moll admits that in her younger days she was "apt to stray," the admission is more an explanation of her thorough knowledge of the tricks of the criminal trade than a confession of guilt (5.1.291). Since any need for penance on the street-wise Moll's part is long since past, the audience gets both the good-natured, morally upright heroine and the vicarious pleasure of innocuous roguery. So virtuous is this protagonist that the sheer discrepancy between the staged Moll Cutpurse and the real one may well have brought about Mary Frith's arrest and trial. One way to demystify the idealized Moll Cutpurse would be to humiliate Mary Frith in public. Whether the humiliation successfully contained her subversive potential is an open question, but the strong likelihood remains that Frith's arrest and public penance were precipitated by the play.

The Roaring Girl itself contains potentially subversive elements. The cross-dressed (but, significantly, undisguised) title character repeatedly flouts authority.[8] According to Jean E. Howard, in this play "the resistance to patriarchy and its marriage customs is clear and sweeping" (439). Not only does Moll expose prostitution as more patriarchal exploitation than woman's tendency to sin; she also roundly denounces the criminal justice system. As she physically rescues Jack Dapper from unjust imprisonment at the hands of his politically influential father, she declares, "If any gentleman be in scrivener's bands / Send but for Moll, she'll bail him by these hands" (3.3.216–17). It would seem, then, that the cross-dressed, defiant Moll Cutpurse of The Roaring Girl embodies the threat to authority that led King James himself to attempt to eliminate transvestitism from London. As Chamberlain writes in a 1620 letter to Dudley Carleton,

> Yesterday the Bishop of London [John King] called together all his clergy about this town, and told them he had express commandment from the King to will them to inveigh vehemently and bitterly in their sermons against the insolency of our women, and their wearing of broad brimmed hats, pointed doublets, their hair cut short or shorn, and some of them stilettos or poniards, and such other trinkets of like moment, adding withal that if pulpit admonitions will not reform them he would proceed by another course. (2.286–87)

About three weeks later Chamberlain elaborated on the dark intimation of "another course":

> Our pulpits ring continually of the insolence and impudence of women: and to help the matter forward the players have likewise taken them to task . . . and if all this will not serve, the King threatens to fall upon their husbands,

parents, or friends that have or should have power over them and make them pay for it. (2:289)

It may not be overstating the case to say that the example of Moll Cut-purse, together with her idealized depiction in *The Roaring Girl*, played a significant role in setting in motion the vogue of cross-dressing that so infuriated King James.

But Marjorie Garber disputes the subversive force of *The Roaring Girl*, debunking what she calls the "positive-role-model-challenge-to-the-sex-gender-system-disruption-of-the-old-verities view of the play" (230). Garber has in mind readings like Mary Beth Rose's, Linda Woodbridge's, Jonathan Dollimore's, and Jean Howard's.[9] For Garber,

> that Moll "unmasked" (SD 5.2.142) is Moll in transvestite garb suggests that the appropriation of "transvestite" and "masquerade" as enabling figures for women—for feminist critics as well as female spectators—is itself an act of phallogocentric mastery. The pleasurable tease of being a woman in masquer-ade, a "transvestite" in imagination, still refers back to the male as norm and hence is still itself a hegemonic move. (232)

My point here is not to assess the relative merits of these arguments for and against the play's subversive potential but to suggest the significance of the play's lending itself to analysis along the lines of subversion and containment. For the play *does* ask to be interpreted in such terms; Rose, Wood-bridge, Dollimore, Howard, and Garber have implicitly agreed—rightly, I think—on the play's ethical axis. *The Roaring Girl* is undeniably about the need for interpretive judgment of the dominant gender/class system, and all five scholars offer such judgments. My own interest involves the broader cultural context in which such judgments were voiced in the seventeenth century. Specifically, I want to cast the development of Jacobean satire in the context of the development of Puritanism.[10]

III

A century before Middleton and Dekker wrote *The Roaring Girl*, the words "Puritan" and even "Protestant" had not yet gained currency. In 1510 Martin Luther had yet to sever his ties with Rome. Henry VIII could still go on a pilgrimage to the town of Boxley to make an offering to a miracle-working icon: the Rood of Grace.[11] An image of the crucified Christ, the

Rood was an ingenious device made of wood, wires, and paste. The eyes and lips could be manipulated from the rear, so that the faithful who made sufficient offerings could directly perceive the workings of divine favor.

The three decades after Henry's pilgrimage to Boxley brought sweeping change to the English church, culminating in the break from Rome, the dissolution of the monasteries, and a wave of officially sanctioned iconoclasm. On February 24, 1538, John Hilsey brought the Rood of Grace with him onto the wooden platform at Paul's Cross, where he preached a sermon exposing the device as a sham. He showed his audience how the crucifix could be manipulated, one eyewitness reporting that during the sermon, "it turned its head, rolled its eyes, foamed at the mouth, and shed tears." [12] Hilsey proceeded to break this body of Christ and distribute the pieces among the audience, who enthusiastically completed the work of demolition. Of course, this bizarre parody of the sacrament of the Eucharist was meant to solidify anti-Roman sentiment by exposing the Catholic deception. But in teaching the audience a reformed version of the sacrament—that the true body of Christ was invisible, not something that could be perceived with the senses, much less localized in a monastery—it also imposed on them an interpretive burden that outweighed even the strain of choosing between denominations. Hilsey did not replace the mechanical crucifix with an ordinary one, a motionless and therefore appropriately evocative icon. Instead he destroyed the rood as an idol, replacing it with the words of his sermon.

Hilsey was not content simply to expose and destroy the false body of Christ; on November 24 of the same year he exposed the blood, too. It seems that a Cistercian monastery in Gloucestershire had been turning a tidy profit by exhibiting for adoration the Blood of Hailes, a crystal vessel purported to contain the actual blood of the Lord: blood that was visible only to those whose liberality to the monastery attested to the sanctity of their souls. Edward Lord Herbert of Cherbury, elder brother of the poet and preacher George Herbert, describes the method of display:

> It was said to have this property. That if a man were in mortal sin, and not absolved, he could not see it; otherwise, very well: Therefore every man that came to behold this miracle, confessed himself first to a priest there, and then offering something to the altar, was directed to a chapel where the relic was shewed; the priest who confessed him (in the mean while) retiring himself to the back part of the said chapel, and putting forth upon the altar a cabinet or tabernacle of crystal which being thick on one side . . . but on the other thin and transparent, they used diversly: For if a rich and devout man entered, they

would show him the thick side, till he had paid for as many masses, and given as large alms, as they thought fit; after which (to his great joy) they permitted him to see the thin side, and the blood.[13]

The Protestant authorities who examined the Blood of Hailes after its removal from the monastery variously reported that it was actually "honey clarified and coloured with saffron" or the blood of a duck.[14]

Staged incidents like the destruction of the Rood of Grace and the Blood of Hailes raise questions similar to the ones implicitly posed by performances ranging from Moll Cutpurse's drunken penance to the staging of Jacobean satire. What sort of rhetoric is in force when the stage— whether at Paul's Cross or the Fortune—is used to parody popular forms of devotion? With what are audiences being asked to replace their old devotional habits?

As Huston Diehl argues, the social drama of the Protestant Reformation evoked, examined, and reinterpreted the paradox of the Eucharist.[15] Hilsey's iconoclastic acts at Paul's Cross, for example, were designed to remind the audience of their Catholic habits, to question the value of literal-minded devotion—both in the Eucharist and in the adoration of images— and to reinforce a new, Protestant epistemology: one that responded to the root paradigm of Christ's martyrdom not with the eye but with the interior faculty of faith. By asking his audience to follow his lead (and he did ask them to) in destroying Catholic "idols," Hilsey was, from one point of view, liberating the people from their former superstitions. But from another, he was laying on them an enormous burden: the burden of interpretation, of discrimination between true and false spirituality, of developing a new epistemology. The demand that individuals learn to discriminate between legitimate and illegitimate images was but one aspect of this widespread Protestant emphasis on the power of discernment. This emphasis on individual interpretation, on definitive knowledge, meant for ordinary English people a whole new way of orienting themselves in the world. By 1598, John Howson could speak of the extent to which the new epistemology had incorporated itself into the liturgy: "In a word, I complain, and I complain not alone, that all the service of God is reduced only to hearing of sermons; and our hearing applied to knowledge only."[16]

Faith itself was defined as a species of knowledge. According to Calvin,

Now we shall have a perfect definition of faith if we say that it is a steadfast and assured knowledge of God's kindness toward us, which being grounded on the truth of the free promise in Christ, is both revealed to our minds and sealed in our hearts by the holy ghost. (*Institutes*, 3.2.7)

Or as George Gifford puts it, "faith is sure what God meaneth, or else it is no faith."[17] An index of the premium placed on assurance of doctrinal knowledge is the Puritans' insistence that all believers be able to recognize sound doctrine. As Patrick Collinson says,

> It is . . . abundantly clear that the puritans repelled intending communicants as much on the grounds of insufficient knowledge as of evil life, so exceeding the powers entrusted to them in the Prayer Book.[18]

One's very status as a member of the believing community, then, depended on knowledge; the sixteenth century witnessed a shift in focus from Calvin's "steadfast and assured knowledge of God's kindness toward us" to knowledge of the self as a member of the readily identifiable community of God's elect. The doctrine of justification by faith directly affected social definition.

The use of knowledge as a means of social discrimination is apparent in the late sixteenth-century controversy arising over the idea of "edification." The opposing positions are highlighted in the Admonition Controversy, the polemic exchange between John Whitgift and Thomas Cartwright arising out of the daring Puritan manifesto *An Admonition to Parliament*.[19] Peter Lake notes that while Whitgift held that edification meant simply moral instruction, Cartwright insisted that it implied the building up of the identifiable body of true believers. According to Cartwright, the "discipline" (the perfect use of each believer's gift in its proper office within the presbyterian system) would guarantee proper edification, so that the true body of the elect would soon be roughly equivalent to the membership of the visible church. Whitgift attacked this idea, arguing that Cartwright's spiritual perfectionism applied to the invisible church only, where the elect would always be united with Christ regardless of circumstances. According to Whitgift, no system of church polity could arrange to isolate the godly community from the ungodly.[20]

The Admonition Controversy thus centered on epistemology. Whitgift's "Who can tell whether he be . . . elect or reprobate?" was a key question of the age, one that Cartwright felt every Christian ought to be able to answer with certainty.[21] Cartwright's vision of a church based on this certainty and perfected by edification posed a radical threat to the precarious ecclesiastical compromise worked out by Elizabeth. Lake notes that in fact both sides saw the presbyterian program as a matter of national security; Cartwright claimed that the discipline would strengthen the state, and Whitgift countered that it would divide the realm in two (50). Both sides enlisted the printing press to educate the public, increasing the pressure for definitive interpretation of theological matters that had implications for the structure of the whole society.

What one could know, especially in matters of salvation, and how one could know it were thus extremely important questions in Elizabethan England. The new centrality of edifying knowledge had its impact not only on church liturgy, with the explosive popularity of late sixteenth-century sermons, and on domestic devotion, with the proliferation of catechisms and devotional handbooks, but also on a broader cultural level. In fact, some polemical writers questioned the value of any mode of discourse that did *not* center on epistemology. Stephen Gosson, for example, was hardly alone in his insistence that stage plays should be as edifying as sermons. In 1582 Gosson complained of the lack of edification in the popular romantic comedies of the 1570s:

> Sometime you shall see nothing but the adventures of an amorous knight, passing from country to country for the love of his lady, encountering many a terrible monster of brown paper. . . . What learn you by that? When the soul of your plays is either mere trifles, or Italian bawdry, or wooing of gentlewomen, what are we taught? [22]

There was no question that such plays produced pleasure, but was the pleasure legitimate? That is, did such romances not only delight but also instruct?

Despite the antagonism of critics like Gosson, romantic comedies flourished through the 1580s and into the 1590s. Toward the end of the century, though, the romantic comedy began to give way to the satire, a genre that promised to make the audience better. According to Alfred Harbage's count, 43 of the 55 surviving plays first produced in the private theaters between 1599 and 1613 are satirical comedies.[23] Nor was satire restricted to the private theaters. As the Bankside player Histrio boasts in Jonson's *Poetaster*, one Demetrius (Dekker) has just been hired to write a satire for the company: "O, it will get us a huge deal of money. . . . [Demetrius] has one of the most over-flowing rank wits in Rome. He will slander any man that breathes, if he disgust him" (3.4.323, 327, 338–40). Critics who comment on the origins of Tudor/Stuart satire are generally content simply to point to classical precedents, noting perhaps that English playwrights began to prefer the "Old Comedy" of Aristophanes to the more romantic "New Comedy" of Menander, Plautus, and Terence.[24]

But why the sudden change in taste? What are the cultural circumstances that make satire palatable to London playgoers? It seems to me that one factor is the explosion of interest in edifying knowledge that grew out of the Protestant Reformation. My claim is that, self-consciously or not, a playwright like Ben Jonson partakes in the very mentality he denounces. In his adaptation of classical forms to current situations, he participates in the Puritan interest in epistemology even as he inveighs against Puritanism. A 1611 Paul's Cross sermon by Robert Milles registers the relative success with which the defenders of the theater argued their case: "Yea, plays are grown nowadays into such high request (*Horresco referens*) as that some profane persons affirm they can learn as much both for example and edifying at a play as at a sermon. *O tempora, O mores!*"[25] As Milles continues, he launches an attack on Jonson himself:

> Did the devil ever speak thus impiously in this conflict with Archangel? To compare a lascivious stage to this sacred pulpit and oracle of truth? To compare a silken counterfeit to a prophet, to God's angel, to his minister, to the distributor of God's heavenly mysteries? And to compare the idle and scurrile invention of an illiterate bricklayer to the holy, pure, and powerful word of God, which is the food of our souls to eternal salvation? Lord, forgive them, they know not what they say. (D6^{r-v})

The "illiterate bricklayer" is undoubtedly Jonson, a playwright as insistent that his plays were edifying as that Puritans were hypocrites.[26]

It is probably a coincidence that Jonson's *Catiline*, first performed in the same year as Milles's sermon, contains an extended translation of the passage Milles quotes from *In Catilinam*, the passage beginning, "*O tempora, o mores!*"[27] But if Jonson got wind of Milles's affront (and there is little reason to doubt that a playwright as engaged in public controversy as Jonson would hear of a barely disguised insult hurled from Paul's Cross and published in the following year), it may well be that the playwright got his revenge in *Bartholomew Fair* (1614), an even more scathing attack on Puritanism than *The Alchemist* (1610). In *Bartholomew Fair* it is Zeal-of-the-land Busy who rails against the stage most vehemently:

Down with Dagon, down with Dagon; 'tis I, will no longer endure your pro-
fanations. . . . I will remove Dagon there, I say, that Idol, that heathenish Idol,
that remains (as I may say) a beam, a very beam, not a beam of the sun, nor
a beam of the moon, nor a beam of a balance, neither a house-beame, nor a
weaver's beam, but a beam in the eye, in the eye of the brethren; a very great
beam, an exceeding great beam; such as are your stage-players, rhymers, and
morris-dancers, who have walked hand in hand, in contempt of the brethren,
and the cause; and been borne out by instruments of no mean countenance.
(5.5.1–13)

Busy is not the only opponent of the theater in *Bartholomew Fair*. There is
also the pompous justice Adam Overdo, who visits the fair in disguise in
order to discover and denouce its "enormities." Overdo says of the acting
profession, "the favouring of this licencious quality is the consumption of
many a young gentleman; a pernicious enormity" (5.3.69–71). It is Overdo
who echoes Milles (and Cicero) in exclaiming, "*O tempora, O mores!*"
(2.2.113). Between *Catiline* and *Bartholomew Fair*, and very likely in response to Milles's insult, Jonson has moved Cicero's words from the lips
of Cicero himself as he rightly bemoans the corruption of his times to the
lips of a self-important, Latinizing opponent of the theater.

The heat of the controversy between the satirists and the reformers
has its bearing not only on the suddenness with which dramatic satire became popular (and vilified) but also on the extreme seriousness with which
a playwright like Jonson took his craft. Jonson's *Every Man Out of His
Humour*, first staged in 1599 by the Lord Chamberlain's Men in the newly
built Globe theater, is instructive in its justification of the move from
romantic comedy to satire. Midway through the play, the choral characters
Mitis and Cordatus comment on the action:

> Mitis: The argument of his comedy might have been of some other
> nature, as of a duke to be in love with a countess, and that count-
> ess to be in love with the duke's son, and the son to love the
> lady's waiting-maid: some such cross-wooing, with a clown to their
> serving man, better than to be thus near and familiarly allied to
> the time.
>
> Cordatus: You say well, but I would fain hear one of these autumn-
> judgments define once, *Quid sit comoedia?* If he cannot, let him
> content himself with Cicero's definition (till he have strength to
> propose himself a better) who would have a comedy to be *Imita-
> tio vitae, speculum consuetudinis, imago veritatis*; a thing throughout

pleasant and ridiculous, and accommodated to the correction of manners. (3.6.195–209)

Unlikely as it may seem, Jonson and Gosson are in complete agreement here: stage plays ought to teach.

As Jonson would be the first to point out, there is nothing new in the idea that art should instruct as well as delight. Whether one looks to English versions of the Horatian ideal such as Sidney's *Defence of Poetry*, or to the native English tradition of morality and mystery plays, one finds widespread agreement in Renaissance England that art should edify. What is new on the English scene with the late Tudor and early Stuart interest in satire is the method of edification. For the first time on the English stage, the mode of edification is "near and familiarly allied to the time," ridiculing contemporary individuals or groups, often ones with a high degree of social respectability. So it was that despite its socially conservative moralizing about "degree," a play like *Eastward Ho!* could land Jonson, Marston, and Chapman in prison, threatened with having their ears cut off and their noses slit, for seeming to be too near and familiarly allied to King James himself.

At times the familiar figures satirized were the playwrights themselves, as was the case in the quarrel that culminated in Jonson's *Poetaster* and Dekker's *Satiromastix*. In these plays the allegorical veil is thin; there is no doubt that in *Poetaster*, for example, Demetrius is Dekker, Crispinus is Marston, Horace is Jonson, Rome is London, the Tiber is the Thames, and so forth. Satire is also directed against contemporary separatist groups like the Family of Love, as in Middleton's play of that title and in Marston's *The Dutch Courtesan*.

One finds this divisive mentality not only on the stage but also in the pulpits, where groups as well as individuals were ridiculed. Throughout Elizabeth's reign, Roman Catholics and Anabaptists were regularly attacked in official sermons, but as the sixteenth century progressed even bishops in the Church of England were increasingly singled out for abuse.[28] The radical Protestant press reflects this development. As Collinson points out, it was not until the early 1580s that the battle lines between the Puritans and the established church were clearly drawn:

> as if to convince the queen that the spirit of Calvinism was irrepressible, the puritan press at this point broadened its attack and began to assert the distinctive social morality with which puritanism has been associated ever since. (208)

No doubt the most derisive of all the Puritan attacks on the bishops came in 1588 and 1589 with the anonymous Marprelate tracts, peculiar combinations of fiercely humorous ridicule and Puritan earnestness. Francis Bacon disliked the tracts, calling their style an "immodest and deformed manner of writing . . . whereby the matter of religion is handled in the style of the stage."[29] The Marprelate tracts were so shocking, even by Elizabethan standards, that it can be doubted whether they advanced the Puritan cause or merely solidified the opposition. In any case the very divisiveness of their rhetoric is instructive since the English satiric comedy developed and gained popularity precisely at the time when the rhetoric of Puritanism was becoming increasingly divisive.

Puritan polemics like the Marprelate tracts were in part responsible for the bishops' 1599 decision to ban the printing of prose and poetic satires. This decision, in turn, led John Marston and Ben Jonson to develop the comical satire for the stage. It seems that the social drama of the Protestant Reformation encouraged a pervasive cultural need, among Puritans as well as anti-Puritan playwrights, to conquer by dividing. Puritan polemics and satiric drama, then, share a rhetorical principle: both hold up for ridicule the caricatures of contemporary opponents in order to edify an audience. In both cases, as a result of the audience's self-definition in contrast to someone perceived as a member of a competing social group, edification comes to mean exclusion.[30]

To be sure, there is disagreement about what the edified audience is to believe; Ben Jonson and Stephen Gosson would no doubt have their differences about any number of topics. The point here is that they disagree in rhetorically similar terms. Both hold that plays should instruct, should provide social definition, even if the terms of this definition are so different for Jonson and Gosson that their ideological descendants were to take opposing sides in the Civil War.

In one sense, then, the satiric playwright and the Puritan polemicist could hardly be more different—as both sides insisted. But in another sense the very insistence belies the difference. By the turn of the seventeenth century the satiric playwrights and the Puritans had developed a symbiotic relationship; each side needed the other in order to be rhetorically effective. In fact, the well-known antitheatrical invectives hurled by Puritans like William Rankins, Phillip Stubbes, John Rainolds, and William Prynne are rhetorically of a piece with the vituperative counterattacks by playwrights like Marston, Jonson, Beaumont, and Middleton. In a sense the Puritans and the playwrights occupied the stage at the same time in the disruptive cultural crisis that gave birth to the modern age. As in the verbal fencing of two antagonistic characters in a play, each side developed a sense of self by railing against the other. Both, though, were caught up in the action of the whole.

IV

The Puritan polemicists and the satiric playwrights share an either/or mentality—a vision of a world clearly divided into sheep and goats, believers and infidels, insiders and outsiders. The tendency toward exclusiveness among the Puritans is well known from contemporary satiric portraits of them. Ben Jonson alone gives us numerous self-righteously exclusive Puritans, such as Ananias, Tribulation Wholesome, Zeal-of-the-land Busy, and Dame Purecraft. Littlewit's claim in *Bartholomew Fair* that his mother-in-law, Dame Purecraft, is a "most elect hypocrite" is borne out by Purecraft herself, who enters a moment later saying, "Now the blaze of the beauteous discipline fright away this evil from our house!" (1.5.163; 1.6.1–2). Dame Purecraft eventually reveals herself as a thoroughgoing hypocrite whose habit of "pronouncing reprobation and damnation" is part of a money-making scheme (5.2.65).

It may well be that in ridiculing the hypocrisies of characters like Purecraft, Jonson is upholding the Christian values that she perverts. Thus, when Quarlous says that Purecraft and company are "the only privileged church-robbers of Christendom," Jonson is very likely defending Christendom and church (5.2.45–46). The point here, however, is not to locate Jonson's theological beliefs in relation to Puritanism but to point out that in exposing Puritan hypocrisy Jonson's rhetoric functions similarly to that of the Puritans he satirizes. In one sense, then, when Jonson attacks Puritan ideas like edification or church discipline he is simply giving tit for tat: if the godly brethren choose to rail against the theater, Jonson will ridicule the godly brethren. But there is more involved here than a simple clash between ideologies. When, for example, upon entering Ursula's booth Busy says, "We scape so much of the other vanities, by our early entering," and Purecraft replies, "It is an edifying consideration," Jonson's satire both attacks a Puritan idea of edification and seeks to edify the audience (3.2.90–92). The same is the case with his satiric attack on Puritan "discipline" in *The Alchemist* when Tribulation expresses hope that Subtle may one day "stand up for the beauteous discipline, / Against the menstruous cloth, and rag of Rome" (3.1.32–33). Here Jonson's irony turns Tribulation's anti-Roman polemic into an anti-Puritan one. One ideologically exclusive discipline replaces another. Such polemic strategy is common in Jonson; his dialogue is consistently fueled by an exclusivist rhetoric, something like partisan politics.

Nor is Jonson alone in this rhetorical tendency. The same might be said of satirical playwrights like Middleton and Beaumont.[31] In Middleton's *A Chaste Maid in Cheapside*, for example, when Yellowhammer cannot decipher the Latin of his son's letter from Cambridge, Maudlin suggests that he ask the parson. Yellowhammer replies, "Nay he disclaims it, calls Latin Papistry, he will not deal with it."[32] Of course, this is not a jab at Papistry at all, but one at the narrow-mindedness of the pervasive Protestant tendency to denounce all things Roman. Again, one denunciation replaces another.

Or as Rafe the "grocer-errant" says to Pompiona in Beaumont's *Knight of the Burning Pestle*,

> I am a knight of a religious order,
> And will not wear a favour of a lady's
> That trusts in Antichrist and false traditions.[33]

The Citizen, eager to see his apprentice-turned-actor do well, shouts from the audience, "Well said, Rafe! convert her, if thou canst" (4.95). Beaumont's parody of the Puritan emphasis on sudden, ideologically exclusive conversion continues as Nell expresses her concern that Rafe will be unable to convert the giant Barbarossa: "a giant is not so soon converted as one of us ordinary people" (3.426–27). In thus satirizing the "ordinary people" whose readiness to be converted really implies their readiness to be gulled, Beaumont of course encourages the audience to define themselves in contrast to the Citizen and Nell. But he does something more. By choosing the idea of conversion as the focus of his satire, Beaumont goes beyond merely poking fun at a simple-minded segment of society. While he is lightly ridiculing a Protestant zeal to gain converts from Roman Catholicism, he is also making it difficult for the audience to embrace the Christian paradigm of conversion.[34]

While Orthodox Christianity (both Eastern and Western) has always held that a conversion of the will is a condition of salvation, in popular devotion during the Middle Ages sacramentalism often received greater emphasis than conversion. The paradigm of conversion, then, tended to stay beneath the surface. A central impulse of the Reformation was to reverse the medieval emphases, to reassert the need for individual conversion. Toward the end of the sixteenth century such assertions often became particularly strident, as did the counter-assertions of those who disagreed. A Puritan insisting on a certain sort of conversion leading to readily identifiable behavior and a playwright ridiculing this kind of conversion are participating in the same kind of rhetoric; both are evoking a central paradigm in order to define an "elect" in ideologically exclusive terms.

This tendency is reflected in the satiric playwrights' handling of repentance. Beaumont, Middleton, and Jonson all provide portraits of characters whose contrition for wrongdoing is satirically undermined. In *The Knight of the Burning Pestle*, the "ghost" of Jasper—actually Jasper "with his face mealed"—frightens Venturewell into contrition for blocking the marriage of the young lovers (5.4 s.d.). Jasper demands that Venturewell beat the rival suitor Humphrey and make amends to Merrythought. After heartily pummeling Humphrey, Venturewell hastens to complete his penance:

> O Master Merrythought, I am come to ask you
> Forgiveness for the wrongs I offered you
> And your most virtuous son. They're infinite;
> Yet my contrition shall be more than they.
> I do confess my hardness broke his heart,
> For which just heaven hath given me punishment
> More than my age can carry. His wandering spirit,
> Not yet at rest, pursues me everywhere,
> Crying, "I'll haunt thee for thy cruelty." (5.249–57)

Venturewell's fearful repentance is undermined not only by the audience's knowledge that Jasper has gulled the old man but also by Beaumont's metadramatic handling of the play-within-the-play. Just as Jasper and Luce are "reborn," just when Venturewell has a chance to prove the sincerity of his conversion by forgiving the lovers, the Citizen interrupts the action:

> Citizen: I do not like this. Peace, boys; Hear me, one of you! Everybody's part is come to an end but Rafe's, and he's left out.
> Boy: 'Tis long of yourself, sir; we have nothing to do with his part.
> Citizen: Rafe, come away.—Make an end on him as you have done of the rest, boys; come.
> Wife: Now, good husband, let him come out and die.

> Citizen: He shall, Nell. — Rafe, come away quickly and die, boy.
> (5.276–85)

Rafe enters with a forked arrow through his head and obliges by dying — and at great length. The absurd death of Rafe, followed by his rising to take his bows, undermines the spiritual death and rebirth implicit in Venturewell's conversion.

Of course, comedy is generally conducive to conversions, to happy endings; it is in a tragedy like *Doctor Faustus* that the tragic figure finds himself unable to repent. While a comedy like Middleton's *A Chaste Maid in Cheapside* doesn't satirize Puritans in the way that, say, *The Alchemist* does, it does work to unsettle the paradigm of conversion. When the wounded Sir Walter Whorehound finally realizes the enormity of his offenses, a conversion would seem to be in order. In fact Sir Walter flirts with repentance:

> I am o'er grown with sin;
> O how my offenses wrestle with my repentance,
> It hath scarce breath — (5.1.74–76).

Middleton thus sets up the expectation of conversion, but Sir Walter never repents. Terrified by the prospect of death, he turns his self-pity into spite, cursing everyone around him as he exits for the last time.

Just as Sir Walter might have been stirred to repentance by his own impending death, it would seem that Moll's apparent death might bring about the Yellowhammers' conversion from their unfeeling acquisitiveness. In fact, though, Yellowhammer is more worried about his own reputation than the death of his daughter, and he remains resolutely mercenary even after she rises from her coffin. In short, Middleton thwarts any expectation of conversion he sets up, leaving the audience to question whether sincere repentance is even possible in the world of the play. Even when a character seems sincerely penitent, it is hard to take him seriously. In *A Mad World, My Masters*, for example, Penitent Brothel's very name registers the difficulty. His speech of contrition for adultery is accompanied by the rather desperate expedient (desperate for an otherwise ordinary City comedy, anyway) of a comic succubus.

Jonson's *The Alchemist* also implies a critique of the basic Christian paradigm of conversion. When Sir Epicure Mammon learns that an explosion has destroyed all his hopes of gold as well as the considerable investment he has made, he seems to see the error of his ways: "O my voluptuous mind! I am justly punished / . . . Cast from all my hopes / . . . By mine own base affections" (4.5.74–76). But the audience is given no chance to recognize the validity of Mammon's conversion, no opportunity for empathy. The focus remains on the con game, as Face manages to use Mammon's contrition to dupe the knight out of yet another hundred pounds.

All these dramatic undercuttings of the stage *topos* of conversion imply an exclusivist rhetoric in that they provide no quarter for any communal reception of a basic cultural paradigm. The appeal is rather to the audience's self-definition in contrast to the gulls depicted on the stage. This is not to say that such plays preclude individual audience members' seeking some alternative, unifying vision that contrasts with the world of the play, but only that the plays themselves tend not to invite such a response. One scholar's claim that "Only by forcing the viewer to see himself in the glass of satire can moral comedy succeed" [35] may be less to the point than Jonathan Swift's comment: "Satire is a sort of glass, wherein beholders do generally discover everybody's face but their own." [36]

The same principle holds in Jonson's use of phrases like "elect hypocrite" and "pronouncing reprobation" (*Bartholomew Fair*, 1.5.163; 5.2.65). By highlighting the doctrine of election in such a context, Jonson is calling into question a doctrine so central to Calvin's thought that well before Jonson's day it had become the identifying feature of Calvinism and was enormously influential not only among dissenting Puritans but also among theologians at the heart of the Church of England. Jonson is not, then, merely ridiculing some fringe group in order to endorse the status quo; he is encouraging his audience to question a widely held theological tenet.

The doctrine of election, of course, implies an absolute, unalterable exclusiveness. One might satirize or question the doctrine in order to impugn the whole idea of social stratification, but this is not what Jonson's plays do. Rather, they assert a new sort of exclusiveness by reinterpreting ideological categories. In depicting characters whose indomitable credulity is not endorsed as faith but condemned as stupidity, Jonson's comedies encourage an exclusiveness based on wit, common sense, shrewdness, and learning—all characteristics that Jonson himself possessed in abundance.

This perhaps explains why Bonario and Celia, the only morally upright characters in *Volpone*, have so little appeal in contrast to Volpone and Mosca. Upon first meeting Mosca, Bonario says, "I would be loth to interchange discourse / With such a mate as thou art" (3.2.5–6). Perhaps Bonario's repugnance is justified by Mosca's habitual behavior, but that behavior has been extraordinarily entertaining to the audience for two acts.

And it is entertaining to see Mosca's trickery work yet again—this time on the too-credulous Bonario, who has just accused the parasite of baseness, sloth, and flattery. Mosca cries as he protests,

> These imputations are all too common, sir,
> And eas'ly stuck on virtue when she's poor. (3.2.12–13)

Bonario responds in an aside,

> What? does he weep? the sign is soft and good.
> I do repent me that I was so harsh. (3.2.18–19)

To be sure, the virtue of Bonario and Celia wins the day in the end, but given the dramatic energy invested in Mosca and Volpone, it is difficult for simplicity, faith, and justice to compete with shrewdness, trickery, and vice. Even in a play that condemns avarice, then, Jonson makes it difficult for the audience to appropriate the opposite virtue of generosity.

The same might be said of Middleton. In *A Trick to Catch the Old One*, for example, it is by virtue of his wit and shrewdness, his readiness to con others, that Witgood is able to arrange his marriage to a rich girl. What distinguishes Witgood from the other scoundrels in the play is not superior moral character in any traditional sense but superior cunning. It is only by virtue of his shrewdness that it seems fitting for him rather than someone else to win the usurer's wealthy niece as a sort of grand prize in a contest of wits.[37]

One might argue that the satiric bent of these plays leads audiences to denounce such commodification of human relationships along with other abuses if it were not that commodification is at the heart of the satiric enterprise. The relentless consumption of *things* that Katharine Maus has identified as a central feature of Jonson's plays is emblematic of an exchange that involves audiences as well as characters in Jacobean satire generally.[38] What is advertized in these plays—what the audience pays for and gets—is a sharpening of boundaries, edification, a kind of epistemic demystification.

Just as pulpit performances like the destruction of the Rood of Grace and the Blood of Hailes expose the trickery of mercenary churchmen by teaching the audience to look beyond appearances, these satires almost invariably center on the exposure of trickery. Quomodo in Middleton's *Michaelmas Term* describes the process as a kind of epistemic transaction: "for craft, once known, / Does teach fools wit, leaves the deceiver none."[39] The rhetoric of trickery exposed leaves the audience member feeling like one of the insiders, a non-gull, a recipient of the "wit" that the deceiver loses upon being found out. A transaction has been completed.

Jonson's comedies in particular are designed to promote an economic/ epistemic partisanship, an awareness that resists the audience's communal reception of non-mercantile paradigms. *The Alchemist* ends with a sort of communal celebration, but it is one in which the audience cannot participate wholeheartedly without sharing in mercenary qualities like Face's dishonesty, not to mention Lovewit's opportunism. The rhetoric of *The Alchemist* keeps the audience at a distance, allowing identification with no character whose vision transcends or replaces the values under attack. Such a strategy makes for excellent entertainment; compared with a play like *Poetaster*, which provides a thoroughly upright satirist in the person of Horace, *The Alchemist* successfully completes the epistemic exchange. But the play leads the audience to recognize the hopelessness of fighting for all the values that greed obscures, allowing identification with entertaining characters like Face, Subtle, and Dol only at the cost of rejecting those values. The same principle holds in the epilogue to *Volpone*, in which the audience is explicitly asked to applaud the villain.

It might be argued that *Bartholomew Fair* tends toward a less exclusive rhetoric since in the end Justice Adam Overdo lets various scoundrels off the hook.[40] It is Quarlous who advises Overdo, "remember you are but Adam, flesh and blood! you have your frailty, forget your other name of Overdo, and invite us all to supper" (5.6.96–98). Overdo does just that, assuring the assorted malefactors that his intentions are "*ad correctionem, non ad destructionem; ad aedificandum, non ad diruendum*" (5.6.112–113). But has Overdo really come to terms with his own frailty? And even if he has, given the play's vision of pervasive human greed, one cannot help wondering whether this throwback to the *pedante* of Italian comedy will really make much headway in his project of edification. After all, not one of the characters to be edified has shown the slightest interest in receiving instruction. And a great deal of the play's rhetoric dictates that even for the audience, edification is based not on any vision of shared human frailty but an exchange of epistemic currency between character and spectator.

V

This analysis charges the satiric plays, and Jonson's in particular, with a more volatile ethical investment than is sometimes seen in them. But given the frequently hostile reactions to early performances of the plays, the claim seems justified; it is fair to say that the plays are at least as much partisan manifesto as they are pastime. Such a view of the plays' rhetoric helps to account for Jonson's hostility as well as that of his detractors. In the Epistle to *Volpone*, for example, Jonson complains of the "supercilious politics" who accuse him of "sharpness," of "a pride, or lust, to be bitter" (49, 51). The playwright protests,

> What broad reproofs have I used? Where have I been particular? Where personal? except to a mimic, cheater, bawd, or buffoon, creatures for their insolencies worthy to be taxed? (55–58)

Jonson's self-defense resides in an appeal to the reader's sense of justice; the satires have attacked only those who deserve attack. Even if Jonson's bitterness is justified, the rhetorical mode remains that of ideological definition: the aesthetic and intellectual (and therefore, in Jonson's view, the moral) isolation of the insiders from the outsiders.

The same rhetorical tendency is evident in the Induction to *Bartholomew Fair*, in which the Scrivener reads some "articles of agreement" penned by the author. The articles claim that the play is "made to delight all, and to offend none. Provided they have either the wit or the honesty to think well of themselves" (Induction, 82–84). As in the Epistle to *Volpone*, Jonson claims to be inoffensive, only to subvert that claim by qualifying it. Those who "think well of themselves," Jonson says, will be delighted by *Bartholomew Fair*. But the play itself relentlessly satirizes those who think well of themselves. After all, who has more self-esteem than Cokes? Or Overdo? Or Zeal-of-the-land Busy? It is Busy who declares that the "reformed mouth" may lawfully eat Ursula's roast pig, especially if it is done to express "hate and loathing of Judaism" (1.6.74, 95–96). Jonson's satire is here so effective that it is easy to lose sight of the similarity of his rhetoric to Busy's; Jonson's Puritans are Busy's Jews.

As Jonas Barish has argued, Jonson's attitude toward the stage involves "a deeply rooted antitheatricalism":

> He belongs, in spirit, among a galaxy of talented playwrights who at a given moment in their careers have seen their whole enterprise as hollow, and proceeded to renounce it, or else reform it.[41]

According to Richard Helgerson, this antagonism to the stage is in part an outgrowth of Jonson's allegiance to humanism.[42] But "humanism" here must not be understood in any narrowly secular sense. The relation between humanism and Protestantism is notoriously complex; certainly it would be simplistic to see the two movements as radically separate.[43] Both center on the word, eschewing merely visual allure, and Jonson is heir to both. Jonson's preference for the printed version of his plays to their staged presentations finds its counterpart in the Protestant preference for the word to the image.[44]

It is instructive that the two poets in addition to Jonson treated in Helgerson's study of "self-crowned laureates" are Spenser and Milton. Like the classicism of these two undeniably Protestant poets, Jonson's humanism is shaped by the Protestant discourse of his time. The playwright's antitheatricalism is in large part a function of the peculiar sort of rhetoric fostered by the Protestant Reformation. This is not to make Jonson (or Middleton, Marston, or Beaumont) into another Spenser or another Milton, but only to note the rhetorical indebtedness of Jacobean satire to the Reformation. Classical precedents existed for the satiric playwrights' rhetoric, but it took the peculiar cultural situation of late Tudor and early Stuart England to allow this rhetoric to flourish.

In their rhetorical challenges to the central paradigms that had informed Western European culture for 1500 years, the satiric playwrights and the Puritans were arguing in similar terms, even when they argued on opposite sides. Both sides were straining for definition at a time when all social institutions seemed threatened. It would be simplistic to label this straining either politically conservative or subversive. In fact both sides took a radically ambivalent view of existing social structures. Both the satiric playwrights and the Puritans longed for social change even as they inveighed against those who seemed to threaten order and discipline.[45] In the end, of course, a new order replaced the old. Although neither side would have claimed allegiance to the secular, self-assertive mentality that developed over the course of the next two centuries, both sides played their parts in ushering in the new epistemology.

VI

To end where we began: Mary Frith is lifted from the London underworld to the stage at Paul's Cross, where she puts on a maudlin display of penance. Meanwhile, the Moll Cutpurse of *The Roaring Girl* displays that she has nothing to repent. Is it possible to draw any conclusions about the ethical relation between the two performances? The play makes overtures to a kind of moral that apparently points to one possibility: in the end Sir Alexander Wengrave, who has all along taken Moll's promiscuity for granted, swears, "I'll never more / Condemn by common voice" (5.2.248–49). It would seem that Wengrave has learned his lesson; he will no longer believe idle gossip. But what does this new moral awareness imply? In asserting his control over the "common voice," Wengrave posits a new kind of hierarchy, one based not on uncommon socioeconomic but on uncommon epistemic status. He invites the audience to join him in a sort of edified elite. The heady shrewdness in which satires like *The Roaring Girl* traffic is the commodity that the price of admission buys. Whether the purchase would help the playgoer learn how to respond—not just to Moll Cutpurse but also to Mary Frith—is quite another matter.

5. "Strange Tempests": The Rhetoric of Judgment in Field and Shakespeare

I

It was Macaulay who said that Puritans hated bearbaiting not because it gave pain to the bear but because it gave pleasure to the spectator.[1] Thanks in no small part to Ben Jonson, we are all familiar with dramatic depictions of this sort of Puritan. The real sort, though, were often more favorably disposed to human pleasure than the caricatures would lead us to believe. A case in point is John Field, a Puritan if ever there was one. Co-author (with Thomas Wilcox) of the 1572 *Admonition to Parliament*, a document that breathlessly demanded immediate and sweeping reformation of the Church of England, Field embodied for many of his contemporaries the spirit of Church purification—that is, Puritanism. Needless to say, Elizabeth was less than pleased with the *Admonition*, but a year after its publication, Field was out of the Tower. Within a decade he was back in the pulpit.

Early in 1583, a Sunday accident at the Paris Garden bearbaiting pit in the burgeoning theater district of the Bankside gave this popular preacher fuel for a characteristically fiery sermon: *A Godly Exhortation, by occasion of the late judgment of God, shewed at Paris-garden, the thirteenth day of January: where were assembled by estimation; above a thousand persons, whereof some were slain; and of that number, at the least, as is credibly reported, the third person maimed and hurt.*[2] As the title indicates, Field saw the collapse of the scaffolding at Paris Garden as a direct judgment of God on those who spent their Sunday at a bearbaiting pit instead of a church.

So far, it seems that Field fits perfectly Macaulay's stereotype of the Elizabethan Puritan; he seems to be the sort who would feel at home exchanging platitudes with Tribulation Wholesome or Zeal-of-the-land Busy. But a reading of the *Godly Exhortation* reveals not only that Field is a vigorous, earthy prose stylist, but also that he is no enemy of human pleasure. In fact this preacher, often cited as one of the primary opponents of the theater, employs a rhetorical strategy remarkably similar to that of some Shakespearean comedy.[3]

All four works treated below—Field's sermon and Shakespeare's *Measure for Measure*, *The Tempest*, and *The Winter's Tale*—focus on the problem of delayed judgment. In their rhetorical similarity, the four works reveal something of an abiding cultural concern. Both in the pulpit and on the stage, the frequent Renaissance treatments of the interrelations among judgment, mercy, and time address the question of how to orient the self in a radically changing world, a world that appears both threatening and promising. Central to the process of identity formation in the Renaissance is the mystery of a God who is simultaneously judgmental and merciful. The idea is a common topic among not only Renaissance playwrights but also Reformation preachers, especially those who habitually explore theological paradoxes.[4] Sampson Price's formulation is typical: "It's a fond conceit of the profane vulgar to make God all of mercies, a gross ignorance to disjoin mercy and justice in him to whom they are both essential."[5]

Like other expressions of contrariety that arise out of the central paradigms of Renaissance culture, performances centered on the paradox of simultaneous judgment and mercy carry the potential to evoke either partisanship or inclusiveness. Particularly if the paradoxical tension is lessened —if judgment is advanced at the expense of mercy (as in, say, *The Spanish Tragedy*), or if a sentimental mercy effaces judgment (as in *The Faithful Shepherdess*), the rhetoric tends toward ideological partisanship. Whether one reads such plays as subversive or conservative of dominant power relations, the plays lend themselves to analysis along party lines. If the playwright (or the preacher) is able to evoke a state of receptivity to judgment and mercy simultaneously, as is the case with the four performances examined here, the audience's impulse toward definition and exclusion is frustrated, replaced with an inclusive sense of human solidarity.

II

The biblical roots of the judgment/mercy paradox are fairly complicated, particularly because the Bible sometimes depicts judgment as desirable and sometimes as utterly fearsome. The Hebrew and Greek words translated "judgment" in the Geneva and King James versions of the Bible cover some range of meaning, but in all cases the concept of judgment involves a reliable authority's equitable decision or sentence.[6] The widely diverg-

ing biblical views of judgment result from differing views of human culpability. In the Hebrew Bible, judgment is almost invariably seen as an
alternative to judicial corruption and is therefore almost invariably desirable. This is the case because the legal disputes conceived in the Hebrew
Bible, especially in the Psalms, tend to be civil cases with the author as
victimized plaintiff. A fair judgment, then—and whose could be more fair
than God's?—is a welcome prospect. So it is that the Psalmist can express a wish that would be horrifying to many Reformation preachers and
their congregations: "Judge me, O Lord my God, according to thy righteousness" (Ps. 35:24). Or, equally frightening from a Calvinist point of
view, "Judge thou me, O Lord, according to my righteousness" (Ps. 7:8).[7]
As the doctrine of original sin is not explicitly developed in the Hebrew
Bible, it is not surprising that the idea of universal human culpability and
therefore the fearfulness of God's judgments is very nearly absent from the
Psalms.[8] When the Psalmist says, then, "I will sing of mercy and judgment"
(Ps. 101:1), the author is not really expressing a paradox; "judgment" here
means fairness—a lack of judicial corruption—and so it means mercy for
any innocent party involved in a legal dispute.

The New Testament at times appropriates this usage, as when Jesus
says, "Woe be to you, Scribes and Pharisees, hypocrites: for ye tithe mint
and anise and cumin, and leave the weightier matters of the Law, as judgment and mercy and fidelity" (Matt. 23:23). At other times in the New
Testament, though, judgment is a fearful prospect for all human beings
since all are guilty in God's eyes. In these passages God is the judge in a
criminal case, and the human defendant, no matter how morally upright,
is inevitably guilty. The individual is no longer the victim looking for just
compensation but the criminal, subject to God's full vengeance for breaking the divine law. Jesus' Sermon on the Mount, for example, replete as
it is with promises of mercy, also intensifies the concept of criminal judgment, allowing no one to claim innocence. It is not only the murderer who
is "culpable of judgment" (Matt. 5:21) but also the one who is angry with
his brother. Judgment awaits not only the adulterous man but also the one
who "looketh on a woman to lust after her" (Matt. 5:28). No human being,
then, can escape guilt. In Paul's formulation of the idea, "all have sinned
and are deprived of the glory of God." The next verse, though, completes
not only the sentence but also the paradox: "and are justified freely by his
grace, through the redemption that is in Christ Jesus" (Rom. 3:23–24). In
short, all believers are subject to judgment and mercy simultaneously.

The Protestant reformers make much of this paradox, stressing both human depravity and human sanctity, both divine judgment and divine mercy. The writings of Martin Luther in particular go a long way to promote this mentality. Luther's habitual use of theological paradox derives in large part from his own powerful experience of remaining subject to God's wrath and mercy simultaneously.[9] Although Calvin is less congenial than Luther to the idea of advocating paradox as a habitual state of psychological tension, like Luther he relentlessly stresses both the mercy of human participation in divine glory and the judgment attendant upon universal human culpability.

Following the leads of Luther and Calvin, English Reformation preachers who speak of God's mercy habitually couple the idea with that of God's judgment—not judgment in the Psalmist's sense but the sort of righteous sentence that condemns every human being. As the marginal glosses in the Geneva Bible reveal, Reformation theologians often stress the latter sort of judgment even in biblical passages that seem to call for the former. In Isaiah 30:18, for example, the prophet uses the word "judgment" to express God's equitable restraint:

> Yet therefore will the Lord wait, that he may have mercy upon you, and therefore will he be exalted, that he may have compassion upon you: for the Lord is the God of judgment: Blessed are all they that wait for him.

The marginal comment on "judgment" refers the reader to Jeremiah 30:24: "The fierce wrath of the Lord shall not return [turn back], until he have done, and until he have performed the intents of his heart." The reader of the Geneva Bible, then, is not allowed to forget God's wrath even in a passage that focuses on God's mercy. Both ideas—wrath and mercy—are to be present in the reader's mind simultaneously. A good deal of Reformation rhetoric aims to instill in the believer this paradoxical mentality.

At times the preachers negotiate the paradox of a judgmental and yet forgiving God by explaining the matter as a temporal process, by contrasting past culpability and the possibility of future judgment with the present offer of mercy. In these terms, God's mercy consists in his delaying the hour of judgment. It might seem that such a paradigm would resolve the paradox into a comprehensible temporal scheme, but such is not the case. In the audience's experience of the preacher's rhetoric, as well as in the theology that informs the sermon, the tension of the paradox is maintained; the believer stands simultaneously condemned and pardoned. The sinner who is somehow accounted righteous in an omniscient God's eyes remains in fact a sinner. Such paradoxical rhetoric, in collapsing the redemptive process into a simultaneous perception of judgment and mercy, invites a peculiar state of moral and aesthetic receptivity, one that is hard to describe except in terms of negation: it makes exclusiveness unpalatable without resorting to a merely sentimental inclusiveness.

This rhetorical effect is possible in part because a sermon or a stage play unfolds through time. These modes are particularly well adapted to paradoxes involving time because they can both assert temporality by narrating a series of events and undermine temporality by generating a state of receptivity in which opposing elements are perceived simultaneously. In the case of artistic presentations of the paradox of judgment and mercy, such rhetoric holds in check the audience's ordinary, temporally experienced concerns and yields a paradoxical awareness: a liberating sense of responsibility. All four works treated below evoke in the audience this peculiar state of moral and aesthetic receptivity. In their rhetorical complementarity, the works by Field and Shakespeare point to the cultural interdependency of Renaissance modes of discourse as different as the sermon and the stage play.

III

The opening sentence of Field's sermon immediately puts the audience under pressure:

> There is no man will deny, as I suppose, dearly beloved in Christ, but that the more a man hath received of the graces and gifts of God, the more is he bound by duty unto his obedience. (A4ʳ)

Surely for everyone in the audience the "graces and gifts of God" are devoutly to be desired, but Field makes it clear that the price of such gifts is increased responsibility, increased obedience. And who among the hearers can claim obedience commensurate with the blessings bestowed by God? To reinforce the point, Field speaks of the blessing that "hath this little island as a garden of the Lord been decked and garlanded with sundry most gracious and excellent gifts" (A4ʳ). England is "the paradise of the world," where

> Every man enjoyeth his wife, children, goods, cattle, and possessions. Every man sitteth under his own vine, and heareth the voice of his children in the streets. Our young men and our maidens rejoice in public places, and the

> noise of music is heard in our assemblies. We drink in bowls of gold, and in cups of silver: our heads are anointed with sweet ointments, and our faces are cheerful, because our hearts are merry. (A4ᵛ–A5ʳ)

Quite apart from the casually proprietary linkage of family members with other "possessions" is the earthy appeal of the children's voices, the music, and the merriment. These images are designed to make the hearer thankful, but they are also unsettling: if not because of the implicit reminder that the hearer has not been thankful enough, then because of the disjunction between the imagery and actual conditions. After all, only a few in England actually enjoy all the blessings enumerated. Field gradually increases the tension of this multiple perception by making his claims more and more fantastic:

> The voice of mourning is not heard amongst us, neither hath terror and fear amazed us. Our weapons are turned into plowshares, and lions and lambs play together without hurting one another. (A5ʳ)

Here the evocation of an England that fulfills biblical prophecy is at once comforting and disconcerting. No doubt it is good to find oneself in paradise, to imagine Elizabethan England as the promised millennial community, but does anyone in the audience really believe that the Millennium has arrived? Has fear really been banished? Are there really no more swords in England?

The strategy of the sermon so far has been to offer the hearers the voice and vision of present mercy but simultaneously to undercut that presentation by forcing an awareness that the full consummation of that mercy is unavailable in the present. To an Elizabethan audience, steeped in the popular eschatology of the day, this rhetoric would be decidedly forceful. Reformation preachers frequently stress the idea that present acts of obedience to the will of God will immediately usher in a time of unheard-of blessings, as acts of disobedience will lead to devastating plague and famine.[10] The present moment, then, is always crucial. The future, which will consist of either absolute joy or absolute sorrow, is folded into the present, which contains elements of both.

Field increases the tension by going on to enumerate God's spiritual blessings, which of course far exceed the temporal. These "infinite" spiritual blessings, though, must be expressed in abstract terms; it is less easy to appreciate "glory," "righteousness," and "grace" than the voices of children

in the streets or lions playing with lambs (A5^{r-v}). Since the demand is that
the hearers appreciate the spiritual blessings *more* than the physical, not
less, Field has now prepared the audience for his next move. Having used
Isaiah to evoke a millennial vision, he now draws on the same prophet to
call down judgment on the unthankful congregation:

> You see how the Prophet setteth forth the large liberality and goodness of
> God towards his people: and again their unthankfulness, with those judg-
> ments that it drew upon them. The benefits no doubt that God had bestowed
> upon them were excellent, but their abuse was likewise intolerable, and there-
> fore for the one, there is threatened the taking of them away, and for the
> other, what horrible punishments he would bring upon them. (A7^{r})

Punishment of the unthankful is certain; the only question is when it
will come.

By evoking simultaneously the uneasiness of impending judgment
and the comfort of present mercy, Field's rhetoric continues to draw the
future into the present. Citing the parable of the fig tree in the vineyard
(Luke 13:6–9), in which the dresser of the vineyard begs the owner to give
him one more year to make a barren fig tree produce fruit, Field simultaneously warns his hearers that judgment is imminent and offers them the
present consolation of God's merciful patience:

> And as he waited for fruit in great patience before his judgments were exe-
> cuted, so he hath waited upon us these many years: he sits looking to that
> tree mentioned in the Gospel, which long since had been plucked up by the
> roots, had not he in a wonderful patience expected our conversion and better
> fruits. (A7^{v})

According to Field, God will not long delay the day of wrath. The preacher
compares the world, "laden with sins and abominations," to a ship about
to wreck (A8^{r}). As yet the ship of the world has not quite capsized, but it
has taken on a good deal of water. Lest anyone doubt that God *will* wreck
the ship, lest anyone think that it is possible to hide from God's wrath,
Field is quick to point out that since all have sinned, no one can escape divine judgment:

> [God] will find out all his enemies. He will strike them upon the hairy scalps,
> and their cheek bones shall be broken, he will bow their backs, and his judg-
> ments shall declare his justice from generation to generation.[11]

On first glance it may seem strange that such a graphic depiction of divine vengeance is followed shortly by the question, "Is there no thankfulness in us, to return unto him the praise of his mercies?" (B1ᵛ). But of course God's mercy consists in his delaying the hour of vengeance.

God's withholding judgment has implications for the rhetorical structure of the sermon itself. Field, too, has been withholding judgment—waiting for the proper time to make his own pronouncement specific. He speaks in general terms of "profane persons" who engage in "wicked exercises" before he begins to mention these pastimes by name:

> There is gadding to all kind of gaming, and there is no tavern or alehouse, if the drink be strong, that lacketh any company: there is no dicing house, bowling alley, cock pit, or theater that can be found empty. These flags of defiance against God, and trumpets that are blown to gather together such company, will sooner prevail to fill those places than the preaching of the holy word of God, the catechizing and instructing of children and servants, can be to fill churches. (B4ʳ⁻ᵛ)

Field makes it clear that the full force of God's judgment will be visited on those who frequent such places on Sundays. Already, in fact, there have been "tokens" of divine displeasure:

> And yet God hath shewed us within these few years many fearful signs and tokens of his heavy anger and displeasure, and one judgment doth even overtake another, and yet nothing can move us. He hath spoken to us from heaven by comets, eclipses, and fiery impressions, he hath set stars in unwonted places, and sent upon the world strange tempests. (B6ᵛ)

These judgments of cosmic proportions serve as the context for the single judgment that is the focus of Field's sermon: the Paris Garden bearbaiting accident.

On Sunday, January 13, 1583, an overflow crowd filled the yard and galleries at Paris Garden. Field describes what happened:

> Being thus ungodly assembled to so unholy a spectacle and specially considering the time, the yard, standings, and galleries being full fraught, being now amidst their jollity, when the dogs and bear were in the chief battle, lo the mighty hand of God upon them. This gallery that was double, and compassed the yard round about, was so shaken at the foundation that it fell as it were in a moment flat to the ground, without post or piece that was left standing so high as the stake whereunto the bear was tied. (B8ʳ)

One pictures the bear and the dogs in the middle of the ruined arena, the only creatures unscathed in a bizarre reversal of the usual course of bear-baiting.

There are some, says Field, who say that the galleries collapsed because the wood was old and rotten. Perhaps so, he admits; but the level to which the rubble was reduced is evidence that the collapse, if not strictly a miracle, was

> an extraordinary judgment of God, both for the punishment of those present profaners of the Lord's day that were [there] then, and also [to] inform and warn us that were abroad (B8^r).

The rhetoric of Field's sermon, then, involves the simultaneous recognition that God's judgment has taken place and that it has not yet taken place. The point is driven home by a single chilling image: "You have heard that the father bringing his child alive thither carried it home again dead, which came not to pass by chance but by God's providence" (C1^v). It is the same God who caused the child's death who is mercifully withholding his judgment from the listeners.

One can even say that on a larger scale, it is God's decision to delay judgment that has made the whole drama of human history possible. The audience at Field's sermon vicariously experiences judgment in the form of the death of a child, just as the audience at a theater vicariously experiences the trials of a character on the stage. But of course in both cases the full force of judgment is withheld; no one in the audience is at that moment as unfortunate as the man in the sermon or the character in the play. In both cases the audience simultaneously experiences judgment and escapes it.

Field recounts the experiences of a lucky few at the bearbaiting pit to demonstrate that God's mercy works in concert with his judgment. It is "miraculous providence and mercy," says Field, that spared some at Paris Garden: "there was one woman that being in the Gallery threw down her child before her and leaped after herself and yet thanks be to God neither of both had any manner of hurt" (C2^v). It is not chance but providence that one child is spared and another killed; God's mercy is real and available, but his judgment is equally real and impending. Particularly those who frequent theaters on Sundays would do well to take warning:

> For surely it is to be feared, besides the destruction both of body and soul that many are brought unto by frequenting the *Theater*, the *Curtain*, and such

like, that one day those places will likewise be cast down by God himself, and being drawn with them a huge heap of such contemners and profane persons utterly to be killed and spoiled in their bodies. God hath given them as I have heard many fair warnings already. (C3ᵛ)

Field himself, of course, is also giving fair warning, but the rhetoric of his *Godly Exhortation* is not one-sided. Unpalatable as the sermon may be in the twentieth century, it is important to note its rhetorical balance. The warnings evoke fear, but they are also "fair." That is, Field's claim is that his warnings are simultaneously just, clear, and beautiful. As such, the warnings call attention to the present possibility of receiving mercy, but the terms of such mercy involve a vicarious experience of judgment. Field's rhetoric engenders a peculiar state of receptivity, a difficult effect to accomplish whether in the sixteenth century or the twentieth: a perception of simultaneous judgment and mercy. The image of the man with his dead child in his arms is balanced by that of the man who hears the voices of his children in the streets.

IV

Several of Shakespeare's plays articulate in a number of different contexts this peculiar simultaneous receptivity. *Measure for Measure*, for example, has for several generations now been classified among Shakespeare's "problem plays." Not only does the play present the moral problem of the proper relation between judgment and mercy, but generations of playgoers have found the ending problematic. The despicable Angelo is spared, and the pairing of Duke Vincentio and Isabella does not seem quite right; the text provides no response for Isabella, who has been outspoken and articulate in voicing her desire for the monastic life, when the Duke proposes. And what are we to make of the Duke himself? Not only are his voyeuristic tendencies unsettling; he has also caused the conflict by his laxity and his use of Angelo as a hatchet man.

The "problem" of *Measure for Measure* may be fully apparent in the last scene, but the tension begins long before the start of the action. Either fourteen or nineteen years before the opening scene (depending on whether one reads 1.2.168 or 1.3.21), a period of lax law enforcement begins. The result is widespread immorality. In short the problem, as Duke Vincentio sees it, is that judgment has been too long delayed:

> Now, as fond fathers,
> Having bound up the threat'ning twigs of birch,
> Only to stick it in their children's sight
> For terror, not to use, in time the rod
> [Becomes] more mocked than feared; so our decrees,
> Dead to infliction, to themselves are dead,
> And liberty plucks justice by the nose;
> The baby beats the nurse, and quite athwart
> Goes all decorum. (1.3.23–31)

Shakespeare's rhetoric leads the audience to expect the satisfaction of seeing order restored. The Duke chooses Angelo, whose credentials are impeccable, to mete out justice after the long delay. But Angelo enforces the letter of the law against fornication by using Claudio, who already has the audience's sympathy, to set an example.

No doubt most in the audience are sympathetic with Lucio's views on Claudio's condemnation. When Isabella asks why her brother has been arrested, Lucio replies,

> For that which, if myself might be his judge,
> He should receive his punishment in thanks:
> He hath got his friend with child. (1.4.27–29)

Lucio's position seems attractive, but his moral laxity eventually emerges as anything but admirable; he has abandoned his bastard child. Even before Lucio's character is fully revealed, though, the trustworthy character Escalus makes it clear that something must be done to restore order in Vienna. The conversation between the Justice and Escalus begins to define the problem of order, the problem of the proper relation between judgment and mercy. The Justice says, "Lord Angelo is severe." Escalus replies,

> It is but needful.
> Mercy is not itself, that oft looks so;
> Pardon is still the nurse of second woe.
> But yet, poor Claudio; there is no remedy. (2.1.282–85)

According to Escalus, there is such a thing as false mercy; mere laxity actually breeds more sorrow rather than assuaging it. Yet he is sympathetic to Claudio. He delineates the moral dilemma, but he can think of no good resolution: "there is no remedy." If a remedy could be found, it would somehow have to combine judgment and mercy—judgment to restore order, and mercy to spare Claudio.

At this point, though, the play has the look of a tragedy; it seems that Claudio will have to be sacrificed for the common good. Yet there are signs that there may be hope for a remedy. In a shrewd rhetorical move that both identifies Angelo with Christ the Judge and reminds him of his subjection to Christ's mercy, Isabella points out that a remedy *has* been found:

> Why, all the souls that were were forfeit once,
> And He that might the vantage best have took
> Found out the remedy. How would you be
> If He, which is the top of judgment, should
> But judge you as you are? O, think on that,
> And mercy then will breathe within your lips,
> Like man new made. (2.2.73–79)

Isabella's argument hinges on the universalizing force of the judgment/ mercy paradox; "all the souls that were were forfeit once," but mercy has been extended to all. But Angelo refuses to acknowledge judgment in the sense of universal condemnation, invoking instead judgment in the Psalm-ist's sense—judgment that uses the law to discriminate between innocent and guilty parties: "It is the law, not I, condemn your brother" (2.2.80). In this reply he simultaneously absolves himself of responsibility and ac-knowledges that he, like Escalus, can see no way out of the moral di-lemma—no way out, that is, except one that both implicates him in a foul crime and forces on Isabella another moral dilemma: the choice between her chastity and her brother's life.

In light of the way Isabella has been treated, it is certainly not surpris-ing that after her brother has been executed (or so she thinks), she demands judgment on Angelo. As the undisguised Duke approaches, it is Isabella who invokes judgment in the Psalmist's sense; she calls for "justice, justice, justice, justice!" (5.1.25). Surely most in the audience feel the same way. But Duke Vincentio, gratuitously manipulative as he may appear in this scene, has in mind a sort of mercy—not the false mercy defined by Esca-lus, but the real thing—mercy that can be accepted only by one willing to pay the price. In Isabella's case, the price is a sincere desire that Angelo be forgiven—a desire that we know to be sincere because she still feels the weight of judgment; she thinks that her brother has been executed. Isabella chooses a sort of mercy that does not merely ignore judgment but rather subsumes it. And this choice yields the remedy that eludes Escalus and Angelo, the remedy that makes *Measure for Measure* a comedy.

One reason the play is hard to accept as a comedy is that for many playgoers the Duke evokes such ambivalent feelings. What is one to make of this character who has worked out a sort of solution by spying on and manipulating others? He is, after all, the one who has allowed Vienna to degenerate and who has left the Puritan Angelo to restore law and order. Clearly Angelo is liable to condemnation (as he himself admits), but what about the Duke? Is *he* to escape judgment? Can we simply accept his marriage to Isabella as a happy prospect for the bride? Can *she* accept it?

It is of course impossible to say how Isabella's silence in response to the Duke's proposal was played in the earliest productions, but a glance at major twentieth-century interpretations reveals a variety of possibilities. Some directors have followed the lead of Peter Brook's 1950 Stratford-upon-Avon production, which managed to make Isabella's acceptance of the proposal a spectacularly happy moment. Especially since John Barton's 1970 production at Stratford-upon-Avon, some directors have taken the opposite approach, stressing Isabella's horror at the prospect of marrying the Duke. Still others, especially since Terence Knapp's 1977 Tokyo production, attempt to preserve for Isabella (and for the audience) some sense of ambiguity.

Regardless of how Isabella's silence is portrayed, a further difficulty about the end of the play is that the audience is not allowed the satisfaction of seeing the letter of the law meted out on Angelo. Nor can the audience return to the world of the beginning of the play, the world of Lucio's false mercy that is really only laxity. The playgoers are forced to accept, or consider accepting, the sudden repentance of one who has been truly wicked, while they are not allowed to use the long passage of years as an excuse for license. In short, the audience is not allowed to let Claudio off the hook without letting Angelo off, too.

As twentieth-century critical as well as performative responses to the play indicate, partial interpretations abound. G. Wilson Knight's view of the play as thoroughly Christian, replete with a Jesus-figure in the Duke, is balanced by interpretations emphasizing the play's political and misogynous agenda.[12] No doubt early seventeenth-century audiences similarly experienced the play's difficult rhetorical demands. If they had an interpretive edge over us, it is only that the widespread currency of discourse centered on the judgment/mercy paradox meant that an experiential category for processing the play's rhetoric was more readily available to them. That not only *Measure for Measure* but also Shakespeare's late romances take pains to preserve the category is all the more striking in view of the fact that the theater most in vogue at the time was the satirical comedy, with its tendency to separate judgment from mercy, honing the former at the expense of the latter.

V

In the introductory chapter I mentioned the magic circle Prospero draws with his staff near the end of *The Tempest*. While inside the circle Prospero casts a spell renouncing his magic: a moment simultaneously dramatic, magical, and religious. Presumably the circle is invisible to the audience: Prospero's staff leaves no trace on the wooden stage. Like the "green sour ringlets" made by the "demi-puppets" Prospero calls on to witness his renunciation, the magical circle becomes visible only in the audience's imagination (5.1.36–37). If the magician underscores the ravages of time by compressing all the action into a single afternoon, by having Ariel tantalize Alonzo and company with a disappearing banquet, and by abruptly halting Miranda and Ferdinand's betrothal masque, the circles are even more evanescent, never literally visible at all. Like *A Godly Exhortation* and *Measure for Measure*, *The Tempest* accumulates rhetorical force through its handling of the relations among judgment, mercy, and time.

Despite the compression of the action, judgment is delayed even in this play. It has been twelve years since the usurping Antonio, in league with Alonso the King of Naples, sent Prospero and Miranda away from Milan in a leaky boat. During those twelve years Antonio and Alonso have escaped judgment for their treachery. But now they find themselves within the compass of Prospero's powers. All the elements of a revenge tragedy are in place.

It is worth noting that the long delay in judgment is not a theatrical necessity; Miranda could have been fully grown at the time of Antonio's usurpation, and Prospero could have enacted his revenge almost immediately. But the twelve-year hiatus adds plausibility to Prospero's gradually growing to an awareness of the form judgment should take. If Prospero seems impatient at times, his vexation is balanced against the audience's perception that he has been patient for twelve years.

Shakespeare underscores Prospero's patience by contrasting his imprisonment with Ariel's. When Ariel expresses an impatience for freedom, Prospero responds by reminding the spirit about his release from the pine tree in which Sycorax confined him. Ariel's twelve-year confinement, unlike Prospero's, was spent in constant lamentation. As Prospero says, "thou didst vent thy groans / As fast as mill-wheels strike" (1.2.280–81). When Ariel thanks his master for freeing him from the pine, Prospero's response seems unnecessarily vindictive:

> If thou more murmur'st, I will rend an oak
> And peg thee in his knotty entrails till
> Thou hast howl'd away twelve winters. (1.2.294–96)

This sounds harsh, but upon hearing Ariel's request for pardon, Prospero is quick to follow his threat with a promise of mercy: "after two days / I will discharge thee" (1.2.298–99). Prospero's occasional outbursts of impatience have more behind them than mere vindictiveness; it seems that the threat of judgment is a necessary preparation for Ariel's appropriation of mercy.

The strategy is a familiar one in Reformation pulpit performances. Developing an analogy based on 1 Kings 19:11–12 ("and after the wind came an earthquake. . . . And after the earthquake came fire . . . and after the fire came a still and soft voice"), Samuel Hieron says in *The Preachers Plea*,

> After the same manner, I would not have the still and mild voice of the Gospel come, till the strong tempest of the law hath rent the stony hearts of men, and have made their bellies to tremble, and rottenness to enter into their bones. (204)

Early in *The Tempest*, the element of mercy mixed with Prospero's judgment is not always easy to detect. It appears, for example, that Caliban's punishments come swiftly and painfully, but the punishments are always either delayed or only threatened; the audience never actually sees swift retribution. When Caliban first enters, cursing magnificently, Prospero replies, "For this, be sure, to-night thou shalt have cramps" (1.2.325). Putting off the punishment for a few hours can be seen as Prospero's vindictively increasing Caliban's agony by making him think about it (and also as Prospero's getting a few more hours' work out of his slave before the cramps set in), or perhaps as giving Caliban a chance to repent. The possibility of Caliban's repentance is not made clear to the audience until later in the play, and at this point Prospero himself may have his doubts. By the end, though, delayed judgment involves the offer of mercy to everyone, even Caliban.

Ariel in the form of a harpy makes the point clear to Alonso and company just after the banquet laid before them vanishes:

> But remember
> (For that's my business to you) that you three
> From Milan did supplant good Prospero,
> Expos'd unto the sea (which hath requit it)
> Him, and his innocent child; for which foul deed
> The pow'rs, delaying (not forgetting), have
> Incens'd the seas and shores—yea, all the creatures,
> Against your peace. Thee of thy son, Alonso,
> They have bereft; and do pronounce by me
> Ling'ring perdition (worse than any death
> Can be at once) shall step by step attend
> You and your ways, whose wraths to guard you from—
> Which here, in this most desolate isle, else falls
> Upon your heads—is nothing but heart's sorrow,
> And a clear life ensuing. (3.3.68–82)

"The pow'rs" may delay judgment, but they do not forget. Their sentence on Alonso is terrible: a "ling'ring perdition" that involves the constant reminder of his son's death. Yet even this judgment is not irrevocable; the powers can be appeased by "heart's sorrow, / And a clear life ensuing."

There is hope, then, for Alonso. The audience knows that Ferdinand is alive, but it remains to be seen whether Alonso will accept the offer of mercy. As usual in Shakespeare, the terms of this offer involve a simultaneous acceptance of judgment and mercy. Up to this point Alonso has merely bemoaned his fate. After Ariel vanishes in thunder, though, Alonso begins to acknowledge his guilt:

> O, it is monstrous! monstrous!
> Methought the billows spoke, and told me of it;
> The winds did sing it to me, and the thunder,
> That deep and dreadful organ-pipe, pronounc'd
> The name of Prosper; it did base my trespass. (3.3.95–99)

At this point Alonso's reaction to the judgment against him precludes any vision of mercy; he resolves to drown himself.

Antonio and Sebastian are even more deluded, refusing even to acknowledge their wrongdoing. They rush off after the spirits, vowing to fight them all. In Gonzalo's assessment,

> All three of them are desperate: their great guilt
> (Like poison given to work a great time after)
> Now gins to bite the spirits. (3.3.104–6)

The desperation of Alonso, Antonio, and Sebastian is a judgment effected by Prospero's magic, but it is also a result of their own guilt. As Gonzalo says, the workings of judgment have been long delayed. It remains to be seen whether after all this time any of the three will be open to the workings of mercy. The long suppression of guilt may end with its acknowledgement and simultaneous release from its power, or it may, as Gonzalo intimates, simply poison the spirits of the men.

The uncertainty of this situation is underscored as Prospero abruptly stops the betrothal masque, which might have seemed to promise an unambiguously happy ending for all, in order to punish Caliban, Stephano, and Trinculo for their treachery. Just after setting dogs on the three, Prospero delivers a wonderfully ambiguous line: "At this hour / Lies at my mercy all mine enemies" (4.1.262–63). Does "mercy" here imply retribution or forgiveness? The answer does not come until Ariel, who has immobilized the courtiers, challenges Prospero:

> Your charm so strongly works 'em
> That if you now beheld them, your affections
> Would become tender. (5.1.17–19)

Prospero replies, "Dost thou think so, spirit?" (5.1.19). Ariel says, "Mine would, sir, were I human" (5.1.20). Perhaps Ariel's statement moves Prospero to compassion, or perhaps the magician has already made up his mind to extend mercy as well as judgment to his enemies. In any case, he says,

> And mine shall.
> Hast thou, which art but air, a touch, a feeling
> Of their afflictions, and shall not myself,

> One of their kind, that relish all as sharply
> Passion as they, be kindlier mov'd than thou art?
> Though with their high wrongs I am strook to th' quick,
> Yet, with my nobler reason, 'gainst my fury
> Do I take part. The rarer action is
> In virtue than in vengeance. (5.1.20–28)

Prospero sets up a rhetorical opposition between "nobler reason" and "fury," between "virtue" and "vengeance," as though mercy and judgment were mutually exclusive. Yet his very next words make it clear that his enemies cannot accept mercy without simultaneously accepting judgment:

> They being penitent,
> The sole drift of my purpose doth extend
> Not a frown further. (5.1.28–30)

If Prospero's enemies are penitent, willing to accept his judgment on them, their submission paradoxically restores their freedom:

> Go, release them, Ariel.
> My charms I'll break, their senses I'll restore,
> And they shall be themselves. (5.1.30–32)

It is at this point that Prospero draws his magic circle and calls the petty spirits he has commanded to witness his vow to accept human vulnerability, his rite of dispossession. The brief catalogue of his magical acts implies that if his powers have been impressive, they have not been commensurate with natural human limitations:

> I have bedimm'd
> The noontide sun, call'd forth the mutinous winds,
> And 'twixt the green sea and the azur'd vault
> Set roaring war; to the dread rattling thunder
> Have I given fire, and rifted Jove's stout oak
> With his own bolt; the strong-bas'd promontory
> Have I made shake, and by the spurs pluck'd up
> The pine and cedar. Graves at my command
> Have wak'd their sleepers, op'd, and let 'em forth
> By my so potent art. (5.1.41–50)

It seems that Prospero's "potent art" has taken on cosmic proportions: dimming the sun, rivaling Jove, and restoring the dead to life. In Christian eschatology, all these signs—eclipses, lightning, and the raising of the dead—are properly associated with the Judge of Nations, the returned Christ.[13] Prospero seems to sense that he is no such judge; he must give up his magic to recover his humanity. Far from being merely proprietary, his statement about Caliban, "this thing of darkness I / Acknowledge mine" (5.1.275–76), is both an acceptance of responsibility for his servant and a recognition of his own human fallibility.[14]

Like the characters under his control, Prospero himself has been judged in the last three hours; he along with the others has been tested. In the end the burden of judgment is shifted to the audience members, simultaneously empowering them to judge and asking them to accept judgment on themselves in remembering their own debt to mercy. Prospero says in the last lines of the play,

> As you from crimes would pardon'd be,
> Let your indulgence set me free. (Ep., 19–20)

There is far more here than the usual request for applause at the close of a comedy. As in *A Godly Exhortation* and *Measure for Measure*, the terms of the resolution involve the audience's acceptance of a paradox: since all human beings, including the audience members, are simultaneously liable to judgment and offered mercy, the only appropriate response is a sense of mercy that paradoxically subsumes judgment.

VI

Where *A Godly Exhortation, Measure for Measure*, and *The Tempest* begin in the present and refer to the past during the course of the performance, *The Winter's Tale* is split into two presents separated by sixteen years. This gap has presented a problem to commentators. Like *Measure for Measure*, *The Winter's Tale* seems to contain elements of tragedy and comedy uneasily joined. Roughly the first half of the play is a thoroughgoing tragedy, while the second half is pure comedy—or so it seems at first glance. In fact the division is not absolute. The play ends with Hermione's stunning resurrection, but the awareness of time irrevocably lost and the deaths of Mamillius and Antigonus temper the comic effect. *The Winter's Tale* is difficult to accept as either a tragedy or a comedy. Moreover, the play seems a poor example of tragicomedy; it is not, as Guarini would have it, a judicious mixture of tragic and comic elements in which no one really dies.[15] Some sense can be made of this "problem" play if it is analyzed rhetorically rather than generically.[16]

If the sixteen-year gap in the middle of the play delays mercy for Leontes, his fast and furious judgments in the first half also follow a long span of time before the action begins. Camillo speaks of the peaceful childhood shared by Leontes and Polixenes: "They were train'd together in their childhoods; and there rooted betwixt them then such an affection, which cannot choose but branch now" (1.1.23–25). The sort of growth that Camillo expects, the branching of an old, firmly rooted friendship, must be a natural, unhurried process. Leontes's sudden eruption of jealousy, though, his "branching" from Polixenes in quite another sense, cuts off the possibility of natural growth. His hurried, fragmented speech patterns reflect his unnatural cast of mind:

> Too hot, too hot!
> To mingle friendship far is mingling bloods.
> I have *tremor cordis* on me; my heart dances,
> But not for joy; not joy. (1.2.108–11) [17]

Despite Camillo's intercession on Hermione's behalf, Leontes remains firm in his judgment.

The next act underscores the point by associating unthinking judgment with bestiality. When Paulina stands up to Leontes, he complains that she "baits" him (2.3.93). And when Antigonus regretfully accepts the task of carrying the infant Perdita to "some place / Where chance may nurse or end it," he says,

> Come on, poor babe.
> Some powerful spirit instruct the kites and ravens
> To be thy nurses! Wolves and bears, they say,
> Casting their savageness aside, have done
> Like offices of pity. (2.3.182–83, 185–89)

Antigonus's speech expresses a compassionate (if somewhat wistful) desire that the beasts of the natural world may be more kind than the beast Leontes. Of course, the speech is also a rather arch bit of foreshadowing on Shakespeare's part.

In short, it seems that the world has been left to be judged by the

beasts, especially the beast Leontes. (His name, after all, connotes not only
the lion's regality but also its fierce bestiality.) When the oracle confirms
Hermione's innocence, Leontes says rashly, "There is no truth at all i' th'
oracle. / The sessions shall proceed; this is mere falsehood" (3.2.140–41).
Retribution is swift; immediately a messenger enters with the news that
Mamillius is dead. Leontes finally acknowledges his own injustice and begs
Apollo's pardon, but his son has already died. Paulina then brings the news
that Hermione too is dead. The King's crimes are too grievous, Paulina
says, to be expiated by any amount of penance:

> But, O thou tyrant!
> Do not repent these things, for they are heavier
> Than all thy woes can stir; therefore betake thee
> To nothing but despair. A thousand knees,
> Ten thousand years together, naked, fasting,
> Upon a barren mountain, and still winter
> In storm perpetual, could not move the gods
> To look that way thou wert. (3.2.207–14)

Despite Paulina's hyperbole, the audience is invited to agree with the sentiment—that is, the audience is invited to judge Leontes. The rest of the
play will deny us that satisfaction, but so far we have seen a nearly complete
tragedy. The impending tempest of the next scene threatens to capsize the
ship, rounding out the tragic action.

Shakespeare sends the storm, but he also sends a bear. As Arthur
Quiller-Couch pointed out some years ago, Shakespeare might easily have
had Antigonus drown with the mariners, but instead we have the famous
stage direction, "*Exit pursued by a bear*" (SD 3.3.58).[18] Why? Quiller-Couch
offers one answer:

> If anyone asks this editor's private opinion, it is that the Bear-Pit in South-
> wark, hard by the Globe Theatre, had a tame animal to let out, and the Globe
> management took the opportunity to make a popular hit. (xx)

Perhaps, but in all likelihood the bear was played by an actor.[19] In any case,
the bear functions well at the thematic and rhetorical crux of the play. As
one commentator says,

> the terrible and the grotesque come near to each other in a *frisson* of horror in-
> stantly succeeded by a shout of laughter; and so this bear, this unique and per-
> fect link between the two halves of the play, slips into place and holds. (204)

The bear's action is simultaneously tragic and comic. It should not be forgotten that those Jacobean playgoers who frequented bearbaiting pits would probably be more familiar than we are with a bear's potential for fury, as the audience would very likely be familiar with the bear as a biblical emblem of judgment.[20] In introducing the bear to dispatch Antigonus, Shakespeare is simultaneously introducing a figure of judgment and indicating that that judgment is not the ultimate one; the bear makes us laugh. The Clown's description of the bear's feast reinforces this rhetorical ambiguity; the scene described is one of horrific torture for an admirable character, but the manner of description precludes any tragic or even fully sympathetic response:

> And then for the land-service, to see how the bear tore out his shoulder-bone, how he cried to me for help, and said his name was Antigonus, a nobleman . . . and how the poor gentleman roar'd, and the bear mock'd him, both roaring louder than the sea or weather. . . . I'll go see if the bear be gone from the gentleman and how much he hath eaten. They are never curst but when they are hungry. If there be any of him left, I'll bury it. (3.3.94–102, 128–32)

The Shepherd's reply to the Clown neatly encapsulates the tragicomic paradox of judgment and mercy: "thou met'st with things dying, I with things new-born" (3.3.113–114).

After a brief exchange between the Shepherd and his son, Time enters as chorus, explaining the sixteen-year gap in the action. The device has been seen as an awkward violation of theatrical unity, but Time's speech actually reinforces the rhetorical paradox of simultaneous mercy and judgment. The chorus begins,

> I, that please some, try all, both joy and terror
> Of good and bad, that makes and unfolds error,
> Now take upon me, in the name of Time,
> To use my wings. (4.1.1–4)

For every human being, good or bad, Time is "both joy and terror," the healer and destroyer, the emblem of mercy and judgment combined.[21] Even the meter reinforces the idea. Time ticks off sixteen couplets: discrete, measured units that contrast with the flowing blank verse and prose of the remainder of the play. Time's rather stiff plodding, then, is metrically transcended by the more natural-sounding speech patterns that follow. In its measured steadiness, Time's speech marks the passage of time as relentlessly real, but Time effaces the force of his own presence even as he asserts it, for the sixteen couplets take the place of sixteen full years. The audience's experience is that all this time has suddenly collapsed into almost nothing.

Emblematic of Time's triumph is the hourglass that he turns during the course of his speech. As this action occurs at the center of the play, and even at the center of the speech, the image of the hourglass deserves some attention. As Ernest Schanzer observes,

> Both parts of the hour-glass look alike, and it may not be fanciful to think that this fact enhances our sense of the similarity of the shape and structure of the two halves of *The Winter's Tale*.[22]

And William Blissett: "call it *enantiodromia* or interpenetration of opposites, it includes a suggestion of yin and yang and of Yeats's gyres."[23] Both of these observations are well-taken; the shape of the hourglass has something to do with the shape of the play. So, too, does the action of turning the hourglass, and even the action within it: surely the sand in the top half is about to run out—the pressure of the first half of the play almost demands it—when Time turns the glass. The pressure is relieved. A whole new store of time awaits. Time must pass, the hourglass tells us, but ultimately time can be redeemed.

This is fitting for a play in which the elements of the second half mirror those of the first. A mirror, after all, both reflects and reverses an image. The two halves of the play, like the two halves of the hourglass, reflect one another, but the play's halves are also reversed. The audience experiences the second half as a whole new world. Or, more accurately, it is a *re*newed world, composed of reversed and redeemed elements of the first half: it is the same sand that was just spent that runs back through the glass. Time's speech serves as a metrical and thematic bridge between the enclosed, hurried atmosphere of the first half and the open, relaxed feel of the long sheep-shearing scene, where the cycles of nature are celebrated. The bear, emblematic of Leontes's bestiality, is replaced by the satyrs that dance at the festival. As Florizel points out, the sheep-shearing festival is a ritual, "a meeting of the petty gods" (4.4.4). Of course, one of the primary functions of ritual is simultaneously to acknowledge time and to arrest it. Ritual provides a sort of aesthetic stasis, a transcendence of the tickings of the clock.[24] The idea is underscored by Perdita's passing out flowers of winter as well as middle summer, by her sympathy with the cyclic movements of "great creating Nature" (4.4.88).

Perhaps because Perdita and Florizel inhabit the idyllic word of natural rhythms and rituals, neither is frightened by Polixenes' unnatural outburst. After the enraged king exits, Perdita's "I was not much afeard" is echoed by Florizel's "I am but sorry, not afeard" (4.4.442, 463). The young lovers admirably (if somewhat naively) refuse to see even a king's judgment as final. In contrast to the fearlessness of Perdita and Florizel is the comical fear of judgment expressed by the Shepherd and the Clown. Autolycus, disguised as a nobleman, explains in graphic detail that the judgment on the two will be severe. The ploy works; the Shepherd and Clown beg Autolycus to intercede for them. As the Clown says, authority is a "stubborn bear" (4.4.802). Perhaps so, but we in the audience know that Autolycus has fabricated the threat. In this case, and in contrast to the first half of the play, a king's beastly judgment is a chimera.

Yet in another sense judgment is real, even in the second half of *The Winter's Tale*. When Paulina remarks that Florizel and Mamillius would have paired well, she is both implying that Mamillius has in some sense been replaced and reminding Leontes (as well as the audience) that Mamillius *cannot* be replaced; he is dead. This realization is balanced by the revelation that Perdita is alive. As the First Gentleman puts it, on hearing the news the Sicilian courtiers "look'd as they had heard of a world ransom'd, or one destroy'd" (5.2.14–15). Of course, the ideas of both the ransom of the world and its destruction recall the Christian story of redemption and final judgment. Just as the paradox of mercy and judgment informs Reformation preaching, it here informs playwriting; the ambiguity of ransom and destruction, of mercy and judgment, is reflected both in isolated lines like the First Gentleman's and in the larger patterns of the play.

The paradox is difficult to express artfully, as the Third Gentleman's account of Paulina's reaction testifies:

> But O, the noble combat that 'twixt joy and sorrow was fought in Paulina! She had one eye declin'd for the loss of her husband, another elevated that the oracle was fulfill'd. (5.2.72–76)

A moment's attempt to visualize Paulina in this posture leaves one grateful that it is Shakespeare, not the Third Gentleman, who has written the play.

In the last scene, Shakespeare brings to a focus his artful handling of the paradox of judgment and mercy. Hermione's statue, a work of art, an object designed to arrest time, actually shows the effects of time's passage. Leontes remarks,

> But yet, Paulina,
> Hermione was not so much wrinkled, nothing
> So aged as this seems. (5.3.27–29)[25]

Paulina replies,

> So much the more our carver's excellence,
> Which lets go by some sixteen years, and makes her
> As she liv'd now. (5.3.30–32)

Had Shakespeare ended the play here, it would have been a somewhat somber but theatrically successful meditation on the mystery of time. But the play does not end here. Even the audience is surprised as the statue comes alive. While Shakespeare's comedies habitually exploit the discrepant awarenesses of character and audience, only in this play is the audience completely deceived by an apparently trustworthy character: Paulina has declared, "I say she's dead; I'll swear't" (3.2.203).[26] In the exceptional case of the resurrection scene in *The Winter's Tale*, the dramatic effect is to place the audience in a position very similar to that of Leontes, transferring to the audience Leontes's reception of simultaneous judgment and mercy. As Northrop Frye observes, there is much talk of magic in the final scene, but there is no magician—no Prospero. As a result, the magic is not localized but diffused, realized in the communal experience of all who witness Hermione's resurrection.[27] In his influential essay "The Purpose of Playing," Louis Montrose offers the following comment on the rhetoric of *The Winter's Tale*:

> It is precisely by means of the boldest theatricality that the climax of *The Winter's Tale* is transformed into a rite of communion. The audience on the stage and the audience in the theatre are atoned by the great creating nature of Shakespeare's art—an art fully realized only when it is incarnated by human players. If we take the attackers and defenders of the theatre at their word, and if we credit our own experiences as playgoers, we may be willing to concede the possibility that a Jacobean audience could experience as intense an emotional and intellectual satisfaction from a performance of *The Winter's Tale* as from a divine service.[28]

Montrose is not overstating the case in his use of the language of incarnation, atonement, and communion. Especially in view of the central myths that inform Renaissance culture, it is clear that in this play's rhetoric, the liturgical and the theatrical merge.

The ending of *The Winter's Tale* is a spectacularly joyous one, but like the mercy celebrated in Field's sermon, even this joy is mixed with sorrow. Herminone and Leontes are reunited, but he cannot deny that his own false judgments have brought down very real judgments on everyone in his world. Mamillius and Antigonus are still dead, and Leontes has lost sixteen years of Hermione's company—years that cannot be replaced. In short, the paradoxical rhetoric of *The Winter's Tale* answers a question posed by Howard Felperin:

> How do you manage to redeem all sorrow and repair all loss . . . while simultaneously bringing home the abiding sense of sorrow and loss as these would certainly linger in life? [29]

Through the audience's experience of judgment combined with mercy, *The Winter's Tale* does precisely that. Central to the play's resolution is the mystery of time. It seems that "this wide gap of time" (5.3.154) has been necessary for Leontes's penance—necessary for time to reveal that judgment is real, but that mercifully, judgment is not the ultimate reality.

This paradoxical awareness informs all of Shakespeare's comedies, but it is perhaps most successfully transferred to the audience in *The Winter's Tale*. While *Measure for Measure* and *The Tempest* present compelling portraits of characters who learn to render mercy along with judgment, *The Winter's Tale* centers on one who learns to receive both, drawing the audience into a similar state of receptivity. In this way the rhetoric of *The Winter's Tale* most closely approximates that of a Reformation sermon like Field's. The unity of *The Winter's Tale* consists not in its adherence to the generic restrictions of tragedy or comedy or even tragicomedy as Guarini defines the form, but in its rhetorical relation to the mythic paradigm of death and resurrection informing English Renaissance culture.

If Reformation churchgoers look to their liturgies for a vicarious experience of death and resurrection, they find that experience not only in the Eucharist but also in sermons like *A Godly Exhortation*. Theater audiences find a similar experience in plays like *Measure for Measure*, *The Tempest*, and *The Winter's Tale*. Field and Shakespeare bring their audiences to feel simultaneously the deathlike weight of judgment and the quickening lift of mercy.

PART III

Tragedy: Watershed and Confluence

6. The Mist and the Wilderness: Protestant Paradox in Gifford and Webster

I

In 1531 John Randall, a pious Cambridge student and kinsman of the English martyrologist John Foxe, was found hanged in his study. Foxe records the incident in his *Acts and Monuments*:

> the young man being studious and scarcely twenty-one years old, was long lacking among his companions; at last after four days, through the stench of the corpse, his study door being broken open, he was found hanged with his own girdle within the study, in such sort and manner that he had his face looking upon his Bible, and his finger pointing to a place of Scripture, where predestination was treated of.[1]

Unwilling to acknowledge that one of the godly would take his own life, Foxe suggests that Randall was murdered by "some old naughty and wicked man," hinting darkly that the murderer was very likely Randall's Catholic tutor.

Whether Randall's elaborately staged death was a murder or a suicide would of course make all the difference to anyone attempting to interpret the incident along ideological lines. But either way, the event reveals on a small scale something of a widespread cultural phenomenon: the tremendous psychological pressure generated by the early Protestant reformers' emphasis on the thorny theological problem of predestination. The English Calvinists' foregrounding of predestination called attention to a whole constellation of Christian paradoxes, none of which could be easily sustained through the sixteenth century's rapid course of theological change.

This chapter briefly traces the development of several related theological paradoxes and examines their rhetoric in two English Renaissance texts: George Gifford's *The Countrie Divinitie* and John Webster's *The Duchess of Malfi*. My aim is to illustrate a rhetorical principle that works similarly in two discursive modes often considered dissimilar: the religious tract and the secular tragedy.

II

One factor in the religious disquiet of Elizabethan England was the Reformation's indebtedness to the Nominalist movement of the late Middle Ages. According to Hans Blumenberg,

> Nominalism is a system meant to make man extremely uneasy about the world—with the intention, of course, of making him seek salvation outside the world, driving him to despair of his this-worldly possibilities and thus to the unconditional capitulation of the act of faith, which, however, he is again not capable of accomplishing by his own power.[2]

The early Protestant reformers saw themselves as breaking from much in Nominalist thought, but one could without much distortion substitute the word "Calvinism" for "Nominalism" in Blumenberg's formulation. Both the Nominalists and the Calvinists emphasized the sovereignty of God's will, and both insisted that only through God-given faith could a human being attain salvation. If only those whom God has chosen to give faith can be saved, the matter is out of human hands—a function of a divine will that is ultimately incomprehensible to human understanding.

One unforeseen result of both the Nominalist and the Calvinist insistence on God's utterly sovereign will was the prospect of God's untrustworthiness—a prospect explored by Renaissance playwrights as well as Reformation theologians.[3] If God's will is completely hidden from human speculation, might not this God do anything at any time? How can such a God inspire one's absolute faith? Yet the believer's task is precisely to take on the paradox of trust in a God whose trustworthiness is open to question. The result in Reformation England was an anxiety of epistemology—a radical disquiet about what one can (or ought to) know.

Calvin attempted to relieve the psychological pressure of the situation by insisting on God's justice; if human beings have no access to the secrets of the divine will, we may at least rest assured that God's decisions are just.

In fact, Calvin says, the Christian is to love God as much for his justice in damning the reprobate as for his mercy in saving the elect. The believer

> embraces him not less as the avenger of wickedness than as the rewarder of the righteous; because he perceives that it equally appertains to his glory to store up punishment for the one, and eternal life for the other. (*Institutes*, 1.2.3)

Love for a God who not only damns the vast majority of the human race but predestines that damnation is a psychologically difficult position to maintain, all the more difficult if adherence to it is seen as a sign of election. As the emergence of the Arminian party testifies, the psychological tension of the Calvinist system could not long remain unopposed even in England, where Calvinism was orthodox.

One Calvinist paradox, then, is that the believer must trust in the mercy of a God whose justice seems willful and arbitrary. The psychological pressure of maintaining this paradox is compounded in Reformation England by Protestant assertions of other paradoxes, such as the insistence that believers are simultaneously saints and sinners. As Steven Ozment says,

> the reformers brought a strange new burden to bear on the consciences of their followers when they instructed them to resolve the awesome problems of sin, death, and the devil by simple faith. . . . The brave new man of the Protestant faith, "subject to none [yet] subject to all" in Luther's famous formulation, was expected to bear his finitude and sinfulness with anxiety resolved, secure in the knowledge of a gratuitous salvation, and fearful of neither man, God, or the devil. But how many were capable of such self-understanding? (*The Age of Reform*, 437)

This psychological anxiety is compounded by yet another paradox: the need for human effort to attain faith, which is a gift that no amount of human effort can procure.

All these paradoxes—trust in a willful God whose justice is incomprehensible, simultaneous sanctity and depravity, and the need for effort to attain a gratuitous gift—are repeatedly urged in sixteenth-century Protestant discourse. The doctrines that underlie paradoxical discourse are of course not exclusively Protestant, but the highlighting of these theological puzzles marks a distinctive feature of Reformation thought. Such apparently dissimilar works as George Gifford's religious dialogue *The Countrie Divinitie*[4] and John Webster's *The Duchess of Malfi* reflect in rhetorically similar terms the psychological anxiety of attempting to maintain the tension of Protestant paradox.

III

Certainly Gifford was no stranger to the literary currents of his day. Admired by literarily sophisticated as well as popular audiences (he was one of only two clergymen named in Sir Philip Sidney's will), this Puritan preacher invests his religious dialogue with an unusually high degree of dramatic tension. In fact *The Countrie Divinitie*, first published in 1581, at times rivals Elizabethan stage plays in the psychological depth of its characterizations. The dialogue's characters are named Atheos and Zelotes; apparently, Gifford wants to leave no doubt about where the reader's allegiance should lie. Not surprisingly, most of the tract consists of Zelotes's correcting Atheos's erroneous notions. What is surprising is the psychological difficulty of siding with Zelotes and rejecting Atheos, whose wit and comfortable, homey religion must have appealed to many of Gifford's readers.[5] Throughout the dialogue Atheos remains affable and accommodating, while Zelotes is often fiercely caustic. At one point, for example, when Zelotes bluntly asks the damning question of whether Atheos has ever been up all night playing cards, Atheos replies, "Yes, that I have, and thought it but a short night, too" (26^r). It is difficult to reject this good-natured gambler in favor of his ill-tempered adversary, but that is precisely what the dialogue demands that the reader do. Of course, the demand can be accepted or rejected, but that is just the point: the take-it-or-leave-it rhetoric has a watershed effect, forcing the ideologies into separate streams of thought.

As the dialogue begins, Zelotes asks about the priest in Atheos's parish. Atheos replies that his curate is

> the best priest in this country; we would be loath to forgo him for the learnedest of them all. . . . He is as gentle a person as ever I see: a very good fellow, he will not stick, when good fellows and honest men meet together, to spend his groat at the alehouse: I cannot tell, they preach and preach, but he doth live as well as the best of them all. I am afraid when he is gone we shall never have the like again. (1^v)

Zelotes suggests that perhaps the priest would be better suited to keeping swine than to shepherding the flock of Christ, and then asks, "doth he not teach them to know the will of God, and reprove naughtiness among the people?" (2ʳ). Atheos replies,

> Yes, that he doth, for if there be any that do not agree, he will seek for to make them friends: for he will get them to play a game or two at bowls or cards, and to drink together at the alehouse. I think it a godly way to make charity: he is none of these busy controllers. (2ʳ)

Atheos insists that he is not alone in his high opinion of the priest; the "best in the parish" agree with him (2ᵛ). Zelotes replies, "like master, like scholar. . . . I smell how unmeet he is, and also how ignorant you are" (2ᵛ). When Zelotes asserts that Atheos is a "carnal man" and the priest a "pot companion," Atheos objects:

> I perceive you are one of those curious and precise fellows, which will allow no recreation. What would ye have men do? We shall do nothing shortly. You would have them sit moping always at their books; I like not that. (3ʳ)

At this point Zelotes invokes a motif frequently employed in Reformation discourse: what I have called the *topos* of the two-edged sword.[6] According to this idea, certain words and actions function as a wedge or watershed, clearly discriminating true believers from infidels. Zelotes claims that what Atheos calls "recreation" has this double-edged effect: "Nay, my friend, I do not allow that recreation, which profane men call so, which is no recreation but a torment to a godly mind" (3ʳ⁻ᵛ). The two-edged force of Zelotes's view of recreation means that Atheos and, by implication, the reader are constrained into an either/or mentality: it seems that recreation must be either wholesome or ungodly. Or, if one disagrees with this premise, this very disagreement places one in the camp opposite to that of Zelotes. Moreover, the stakes are so high that it is difficult simply to shrug off Zelotes as a relatively harmless nuisance. One must either take "these busy controllers" or leave them. If Atheos decides to reject Zelotes, there is always the haunting suspicion that the latter was right all along, that the very rejection is evidence of Atheos's reprobation. And if Zelotes is right, then nothing less than a revolution of Atheos's view of himself and his world is in order. Either way, Atheos is forced to declare allegiance to one camp or the other—the priest's or Zelotes's.

In an attempt to defend himself by defending his priest, Atheos points out that the curate "doth keep a good house, and doth feed the poor," but Zelotes argues that an ungodly clergyman is a thief, and that it is no virtue for a thief to distribute his plunder (5ᵛ). A discussion of pure doctrine follows, Zelotes's implication being that Atheos should be able to spot a wolf in sheep's clothing like the parish priest. Atheos protests, "It is not for us that are simple men for to judge who doth well and who doth not" (11ʳ). At this point Zelotes again invokes the two-edged sword *topos*:

> Our Savior Christ sayeth, "My sheep hear my voice; a stranger will not hear." Whereupon it doth follow that he which knoweth not when pure doctrine and wholesome is uttered is not as yet among the number of the sheep of Christ. (11ʳ)

According to Zelotes, the word of God is essentially divisive; only the few who recognize Christ's calling can be saved. The paradox is that even those who desire salvation but who cannot yet hear Christ's voice must first hear it before making further progress. A sincere doubter like Atheos is left where he started; one hears the voice or one doesn't.

Zelotes employs the rhetoric of the two-edged sword again and again in the course of the dialogue. In response to Atheos's hesitation to claim certainty of salvation, Zelotes argues that in Scripture, "God . . . hath told some men, that is, such as believe, that they shall be saved, and such as doubt of his promise and his oath, they shall be damned" (24ʳ). In other words, Atheos's doubts are evidence that the Scriptures condemn him, while Zelotes's belief is evidence that the same Scriptures promise him life.

Of course, Zelotes does not claim that his status as a member of the elect makes him perfect; even the chosen will continue to sin in this life. Sorrow over these sins, in fact, is one more sign of salvation. Zelotes claims that the words of assurance in the Gospel offer comfort to the elect but have little effect upon the reprobate:

> Therefore to such as have wounded consciences, the Gospel is sweet and comfortable. . . . But such as have no feeling of their sins, or which are blinded and hardened, ye shall perceive small joy or delight in them for to hear the word preached. They had rather be at bear-baiting. (35ᵛ–36ʳ)

The Scriptures as well as their exposition in sermons have a two-edged force, providing clear evidence of each individual's fate.

When Atheos asks, "Are none indued with God's spirit, but such as run to hear preaching?" Zelotes replies,

> Whoever hath the spirit of God cannot but delight in the word of God, which the same spirit hath uttered. . . . Seeing therefore that the holy Ghost doth

get men by the word, it followeth that all those which set light by the word are led, not with the spirit of God, but with the spirit of the devil. (28ʳ⁻ᵛ)

Once again, Zelotes forces Atheos to confront the claim that his attitude about sermons is evidence of his reprobation.

The polarizing force of this kind of rhetoric is in part a reflection of Calvinism's insistent division of humankind into the divinely predetermined categories of the saved and the damned. The key to this discrimination, as Zelotes repeatedly insists, is knowledge. Those who truly know God are a community unto themselves, defining themselves in contrast to the ungodly. The primary vehicle for self-knowledge, according to Zelotes, is preaching; in attending to and applying to one's life the words of the godly preacher, a believer learns to become assured of a divinely ordained role in society. This social self-definition is a reflection of the believer's status as a member of the elect—a society that exists in eternity. It follows that the most essential piece of knowledge one can possess is the certainty of one's own salvation. Without such certainty, no amount of preaching will be of any avail. The paradox is that it is preaching itself that must awaken and encourage this knowledge. If one finds oneself on the "inside," certain of membership among the elect, then the words of the preacher are edifying and reassuring. If, on the other hand, one prefers to leave knowledge of election up to God, then this very preference is clear evidence of reprobation. How does one gain membership among the elect—a matter that has already been decided?

When Zelotes asks, "I pray ye tell me this: are ye sure ye shall be saved?" Atheos replies, "No, nor you neither, nor the best of ye all; we must commit that to God" (20ʳ). Zelotes then explains that his adversary's position is absurd since knowledge of salvation is the only conceivable ground of trust in God:

> What is it that ye put all your whole trust in him for? Is it not this, that God hath promised unto ye eternal life, and that ye believe he will perform his promise? . . . If God cannot lie, when he saith, all that trust in him shall be saved, and you know that you put your whole trust in him, wherefore do ye not then know that ye shall be saved? (20ʳ⁻ᵛ)

Atheos can only assert that he does trust, and that his faith leads to hope rather than knowledge. Zelotes says, "Ye know as well what faith is as doth a goose" (20ᵛ).

This emphasis on knowledge rather than hope or love as the basis of the Christian faith has a tremendous impact on a whole range of sixteenth-century discursive modes; the quest for certain knowledge at once liberates individuals, authorizing them to think for themselves, and constrains them, pressuring them to declare epistemological allegiance to one of two opposing camps.[7] Such rhetoric simultaneously encourages wide-ranging inquiry and collective self-defensiveness, confidence and doubt, hope and despair.

In such an atmosphere a hotly debated topic is what beliefs and behaviors are socially disruptive. Not surprisingly, in Gifford's dialogue Atheos and Zelotes accuse each other of advocating subversion. Atheos insists that pretensions to knowledge of salvation are socially destructive:

> I allow preaching; it is good now and then, but some can keep no measure, nor tell when they have done. Again they be over hot and severe, and preach damnation to the people. Likewise they meddle with such matters as they need not, as election and predestination. What should such matters be spoken of among the people? They make men worse. (24ᵛ)

And Atheos claims that it is not only individuals who are made worse. He goes on to say,

> I know towns myself which are even divided one part against another since they had a preacher, which were not so before. This they gain, that whereas before they loved together, now there is dissension sown among them. (46ᵛ)

Zelotes replies that such divisiveness is to be expected where true knowledge is found:

> Will ye have light and darkness for to agree as companions together? . . . Would ye have God and the devil agree together? Would ye have the godly and the wicked for to be at one? (46ᵛ)

When Atheos objects that such watertight compartments are inappropriate in a world in which all believers are striving to overcome their weaknesses, and that divisive rhetoric like Zelotes's would "drive men into despair and bring them out of belief with the fear of damnation," Zelotes emphatically reasserts his polarizing strategy: "This wedge hath been driven often enough already; nevertheless, because ye are so knotty and crabbed a piece to cleave, I will give it one blow more" (75ᵛ). Atheos gets nowhere with his claim that advocates of love and tolerance have every reason to hope that they are already on God's side, that the real threats to the God-given peace of a community come from the precisions who are "busy in checking every man" (17ᵛ). Zelotes replies,

> I marvel how far you would go if a man should follow ye: ye are like a puddle, which the more a man stirreth it, the more filthy mud ariseth: ye are like a sink, where the more a man stirreth, the more is the stink. (17ᵛ–18ʳ)

Atheos asks, "What mean ye by that?" Zelotes replies, "I mean that your heart is full of foul stinking and rotten matter, which floweth out at your mouth" (18ʳ). When Atheos questions his adversary's holier-than-thou attitude, Zelotes says, "Ye would even pour out your stinking and rotten poison like blasphemous and venomous beasts" (19ʳ). Gifford's dialogue thus presents an uncomfortable choice: the reader must decide between the cross-tempered Zelotes, representing salvation, and the affable Atheos, representing damnation. The reader who favors religious tolerance will tend to side with Atheos, but Zelotes is clearly Gifford's spokesman. There is no question here of authorial irony; Gifford is not satirizing the Puritans.

Interestingly, at one point it seems that Atheos begins to come around. He replies to one of Zelotes's accusations, "Ye say well; I would I could remember your words" (36ʳ). Gifford thus leads the reader to expect Atheos's conversion—his entrance into the body of the elect (or, more properly, his realization that he has been a member of the elect all along). Yet Atheos never does come around. He holds to his doubts about his own salvation, so that the two characters part at the end of their journey no nearer to agreement than they were at the beginning. The dialogue simply reinforces both polemical positions.

In its well-developed characterizations of Atheos and Zelotes, *The Countrie Divinitie* stands as a sort of puritanical precursor to the late Elizabethan and Jacobean stage, where characters of moral and intellectual complexity replaced the stock characters of mid-century drama. While it is conceivable that the secular tragedies of Shakespeare's day could have been written in the absence of the vigorous and often tortured theological speculation arising out of the Reformation, the simpler explanation is that Reformation theology and Renaissance drama were mutually influential. In short, church and stage were no more separate in Elizabethan England than church and state.

If one wanted to find in the drama ideological parallels to *The Countrie Divinitie*, it would be easy enough: the Protestant moral interludes of the mid-sixteenth century or the more dramatically sophisticated Protestant polemical plays of Shakespeare's day (say, the Henslowe dramatists' *Sir John Oldcastle* or Dekker's *The Whore of Babylon*) would furnish examples. What I want to do here is offer a comparison with a play whose ideological stance is by no means as clear as that of *The Countrie Divinitie* but that highlights the same Protestant paradoxes and so occupies the same ideological landscape.

IV

The Duchess of Malfi treats such conventional themes in Renaissance dramatic and religious discourse as the need for integrity in positions of responsibility and the difference between appearance and reality in a corrupt world, but the play's rhetorical strategy is not simply to present ideas in a straightforward, didactic manner. Instead, the play works to unsettle the audience, to present varying and conflicting responses to Protestant paradox, and to compel each audience member to choose among the ideologies represented. *The Duchess of Malfi*, like Gifford's *The Countrie Divinitie*, has a watershed effect on audiences.

This is apparent not only in the internal dynamics of the play but also in the body of critical interpretation that has come down to the present. It would be hard to find a Jacobean play that occasioned more radical disagreement among commentators.[8] On one hand are scholars such as William Empson, Peter B. Murray, D. C. Gunby, Dominic Baker-Smith, and John L. Selzer, who find the play expressive of the values of orthodox Christianity.[9] On the other hand are those such as Ian Jack, Alvin Kernan, Gunnar Boklund, Robert Ornstein, and Alan Sinfield, who view Webster as a spokesman of despair.[10] At times, as Charles Forker remarks, it is difficult to imagine that these two groups can even be talking about the same play.[11] Forker, in fact, offers an intriguing third alternative:

> In suspending us between alternative perceptions, both of which the experience of the individual characters and the larger patterns of the play appear to validate, *The Duchess of Malfi* finally projects a vision of tragic indeterminacy. (367)

It is possible to effect such a suspension between opposing perceptions, with a full awareness of both extremes, but it is questionable that the audience can maintain *this* play's suspension of contraries for long. If such interpretive suspension can be maintained, how does one explain the radically divergent readings—not to mention the radically divergent performances—of *The Duchess of Malfi*?[12] Interestingly, even Forker offers his interpretive preference: "the most admirable posture is stoical" (365).

I will argue that although it is possible to perceive isolated lines as trembling with tension between ideological extremes, in the end the playgoer must decide between the contraries. Since the play's rhetoric compels each audience member to make an independent decision, an interpretive leap (even if the individual leaps are in different directions), Webster's first task is to unsettle the audience members, to prevent them from simply identifying with the protagonists and allowing them to make all the decisive moves. Of course, one hallmark of Jacobean drama is the playwrights' willingness to present a variety of perspectives, to challenge preconceived notions of right and wrong, to overturn the audience's expectations. Webster in particular seems to delight in the possibility of audience subversion. He carefully sets up expectations and almost invariably thwarts them. This strategy is apparent even in the first two scenes, in which Bosola is set up as the villain, and Antonio and the Duchess as hero and heroine. Bosola's wit, though, makes him a curiously attractive villain, as the "fearful madness" of the secret union between Antonio and the Duchess makes their heroism curiously unstable; the tension between their worldly wisdom and their naïveté remains unresolved.[13]

During the first act, then, Webster systematically subverts the audience's expectations: Antonio is something less than a real hero, Bosola is something more than a mere villain, and the Duchess is something other than the celestial creature Antonio makes her out to be. The effect is to leave the audience intrigued but unmoored, uncertain of where allegiances should lie. For all the characters, in fact, external or reputed virtues seem to belie inward natures, and the audience has not yet had a chance to form any clear impression of what truly lies within any character. For one thing, the web of policy and intrigue is thick and tangled. For another, Webster's vision demands that the characters be put to the test before they can rightly understand themselves or be understood by the audience. In the middle part of the play, then, the audience, bereft of any certain reference point, is drawn increasingly into a world of madness, dreams, and suffering. Webster's rhetoric is relentlessly moralistic—the play is riddled with *sententiae* (as is Gifford's tract, in which Atheos frequently invokes conventional moralisms)—but there is no character in *The Duchess of Malfi* whose statements can be trusted. As the action develops, then, each audience member's interpretive faculties are increasingly brought into play even as those faculties are challenged, especially by Bosola.

In the fifth act, when Bosola is asked how his accidental killing of Antonio has come about, he replies, "In a mist: I know not how" (5.5.93). This is the second of Bosola's intimations of a tragic uncertainty figured in a mist. Earlier, disguised as a bellman in his attempt to prepare the Duchess for death, he has described earthly life as a "mist of error" (4.2.185). The phrase is perhaps an echo of Thomas Norton's 1561 translation of Calvin, who describes in his *Institutes* spiritually blind humankind as "compassed with mists of errors" (3.2.4).[14] If there is any interpretive certainty beyond Bosola's mist, it is figured in an apparently similar but actually contrasting image: that of the wilderness.

When the Duchess first reveals her plan to marry Antonio, she says to Cariola,

> wish me good speed
> For I am going into a wilderness,
> Where I shall find nor path, nor friendly clew
> To be my guide. (1.2.277–79)

For the Jacobean audience, the word "wilderness" is charged with theological significance: the Israelites' wandering for forty years in the wilderness of Sinai prefigures Christ's temptation after forty days of prayer and fasting in the wilderness. In both cases the wilderness is a figure for a divine testing ground from which those receptive to God's word will emerge victorious.[15] Yet it is by no means clear that the wilderness will prove salvific for the Duchess; she herself appears to doubt the outcome of her journey. On the other hand, her request for Cariola's blessing indicates that she is not without hope.

Also significant is the Duchess's complaint that she has no "friendly clew" to guide her. In Renaissance iconography, a "clew" is a spool of thread used to find one's way out of a labyrinth, which is in turn an image for the maze of this world, a maze that can be negotiated successfully by only the faithful pilgrim. The Duchess's statement, then, is ambiguous; the evocation of the image may or may not imply successful passage through the labyrinth. It is true that the Duchess considers herself without a clew. But emblem books of Webster's day, especially Protestant ones, indicate that one's "clew" must be something intangible: a faith whose presence can be experienced only subjectively.[16] In denying the presence of any literal, external "clew," then, the Duchess may be expressing either her sense of abandonment or her faith. The question is thus put before the audience: will her negotiation of the labyrinth, her pilgrimage through the wilderness, be successful? In other words, is the Duchess a member of the elect, one who has been called into the wilderness as one stage in the process of sanctification, or is she merely lost in the world's labyrinth—a pitiable victim of her own sensuality and her brothers' senseless cruelty?

Again, the signals from the Duchess herself are ambiguous. As she realizes that she must part from her husband and son, she is torn between outrage at the injustice of her plight and acceptance of its divine purpose:

> Must I like to a slave-born Russian
> Account it praise to suffer tyranny?
> And yet, O Heaven, thy heavy hand is in't. (3.5.73–75)

With which sentiment does the audience sympathize? It seems that a choice is called for; it is difficult, to say the least, to reconcile the ideas of her willful desire to assert her aristocratic rights and her humble acknowledgement of divine guidance and purpose. Can one have it both ways? Can one simultaneously assert that suffering is necessary and that it is not?

The Duchess's troubled ambivalence remains after her capture and imprisonment, as Ferdinand devises a series of excruciating psychological tortures. Feigning a willingness to forgive her, he offers his sister a dead man's hand instead of his own, shows her wax figures that she mistakes for her murdered husband and children, unleashes a company of madmen into her chamber, and finally sends Bosola as bellman to announce her impending execution. After all this, she asks Bosola the simple question, "Who am I?" He replies, "Thou art a box of worm seed" (4.2.122–23). With a flash of regal pride, she retorts, "I am the Duchess of Malfi still" (4.2.139). Is this an heroic assertion of identity hurled at those who have tried to strip her of all that could make her title meaningful, or is it the last trace of worldly pride, the last obstacle to be overcome in her pilgrimage through the wilderness? If by any stretch of the imagination it can be both, can either the Duchess or the audience maintain this radical ambivalence for very long?

The Duchess's last moments before her execution present a similar problem. One commentator has suggested that she continues to the end to take part in a purely worldly power struggle with her brothers, that she maintains pride in her title, and that she fails to call upon the Christian

God, even at the point of death.[17] On this view, she may be Machiavellian to the end, or stoic, or simply confused.[18] Of course, it is also possible that her forgiving of her brothers and her insistence on kneeling for her execution are evidence of her Christian faith.[19]

In fact, these actions can be seen as reconciling all aspects of the characteristically Protestant paradoxes. On this view, the Duchess trusts in a God who has given her no reason to trust. She realizes both her utter dependence on the heavenly powers and the need for human action; she victoriously and humbly accepts herself as simultaneously saint and sinner. In this interpretation the Duchess's faith, despite the utter lack of anything in her external circumstances that could justify faith, is a mark of her successful negotiation of the wilderness.

In short, the Duchess can be seen as embracing whole paradoxes, while Bosola and Antonio can perceive only the opposite sides of them. On this view Bosola is cynical and untrusting, and yet a man of action—a shrewd manipulator whose actions grow out of his vision of utter human depravity, both his own depravity and that of those around him. Antonio, in contrast, is the essentially trusting, passive, stoic object of everyone else's manipulations. He relies on his own integrity, a sanctity that is at times sanctimonious, to see him through. In this interpretation, each of these characters stays on one side of Protestant paradox: Bosola on the side of distrust, the necessity of human action, and a recognition of human depravity—and Antonio on the side of trust, the need for human passivity, and the possibility of human sanctity. Both positions emerge as inadequate in their failure to attain the wholeness of the Duchess's vision.

Yet this is only one view; it is not at all certain that the Duchess's wilderness is really any different from Bosola's mist. In the end she may be just as lost as Bosola, or even more so since she refuses to acknowledge that the mist is all that there is. Her death may therefore be either a glorious martyrdom or a pathetic mistake. Interpretation is clearly called for, and it is futher complicated by the possibility that the Duchess of Malfi is not even the focal character in *The Duchess of Malfi*. After all, the play goes on for a whole act after her death.[20] Is the Duchess's ideological stance— whatever it is—to be taken any more seriously than the statements of stoicism and despair in the fifth act? At the close of the haunting echo scene, Antonio states the stoic position clearly:

> Though in our miseries Fortune hath a part
> Yet, in our noble sufferings, she hath none:
> Contempt of pain, that we may call our own. (5.3.54–56)

Antonio's dying words are less triumphant, but they are consistent with his stoic vision: "Pleasure of life, what is it? only the good hours / Of an ague" (5.4.66–67). The words seem bankrupt if the Duchess's death is viewed as victorious, but authoritative if she is merely a victim of senseless corruption.

Bosola's final vision is even more bleak than Antonio's. Near the end of the play he says, "We are merely the stars' tennis-balls" (5.4.53). The words are taken from Sir Philip Sidney, who may in turn have found them in Calvin.[21] Norton's 1561 translation of *Institutes* 1.17.1 reads, "the flesh stirreth us to murmur, as if God did to make himself pastime, toss [men] like tennis balls." Compare the narrator's comment on a twist of fate in the *New Arcadia*:

> in such a shadow or rather pit of darkness the wormish mankind lives, that neither they know how to foresee nor what to fear, and are but like tennis balls, tossed by the racket of the higher powers.[22]

Webster's sources are apparent, but does *The Duchess of Malfi* reflect the explicitly Christian context of either the *Institutes* or the *New Arcadia*? Some of Bosola's dying words are also borrowed from the Sidney passage just quoted:

> In what a shadow, or deep pit of darkness
> Doth, womanish, and fearful, mankind live? (5.5.100–101)

Interestingly, where Sidney uses the word "wormish," Webster has "womanish." Why the change? Is Webster in effect kicking the Duchess after she is down, or is the irony that it is the woman, the Duchess, who points the way out of the "deep pit of darkness," redefining for the faithful playgoer, but not for Bosola, the word "womanish"?[23] Again, it seems that one interpretation or the other is called for, and again the interpretive situation is complicated as Bosola continues. He seems to express assurance that a truly moral order exists—albeit an order from which he has been excluded:

> Let worthy minds ne'er stagger in distrust
> To suffer death or shame for what is just. (5.5.102–3)

What is one to make of this *sententia*? Given the play's pervasive vision of human depravity, can such a statement be taken at face value?

The final speech in the play is similarly puzzling. Apparently ignoring Antonio's dying wish that his young son "fly the courts of princes" (5.4.71), Delio suggests that the boy be established as the next Duke of Malfi and goes on to imply that the realm has been purged of evil. Is the playgoer meant to believe this? The final couplet of the play, if taken at face value, implies not only that a moral order exists, but that it will prevail:

> Integrity of life is fame's best friend,
> Which nobly, beyond death, shall crown the end. (5.5.119–20)

Upon leaving the theater, is the playgoer resolved to strive for greater integrity of life? Or is such striving hopeless?

The rhetoric of *The Duchess of Malfi* has a distinctly polarizing tendency. The play presents several apparently conflicting ideological voices, placing the burden of interpretation on the playgoer. Since the dramatic force of these presentations decreases as the play progresses (from the Duchess's death to Antonio's to Bosola's to the *sententia* of the final couplet), and since the end of a play traditionally enjoys a rhetorical privilege, the various ideologies come across in the end with something like equal force.

It seems that sense can be made of all these voices only if the playgoer takes one of two positions: that which assumes that there is purpose in human suffering or that which assumes that there is not. The Duchess's Christian faith can make Antonio's merely stoic virtue seem bankrupt, Bosola's despairing of his own salvation a mark of his reprobation, and Delio's final *sententia* an admirable sentiment, but only if viewed from the perspective of faith; if the *sententia* is seen as a channel for virtue apart from faith, it is hopelessly inadequate to effect real moral improvement. From this perspective, *The Duchess of Malfi* intensifies the exclusivist rhetoric implicit in discourse centering on election and reprobation. The paradox of predestination is fully in force, in that the audience must decide what to make of each character; but in effect the choice has already been made since the audience's assumptions determine how each character's language and actions will be received.[24] This circularity leads one both to choose and to question the value of choosing. Thus, the tension generated by the play is something like that generated by the doctrine of predestination: one must choose, but ultimately one's choice has already been made. In both cases— that of the choice and that of a determinism that precludes any choice— the audience is polarized into separate camps.

Even if one rejects the Christian paradigm, the play still exerts its

polarizing force by compelling the playgoer to define an interpretive position in opposition to the exclusively Christian one. Such an interpretation
centers on the absurdity of human suffering. In this view Delio's senten-
tious morality is hopelessly myopic, while the Duchess's tragic passion,
Antonio's stoic resolve, and Bosola's eloquent despair are all at best pitiable attempts to make sense of a meaningless universe.

As evidenced by the body of criticism centering on *The Duchess
of Malfi*, the interpretive options—the Christian and the absurdist—are
clearly delineated and are extraordinarily difficult to embrace simultaneously. To be sure, there are some plays of the period for which this
is not the case; the complex intellectual matrix of Elizabethan and Jacobean England engenders certain tragedies—most notably Shakespeare's—
that present radical inquiries into questions that cannot be definitively resolved.[25] Such plays tend to foster in the audience a communal sense of
wonder, a shared awareness that provides some ground for encompass-
ing the tragic situation without reducing it to an ideological statement.
Such plays short-circuit the ideologically definitive response. The prevailing rhetoric of *The Duchess of Malfi*, though, like that of *The Countrie
Divinitie*, functions as an ideological watershed. At the play's close, two
mutually exclusive interpretive options—the Christian and the absurdist—
remain clearly and insistently delineated.

It would be interesting to know how John Webster interpreted his
own play. He may have been a devout Christian of one stamp or another—
radical Calvinist, proto-Arminian, or even Roman Catholic.[26] He may have
been a thoroughgoing atheist in an age in which almost everyone still professed belief.[27] He may have believed in nothing but John Webster, who
took a perverse delight in manipulating audiences.[28] He may have been
a gifted dramatist but a confused one, perhaps even a schizophrenic.[29] It
would be interesting to know—interesting but not essential. Whatever
Webster's conscious interpretation of Protestant paradox might have been,
it is certain that his play both reflects and intensifies a rhetorical principle
that cuts across the boundary between Reformation theology and Renaissance drama.

A case in point is Bosola's reply to the Duchess's "I could curse the
stars." He says, "Look you, the stars shine still" (4.1.95, 99). Is the reply an
affirmation of a cosmic order that benevolently transcends human caprice,
or a taunting sneer at the impotence of even the most heartfelt human
action? A good actor could perhaps preserve the ambiguity. But can the
playgoer maintain it? *The Duchess of Malfi*'s insistently divisive rhetoric

makes it extraordinarily difficult to remain suspended for long between these extremes.

In his last lines, Bosola reinforces the play's divisive rhetoric by asserting that justice and mercy are attainable, but that they are beyond his own reach. He acknowledges that "worthy minds" exist (5.5.102). His last words, though, are, "Mine is another voyage" (5.5. 104). The audience members, like George Gifford's readers, are invited to contemplate the separate destinations of their own voyages. Both *The Duchess of Malfi* and *The Countrie Divinitie* offer all sorts of advice about getting on the right ship. But the advice seems somehow chilling when one realizes that each voyager's vessel has long ago left port.

7. Donne in on Shakespeare's Stage: The Theology and Theatrics of Renaissance Dying

> Yet have I seen thee in the pulpit stand,
> Where we might take notes from thy look, and hand;
> And from thy speaking action bear away
> More sermon than some teachers use to say.
> Such was thy carriage, and thy gesture such,
> As could divide the heart, and conscience touch.
> Thy motion did confute, and we might see
> An error vanquished by delivery.
> —Jasper Mayne, to John Donne [1]

I

The frontispiece to the first printed edition of John Donne's last sermon is a portrait of the late preacher in his winding sheet. Michael Droeshout's engraving copies the upper portion of a life-size painting that Donne posed for just before his death, elaborately staging the details himself. According to Izaak Walton's 1639 biography (or, rather, hagiography) of Donne,

> Several charcoal fires being first made in his large study, he brought with him into that place his winding-sheet in his hand, and having put off all his clothes, had this sheet put on him, and so tied with knots at his head and feet, and his hands so placed as dead bodies are usually fitted to be shrouded and put into their coffin or grave. . . . He thus stood, with his eyes shut, and with so much of the sheet turned aside as might shew his lean, pale, and death-like face, which was purposely turned towards the East, from whence he expected the second coming of his and our Saviour Jesus.[2]

As Walton remarks, it seems curious that a clergyman as self-effacing as Donne would take such extravagant pains to leave a monument to himself, particularly such a gruesome reminder of his emaciated condition just before death.

But of course that is just the point. Donne is a poet and a preacher of contrariety, of paradox. He delights in offering to his audience unsettling combinations of contrary principles, and so it is perfectly in character that he would assert his bodily presence even as he effaced it, that he would bequeath to posterity a portrait of living death. Walton reports that the actual moment of Donne's death is commensurate with this macabre concern for appearance:

> as his soul ascended, and his last breath departed from him, he closed his own eyes, and then disposed his hands and body into such a posture as required not the least alteration by those that came to shroud him. (55)

Donne had been preparing for the moment of his death for weeks, months —even, he would have said, his whole life. And so when premature reports of his passing began to circulate in London in January of 1631, Donne hastened to dispel the rumors. He wrote to a friend that although his illness had left him in a severely weakened condition, he hoped that arrangements could be made for his usual sermon at Court on the first Friday of Lent. He added a hint that the audience could well be in for a memorable experience:

> It hath been my desire (and God may be pleased to grant it) that I might die in the pulpit; if not that, yet that I might take my death in the pulpit; that is, die the sooner by occasion of my former labors.[3]

Donne was speedily appointed to preach the sermon.

Three years earlier he had explicitly made a connection between deathbed and pulpit: "The pulpit is more than our death-bed; for we are bound to the same truth and sincerity here as if we were upon our death-bed."[4] Now that his death was imminent, there was a strong chance that he could make the point emphatically. Upon his arrival in London, according to Walton,

> many of his friends—who with sorrow saw his sickness had left him but so much flesh as did only cover his bones—doubted his strength to perform that task. . . . And when, to the amazement of some beholders, he appeared in the pulpit, many of them thought he presented himself not to preach mortification by a living voice, but mortality by a decayed body and a dying face. And doubtless many did secretly ask that question in Ezekiel: "Do these bones live?" (49)

Walton goes on to point out that Donne's tears and faint, hollow voice gave rise to the paradoxical impression recorded on the title page of the 1632 Quarto: the performance was *called by his Majesties houshold the Doctors Owne Funerall Sermon.* (10:277)

Deaths Duell is a self-conscious performance piece, one whose rhetorical effectiveness depends in part on its relation to the biblical sub-genre of the "prophetic performance"—a tradition that includes, for example, Jeremiah's preaching with a yoke on his neck to prophesy servitude in Babylon and Agabus's binding himself with Paul's girdle to warn of Paul's impending capture.[5] In short, Donne's sermon is not merely idiosyncratic; it owes something to the biblical tradition of the prophetic performance, something to the *ars moriendi* tradition, and something to the audience's familiarity with the performative paradoxes of the Renaissance stage.

The Quarto editor's epistle to the reader says that although the sermon is perhaps not Donne's best, the occasion of its delivery and the universal applicability of its topic make it compelling (10:277). Subsequent history has confirmed the editor's impression; *Deaths Duell* is probably the best known of Donne's 163 extant sermons. It seems to me that it is from precisely the theatricality of Donne's presentation of the death-in-life paradox, from precisely its status as a staged presentation of funereal ritual, that the sermon derives its affective force. *Deaths Duell* develops the performative potential implicit in another of Donne's funeral sermons, this one delivered in 1626 at the funeral of the wealthy London alderman and former Lord Mayor Sir William Cokayne. The first part of this chapter argues that in both sermons, but in *Deaths Duell* more successfully, Donne systematically plays on the paradoxes arising out of the cultural paradigm of Christ's martyrdom in order to bring his audience to a sense of human solidarity. The rest of the chapter explores a similar rhetorical principle adumbrated in *Richard III* and fully developed in *Othello*.

II

Toward the end of his funeral sermon for Cokayne, Donne remarks that "the funeral is the Easter-eve; the burial is the depositing of that man for the Resurrection" (7:10.575–97). In offering these words of hope, Donne is of course performing the task of comforting the family and friends of Cokayne at a critical time—a time marked out in all human societies for the ritual observance of passage. But Donne is also complicating the moment. According to the theology of Donne's Church of England, Cokayne's soul has been split from his body at the moment of death, and this situation will hold until the General Resurrection. The funeral sermon both offers assurance that body and soul will eventually be reunited and evokes a sense of present irresolution. In fact, in the very first sentence of his sermon, Donne sets up this tension by using the conceit of marriage and divorce to place the blame for the body/soul separation on human sin:

> God made the first marriage, and man made the first divorce; God married the body and soul in the Creation, and man divorced the body and soul by death through sin, in his fall. (7:10.1–4)

Donne says that although Cokayne's soul is "at the table of the Lamb, in Glory," his body is "at the table of the serpent, in dust" (7:10.21–22). In obscuring any facile sense of contraries joined, such a graphic reminder of irresolution serves Donne's rhetorical project of generating a conciliatory sense of mystery.

In *Deaths Duell*, Donne accomplishes the same task by calling attention to the passages between the stages of human life. This attention to the "liminal" phases of life—the transitional points at which social roles are in flux and definitions obscured—serves to unsettle the audience, reminding the mourners that their own lives have been disrupted by the mystery of death.[6] As Donne puts it,

> all our periods and transitions in this life are so many passages from death to death. Our very birth and entrance into this life is *exitus à morte*, an issue from death . . . for this whole world is but an universal churchyard, but our common grave; and the life and motions that the greatest persons have in it is but as the shaking of buried bodies in their graves by an earthquake. That which we call life is but *hebdomada mortium*, a week of deaths, seven days, seven periods of our life spent in dying, a dying seven times over; and there is an end. (10:11.66–68, 160–66)

Just as some thirty years earlier Shakespeare had worked a similarly somber meditation on the "seven ages" *topos* into a romantic comedy, Donne here weaves his thoughts on the finality of earthly death and separation into a sermon that is really about life and reconciliation.[7]

In his equation of death with the liminal phases of life and in his physical embodiment of the death-in-life paradox, Donne's rhetoric involves the persuasive principle that Kenneth Burke calls "identification"— the assertion of common ground between speaker and audience.[8] In part this strategy works by bringing the audience to an unsettling awareness of the reality of worldly corruption and bodily decomposition in order to preclude any facile sense of closure, any merely palliative resolution to the problem of death. For example, in another passage that might have been drawn from Shakespeare (*Hamlet* this time; but the *topos* appears frequently in the Renaissance), Donne invokes the "emperor worm" motif:

> When those bodies that have been the children of royal parents, and the parents of royal children, must say with Job to corruption, "thou art my father," and to the worm, "thou art my mother and my sister": Miserable riddle, when the same worm must be my mother and my sister and my self. Miserable incest, when I must be married to my mother and my sister, and be both father and mother to my own mother and sister, beget, and bear that worm which is all that miserable penury; when my mouth shall be filled with dust, and the worm shall feed, and feed sweetly upon me, when the ambitious man shall have no satisfaction, if the poorest alive tread upon him, nor the poorest receive any contentment in being made equal to princes, for they shall be equal but in dust. (10:11.308–20)

The unsettling imagery is rhetorically necessary for Donne's performance to accomplish its goal. Later in the sermon the preacher says explicitly that a meditation on death *should* be "visceral" (10:11.553). The passage just cited serves the twofold function of viscerally unsettling the audience and introducing the central theme of the "levelling" effect of death.

In the funeral sermon for Cokayne, Donne is careful to stress that it is not only in death that Christians are "levelled," but through the whole of their lives. In true Calvinist fashion (Donne's debt to Calvin has been persistently underestimated)[9] he subverts any impulse toward devotional hierarchy, toward structured, pietistic discrimination, by pointing out that even the best of human works are inevitably tainted: "the man that does them, and knows the weakness of them, knows that they are not good works" (7:10.303–4). Even the most devout Christians, says Donne, are unable to maintain a spirit of devotion for as long as the thirty seconds it takes to say the Lord's Prayer:

> which of us ever, ever says over that short prayer with a deliberate understanding of every petition as we pass, or without deviations and extravagancies of our thoughts, in that half-minute of our devotion? (7:10.259–62)

Donne is quick to include himself among the distracted:

> I throw myself down in my chamber, and I call in and invite God and his angels thither, and when they are there, I neglect God and his angels for the noise of a fly, for the rattling of a coach, for the whining of a door; I talk on in the same posture of praying: eyes lifted up; knees bowed down; as though I prayed to God; and if God or his angels should ask me when I thought last of God in that prayer, I cannot tell. Sometimes I find that I had forgot what I was about, but when I began to forget it, I cannot tell. A memory of yesterday's pleasures, a fear of tomorrow's dangers, a straw under my knee, a noise in mine ear, a light in mine eye, an anything, a nothing, a fancy, a chimera in my brain, troubles me in my prayer. So certainly there is nothing, nothing in spiritual things perfect in this world. (7:10.273–86)

In taking such pains to make it clear that he, the famous Dean of St. Paul's, is no different from his listeners in his inability to reconcile the mundane and the spiritual, Donne is furthering his project of "levelling," of effacing social distinctions. He is working instead to generate a communal sense of mystery.

Having established the idea of universal human imperfection among the living, Donne extends the principle to include the dead. That is, he employs the same strategy we have seen at work in *Deaths Duell*:

> this body must wither, must decay, must languish, must perish. When Goliath had armed and fortified this body, and Jezebel had painted and perfumed this body, and Dives had pampered and larded this body, as God said to Ezekiel, when he brought him to the dry bones, "*Fili hominis*, Son of man, dost thou think these bones can live?" They said in their hearts to all the world, Can these bodies die? And they are dead. Jezebel's dust is not amber, nor Goliath's dust *terra sigillata*, medicinal; nor does the serpent, whose meat they are both, find any better relish in Dives' dust than in Lazarus'. (7:10.551–60)

Donne's imagery forces the mourners to contemplate the physical decay of Cokayne's body. And yet, says Donne, "our brother is not dead" (7:10.606). The mourners, having already been drawn into a liminal social phase by Cokayne's death, are asked to embrace a paradox: "Even he, whom we call dead, is alive this day" (7:10.665). Given the amount of energy Donne has invested in making it clear that Cokayne *is* dead, and given the physical presence of the corpse, the prospect of Cokayne's being alive must be taken on faith. In other words, the terms of embracing the paradox involve the suppression of ordinary sensory and rational categories. This suppression is a key factor in Donne's performative strategy of effacing the differences of opinion, personality, and social role by which the audience members ordinarily define themselves.

In *Deaths Duell*, Donne repeatedly invokes Christian paradox. A few examples: in Christ's passion his joy "filled him even in the midst of those torments, and arose from them"; Christ "died voluntarily, but yet when we consider the contract that had been passed between his Father and him, there was an *oportuit*, a kind of necessity upon him"; Christ said, " 'If it be possible, let this cup pass,' when his love, expressed in a former decree with his Father, had made it impossible" (10:11.531–32, 513–15, 501–3). All these paradoxes work by checking the urge toward discursive thought.

The funeral sermon for Cokayne works similarly, highlighting the Christian paradoxes of time and eternity. Far from serving merely as epideictic ornamentation, paradox is central to Donne's rhetorical project, to his function as a priest playing a pivotal social role in a ritual performance. Donne's riddling rhetoric is effective in large part because it reflects the central cultural paradigm of the sacrificial death of God in Christ.[10] Donne goes so far as to say that although the reunion of Cokayne's body and soul must wait for the General Resurrection, that very resurrection has already taken place. In Christ "we all rose, for he was All in All" (7:10.43). Quoting Ephesians, Donne says,

> "God hath raised us," and "God hath made us to sit together in heavenly places, in Christ Jesus." They that are not fallen yet by any actual sin (children newly baptized) are risen already in him; and they that are not dead yet, nay, not alive yet, not yet born, have a resurrection in him, who was not only the Lamb slain from the beginning, but from before all beginnings was risen too; and all that shall ever have part in the second Resurrection are risen with him from that time. (7:10.45–52)

In short, the sermon unfolds for the mourners a sacred mystery: not only Cokayne, but they themselves have already partaken in a future resurrection. The rhetorical effect is to remove Cokayne from the center of attention, transferring the focus to the mourners themselves. Donne simultaneously reminds the audience that they have already won the battle with death and that the battle is far from over. Such paradoxical rhetoric circumvents discriminatory thought by conflating bodily with spiritual "levelling."

Cokayne's funeral sermon is rhetorically effective, but it is in *Deaths Duell* that Donne fully capitalizes on the sermon's theatrical potential. Of course, any funeral sermon of Donne's day would bear signs of the priest's role in a cultural performance: the clerical garments, the positioning of priest and audience, and the heightened diction all have their counterparts in the theater. In *Deaths Duell*, though, Donne goes so far as to speak through a sort of death mask. His very appearance provides a visually effective, strikingly dramatic confirmation of the Pauline paradox that he makes a point of underscoring: "I die daily" (10:11.194). He then explicitly calls for an emotional release:

> So then this part of our sermon must needs be a Passion sermon; since all his life was a continual passion, all our Lent may well be a continual Good Friday. Christ's painful life took off none of the pains of his death; he felt not the less then for having felt so much before. Nor will anything that shall be said before lessen but rather enlarge your devotion to that which shall be said of his Passion at the time of the due solemnization thereof. Christ bled not a drop the less at the last for having bled at his circumcision before, nor will you shed a tear the less then, if you shed some now. (10:11.474–83)

Having introduced the idea of his audience's participation not only in Easter but also in Christ's Passion, Donne takes on the role of Christ himself in calling for a passionate response:

> If thou didst any thing then that needed Peter's tears, and hast not shed them, let me be thy cock; do it now. Now thy master (in the unworthiest of his servants) looks back upon thee; do it now. (10:11.620–22)

Donne's role-playing is itself paradoxical, simultaneously self-effacing and bold. The dying preacher, "unworthy" though he is, impersonates the stricken Christ on Good Friday. By offering himself as a Christlike embodiment of living death, Donne fully exploits his sermon's dramatic potential.

III

Of course, the occasion of *Deaths Duell* presented Donne with a once-in-a-lifetime opportunity. The Renaissance playwright was in a somewhat more enviable position in that his tragic heroes were reborn for each performance. While such differences between the presentations of death in Donne and Shakespeare are too obvious to require further comment, certain less obvious rhetorical similarities are compelling enough to warrant consideration of the cultural interplay between the pulpit and the stage.

In such an examination of the relations between religion and literature, one does well to heed the warning that Shakespearean tragedy is never reducible to exclusive formulations, including those of Reformation theology.[11] One scholar says of *Richard III*, for example, that the play is "an endorsement of protestant dogma"; like Shakespeare's chronicle sources, it "is designed to exemplify the operation of retributive justice."[12] Clearly, such a formulation is unnecessarily reductive; *Richard III* amounts to much more than a simplistic vindication of divine retribution. But what if there are nonexclusive modes of seventeenth-century religious thought? What if the very purpose of certain theological formulations is to guard against exclusive reduction, to guard against the diminution of mystery? In that case, one could examine the theological implications of a play like *Richard III* without reducing it to any sort of definitive statement.

As this study has argued, such nonexclusive theology is precisely what we find in certain strains of Reformation England's paradoxical discourse. This theology works in a sort of cultural dialectic with the process of definitive ideological formulation. Such nonexclusive theological discourse, grounded in the root paradigms of Christian culture, is pervasive enough to inform and in turn to be informed by all the institutions of early modern England, including Shakespeare's stage. A number of commentators have argued that a play like *Richard III* derives a large part of its peculiar horror and fascination from the paradox of free will and determinism, which was central not only to the classical tragedies revived in the Renaissance, but also to the Protestant discourse of Shakespeare's day.[13] True enough; the confluence of classical and Christian sources engenders a broad receptivity to certain theatrical handlings of this paradox, especially in staged presentations of death. What is not always noticed is the similar effect produced by dramatic and religious performances. Shakespeare's and Donne's presentations use similar strategies to offer the audience the chance for an appropriation of communal vitality—a sense of shared life. To be sure, there are exceptions on both sides: it would be difficult to include a play like *Troilus and Cressida* in this category, and Donne can be resolutely polemic. Moreover, Shakespeare's rhetorical strategies, like Donne's, are richly varied. An examination of the playwright's variations on one such strategy—the embodiment of motiveless evil in Richard III and Iago—sheds light on one aspect of Shakespeare's development as a dramatic artist. It seems to me that this development is a function of the playwright's relation to the complex theology of his day.

In his discussion of *Richard III*, A. P. Rossiter remarks,

> [An] overall system of *paradox* is the play's unity. It is revealed as a constant displaying of inversions, or reversals of meaning: whether we consider the verbal patterns (the *peripeteias* or reversals of expectation); the antithesis of false and true in the histrionic character; or the constant inversions of irony. (*Angel with Horns*, 20)

Richard himself, it might be argued, is the embodiment of paradox: he is viscerally unsettling and at the same time appealing—a "bloody dog" and an admirably inventive performer (5.5.2).[14]

Shakespeare depicts these contraries in part through Richard's soliloquies: this is the only play in the Shakespearean corpus that begins with a soliloquy, and Richard has no fewer than four of them in the first three scenes. The effect of Richard's disarming intimacy is not only to detach the audience from the rest of the characters but also to effect a Burkean identification—to make Richard's voice disturbingly like one's own. Of course, in his witty soliloquies Richard is in part descended from the medieval Vice. Shakespeare's play, however, presents the audience not with an allegorical abstraction but with a decidedly human protagonist, one all the more appealing, somehow, for the unfathomability of his motives. Norman Rabkin argues persuasively that Richard is "inexplicably and gratuitously evil," that he is motivated by "a nihilistic and universal hatred," that his disingenuous self-psychologizing about his physical deformity no more explains his behavior than does his political ambition: "Richard kills his family not because he wants to be king but because he wants to kill his family."[15]

As the play continually reminds the audience, such unmotivated evil clearly marks Richard as diabolical, but dismissing this character as a reprobate "other" is by no means easy; Richard's powers of seduction are undeniably strong.[16] If the audience finds Richard's successful wooing of Lady Anne startling, it is partly because the audience is similarly taken in by Richard's eloquent machinations. As James Calderwood says, "Richard seduces us as he seduces Lady Anne, and by the same device—by announcing his desire."[17] Anne's protest that her "woman's heart / Grossly grew captive to his honey words" cannot easily be dismissed as a merely misogynous sentiment on Shakespeare's part; Richard's honey words seduce audience members irrespective of gender (4.1.78–79). The audience's sense of intimacy and complicity with Richard is all the more unsettling because of the play's repeated intimations that he is a reprobate.

Of all the plays in the Shakespearean canon, only *Othello* contains more references than does *Richard III* to hell, devils, damnation, and despair.[18] According to Lady Anne, Richard is a "dreadful minister of hell" and a "foul devil" (1.2.46, 50). He is by his own mother's own admission her "damned son," destined, according to no fewer than seven ghosts, to "despair and die" (5.3.135–163). And, given the Pauline origin of the doctrine of predestination, surely it is noteworthy that all five of the references to the apostle Paul in the whole corpus of Shakespeare occur in *Richard III*. In each case Richard is swearing "by Saint Paul," "by holy Paul," or "by the apostle Paul" (1.2.36, 41; 1.3.45; 3.4.76; 5.3.216). In view of the currency in Shakespeare's England of discourse centering on the Pauline doctrine of election and reprobation, Richard's invocation of the apostle's name reinforces his status as a reprobate.[19] In Pauline terms, Richard is a "vessel of wrath":

> Hath not the potter power of the clay to make of the same lump one vessel to honor, and another unto dishonor? What and if God would, to shew his wrath, and to make his power known, suffer with long patience the vessels of wrath, prepared to destruction? (Rom. 9:21–22)

If Richard is such a vessel of wrath, a lump of clay formed for destruction (Anne calls him a "lump of foul deformity"), the audience's awareness of his reprobation hardly solves the problem of what to make of him.[20]

It is in these theologically topical terms that the play presents the problem of what to make of a character who seems simultaneously fated and free. The paradox is intimated in the play's opening soliloquy, in which Richard says, "I am determined to prove a villain" (1.1.30). Has he freely made up his mind to be a villain, or has he been "determined," predestined, to villainy?[21] Later in the play, in a brief exchange between Richard and Queen Elizabeth, Shakespeare neatly encapsulates the paradox of predestination. To Richard's "All unavoided is the doom of destiny," Elizabeth replies, "True—when avoided grace makes destiny" (4.4.218–19). Just how many layers of irony are involved here? Does Richard really think he can convince Elizabeth that his marriage to her daughter has been preordained? Or does his rhetorical strategy dictate that Elizabeth catch his irony? Or, on some level, does Richard *believe* that his future has been predestined? If so, does he consider himself a reprobate? In any case, just how is the audience to process this paradox of freedom and determinism? If, as Elizabeth says, "avoided grace makes destiny," does Richard freely choose to avoid grace? If so, how can the result be called "destiny"?

From a Catholic standpoint, and of course the historical Elizabeth Woodville was Catholic, there is nothing inconsistent in the claim that avoided grace makes destiny. In Catholic theology grace is offered to all, and all freely choose to accept or reject it. But Shakespeare is not writing in Catholic England. The Calvinists' highlighting of the paradox of predestination complicates the audience's response. Difficult as it is, the paradox must be processed, for the play makes it insistent.

Not the least of Shakespeare's devices for generating a sense of the mystery of reprobation is his inclusion of Queen Margaret, a presence that the playwright did not find in his chronicle sources. Margaret functions as a sort of Senecan Fury, howling out invectives and prophesying events that inevitably come to pass. In doing so, she enlarges the arena in which the action unfolds; Margaret's disturbing presence makes it clear that Richard's tyranny is not only a matter of local politics—she is a constant reminder of political history—but also that the tyranny has cosmic proportions. As Jean Howard argues, Margaret detaches the audience from immediate situations like the argument between Richard and Elizabeth:

> Oblivious to the doom Margaret cries down upon them, they act out their quarrel in the face of her withering scorn, a situation that makes their fight seem a pointless irrelevancy. Nearsighted players in the drama of history, acting in response to present pressures, they are blind to the larger forces that shape their destinies.[22]

Margaret identifies these larger forces with the "upright, just, and true-disposing God," the Providence informing the theology of Shakespeare's England (4.4.55). The play dramatizes the mystery of a providential deity whose preordained plan involves not only divine vengeance on the wicked but also the murder of children who can by no means be implicated in Richard's wickedness. In highlighting the paradox of divine justice that seems anything but just, Shakespeare's play fully engages his audience's ambivalent response to the problem of evil.

This response involves an acute awareness of evil's pervasive power, an effect intensified by Richard's apparent unstoppability. Significantly, knowledge of Richard's corruption is widespread; ordinary citizens as well as members of inner circles at Court know that Richard's piety is a sham.

The Third Citizen is aware that "full of danger is the Duke of Glouces-ter," and the Scrivener's comment on Richard's trumped-up indictment of Hastings is, "Who is so gross / That cannot see this palpable device?" (2.3.27; 3.6.10–11). The whole kingdom knows that Richard is a tyrant, but nobody seems able to stop him. The ordinary citizens are hardly em-powered to do so, and the influential ones, including Buckingham, Hast-ings, and Stanley, are unwilling. With an eerie sort of ease, Richard's evil insinuates itself into all areas of England's political life.

For the audience, one effect of this horrifying portrayal of the intelli-gence of evil—this mystery of an ingenious tyrant fated to slide into power —is to destabilize any impulse toward accepting an easy political solution. As one asks at the end of *Hamlet* whether a mere Fortinbras can set things right in Denmark, one wonders at the end of *Richard III* whether the pious and relatively colorless Richmond can really purge England of evil. Cer-tainly the play upholds the Tudor ideology that Providence replaced the evil Richard III with the virtuous Henry VII, but the experience of play-goers—many of them, anyway—is that this ideology rests uneasily with the mystery of evil. Rabkin's comment is that in his final moments, Richard "makes his nemesis Richmond sound like a perfunctory bureaucrat."[23]

In one sense, then, the central paradoxes of the play are resolved in terms of official political and theological ideology: an ultimately just God has brought good out of evil. In another sense, the paradoxes are resolved in a sense of wonder—a response that evokes a nonpossessive, simply human rather than a merely national solidarity.[24] If these two sorts of reso-lution rest together uneasily, one explanation is that Shakespeare is more interested in dramatizing problems than in generating a single vision, more interested in asking questions than in answering them. Another explana-tion is that in *Richard III* Shakespeare's tragic vision has not yet come quite into focus, as it will in *Othello*.[25] As Donne's *Death's Duell* draws on the energies of paradox to exploit the theatrical potential implicit in Co-kayne's funeral sermon, Shakespeare's Iago fully embodies the paradoxical force adumbrated in Richard.

IV

From the riddling epigram and the oxymoron to broad compositional techniques, paradox pervades *Othello*. The mock encomia of Iago's epi-grammatic musings on wisdom and folly, fairness and blackness, for example, are far more than what Desdemona naïvely calls them: "old fond paradoxes to make fools laugh i' th' alehouse" (2.1.138–39). As Iago knows, the inversion of wisdom and folly, fairness and foulness, is central to his project. The play's oxymorons are likewise suggestive. Othello's bemused "Excellent wretch," for example, seems a simple expression of endearment, but it also carries prophetic force, encapsulating the hero's notorious inability to resolve contraries and prefiguring all the excellence and wretchedness of Desdemona's death. The words immediately following are

> Perdition catch my soul
> But I do love thee! and when I love thee not,
> Chaos is come again. (3.3.90–92)

Of course, this is prophetic; the play is about all these things—perdition, love, and chaos—elements that are held in tension through the final scene. Iago's "Divinity of hell!" is also enormously suggestive (2.3.350). The oxymoron is set in the middle of a soliloquy that makes Iago simultaneously appealing and horrifying. The same device so effectively employed in *Richard III* is in force again here: the soliloquy that is disarmingly witty, confidential, subtle.

At this point Iago has just suggested that Cassio appeal to Othello through Desdemona. As Cassio exits, Iago addresses the audience:

> And what's he then that says I play the villain,
> When this advice is free I give, and honest,
> Probal to thinking, and indeed the course
> To win the Moor again? (2.3.336–39)

What's he, indeed? As Rosalie Colie says, "Iago is the dramatic figure acting out the duplicity of the Liar paradox, for he lies in speaking the truth."[26] Iago repeatedly uses the truth to lead Othello astray:

> I confess it is my nature's plague
> To spy into abuses, and [oft] my jealousy
> Shapes faults that are not. (3.3.146–48)

This is true enough, as is Iago's ingenious protest, "To be direct and honest is not safe" (3.3.378). The play cultivates a paradoxical awareness of the need for directness and honesty in a world bent on punishing these very qualities.

It is of course Iago who engenders all the play's action, but his own motives, like those of Richard III, remain mysterious, perhaps diabolical. Although there may be some psychological plausibility in Iago's military ambitions and his marital jealousies, these factors no more explain his behavior than do Richard's ambitions and physical deformity. Coleridge's term "motiveless malignity" is not too extreme. And yet Iago is not in every sense at the center of the play. It is, after all, Othello's tragedy. Shakespeare's crucial strategem in developing the tragic potential implicit in *Richard III* is to move the diabolical schemer to one side of the tragic hero, providing on the other side Iago's counterpart in Desdemona. The tragic action thus revolves around Othello, whose inability to reconcile extremes largely defines his character. As Robert Grudin says, Othello compusively polarizes experience; he "characteristically expresses his feelings in terms of juxtaposed but mutually annulling realities."[27] Even before the eruption of his jealousy, Othello speaks of his love for Desdemona as a matter of mythic proportions:

> O my soul's joy!
> If after every tempest come such calms,
> May the winds blow till they have wakened death!
> And let the laboring bark climb hills of seas
> Olympus-high, and duck again as low
> As hell's from heaven! (2.1.184–89)

Of course, Iago fully exploits this insistence on polarizing experience, this inability to reconcile extremes. As Iago is fully aware, his advice "Wear your eye thus, not jealous nor secure" is impossible for Othello to follow (3.3.198).

Just as Iago draws the audience irresistibly into his diabolical world, and partly *because* of our knowledge of that world, Othello's experience of contrariety is wrenchingly compelling. Grudin's comments are instructive:

> Pathological idealism—the faith that builds upon absolutes and founders with them—is a diagnosis that can apply to more than one of Shakespeare's tragic heroes. What makes *Othello* uniquely disturbing, however, is that the play's whole structure tends to realize rather than contradict this radical attitude towards experience. Iago is indeed a kind of devil; Desdemona personifies angelic purity; the drama resounds, on a larger scale, with the same appalling dissonances which affect its hero. Thus, far from being allowed to judge Othello objectively, we are lured into his world and compelled to appreciate intensely the polarities which torment him. (*Mighty Opposites*, 136)

This intense appreciation of Othello's tragic inability to find any middle ground between heaven and hell means that for the audience, as for Othello, the action of the play revolves around a vacuum. As Donne's audience is teased into a community-affirming sense of wonder by the contemplation of apparently irreconcilable opposites, Shakespeare's audience is moved to a similarly disarming confrontation with contraries.

The scene in the very center of the play, a scene in which the word "nothing" is spoken eight times, is really about nothing—mere insinuation, absence of evidence, ignorance. The following exchange comes near the beginning of the scene, just after Cassio's exit:

Iago:
  Hah? I like not that.
Othello:
                    What dost thou say?
Iago:
  Nothing, my lord; or if—I know not what. (3.3.35–36)

Once again, Iago is simultaneously telling the truth and lying. He knows "not what," for there is nothing to know; and yet, in a diabolical parody of the *creatio ex nihilo* paradox, he is leading Othello astray by coaxing him to make a great something of this nothing. Near the end of the scene, when Iago's insinuations have had a chance to run their course, Othello says,

I had been happy, if the general camp,
Pioners and all, had tasted her sweet body,
So I had nothing known. (3.3.345–47)

Of course, the irony is that Othello's desire has already been fulfilled: "nothing" is precisely what there is to know, and so although he is mistaken, Othello knows precisely what is true: nothing. This epistemological paradox makes the play a sort of vortex; the action swirls with increasing force around the vacuum at its center.

And if nature abhors a vacuum, so does an audience. As Othello spins madly from trust to jealous rage, terrified to the point of convulsions by the absence of any middle ground, the audience too strains to find footing. In one sense, Shakespeare's dramatic irony means that the audience and Othello remain on radically different levels of awareness; we know what he doesn't—or, rather, we know the absence of what he thinks he knows. In another sense, though, a strong impulse remains for us, as for

Othello, to resolve contraries—the impulse that Donne so artfully exploits. As Donne's audiences are presented with the twin realities of the death and life of a loved one, of his decay and glory, Shakespeare's audience has felt the allure of the polarized forces embodied in Iago and Desdemona. The play generates sympathy with both the hero's wild vacillation and his demand for a resolution. Othello says to Iago,

> By the world,
> I think my wife be honest, and think she is not;
> I think that thou art just, and think thou art not.
> I'll have some proof. (3.3.383–86)

Our knowledge that the proffered proof of the handkerchief is no proof at all means that the demand for resolution is displaced onto us. If the handkerchief provides a false resolution, what will provide a true one? As is the case in Donne's sermons and *Richard III*, Shakespeare's strategy in *Othello* demands that the terms of this resolution embrace the contraries of Iago's knowledge and Desdemona's innocence.

Shakespeare points the way, I think, in Emilia. Her level of self-awareness contrasts sharply with that of Desdemona, who seems genuinely unaware of her own capacity for deceit. After all, Desdemona lies to Othello about the handkerchief and, as both Brabantio and Iago point out, she has deceived her father. Yet Desdemona herself, in her almost Edenic innocence, shows no awareness of any duplicity. I think she actually believes herself when she says, paradoxically, "I cannot say 'whore'" (4.2.161).

After all this, Shakespeare gives us the moving scene in which Desdemona and Emilia discuss marital infidelity. In contrast to Desdemona, who says naïvely, "I do not think there is any such woman," Emilia acknowledges her own fallibility: "The world's a huge thing" (4.3.69,83). Then, in a meditation that works to dismantle the ideological structure validating the moral absolutes of masculine control and feminine purity, Emilia says simply, "Let husbands know / Their wives have sense like them" (4.3.93–94). This is the kind of sense that, if acknowledged, makes women into neither men's idols nor their whores. Emilia asks for a recognition of shared human vulnerability. It seems to me that this scene begins to provide the terms of a resolution to the contraries that inform *Othello*. Somehow the kind of sensibility Emilia envisions must mediate the extremes figured in Iago's knowledge and Desdemona's innocence. But even Emilia, who comes closest, is not quite able to effect this mediation. At one point she literally has the solution in her hands, but she does not comprehend Iago's villainy until it is too late. Since neither Emilia nor any other character proves able to mediate the play's insistent contrariety, it is the audience who must find a way do so—to be as wise as serpents yet gentle as doves.

If Othello comes to this level of awareness, it is only for an instant; a mind like his, one that habitually vacillates between moral absolutes, cannot hold contraries in suspension for long. The combination kills him. As Robert Knapp says, "No other Shakespearean tragedy works out so exact a coincidence between a moment of recognition and the extinction of the hero's revealed being."[28] In order for Othello's tragic recognition to live beyond the moment of his death, it must live in the audience's experience of the tragic action.

As Donne's funeral sermons bring to a focus the contrary states of awareness attendant upon the death of a loved one, Othello's death similarly sets up a communal sense of mystery by drawing the audience toward a resolution of paradoxical terms. While the word "resolution" is appropriate in this context, it must be remembered that in Shakespeare's staged presentations of death, like Donne's, this resolution resists ideological definition. In the case of *Othello*, any attempt to reduce the play to ideologically exclusive terms is inadequate to the experience of the tragedy.[29] What the play does is bring about an excruciating sense of what it means to live in a world in which Desdemona is dead and Iago is alive. One thing this means is that in simply human terms, there can never be too much compassion. But it also means that simply human responses are utterly inadequate to cope with this world's evil. The action of the play calls for the audience to respond by embracing contrary terms—a response that the exclusive ideological categories of this world seem unable to supply.

Conclusion

This study's Preface noted the tendency in literary scholarship of the last fifteen years or so to treat religious language as encoded discourse of power—to remove the theological maskings that disguise economic and political motives. There are now signs that religious language is once again coming into its own. Once again it seems possible to talk of religious belief as a primary mode of intent. These signs extend to historical as well as literary studies of the early modern period: once again historians seem willing to discuss, for example, not only socioeconomic but also religious causes of the English Civil War.

This is not to say that anyone supposes—or ought to suppose—the meaning of religious language to be transparent or stable. While preachers are by vocation forthcoming about their beliefs in a way that playwrights are not (or not necessarily), the content of those beliefs is notoriously volatile. By dint of both its resistance to definitive formulation and its potential for engendering passionate commitment, religious belief fuels cultural performances that rival the dramatic intensity of Elizabethan plays. It is heartening to see students of early modern culture once again taking such a force seriously.

Or almost seriously: a case in point is Gary Taylor, a scholar whose passionate insistence on reopening the question of religious intent in Shakespeare and Middleton is sure to provoke response. It's an important enough question, Taylor says, that we should be arguing about it, and he's right ("Forms of Opposition," 296). Part of Taylor's aim is to debunk the idea that the contradictory impulses in Shakespeare's plays imply a transcendence of partisan ideology, a transcendence marked by the reconciliation of all opposites (313). The Shakespeare of such uncanny negative capability, in Taylor's view, is itself an ideological construction, one begun by the playwright himself: "Shakespeare's apparent invisibility is not a simple fact; it is an *act*" (314).

Despite Taylor's acknowledgment that such an act is not only *intentional* but also *performative*, his analysis as a whole serves to reify the former and demystify the latter. It is as though the thing to do in a theater were to stand up from the audience in the middle of a play and shout, "Wait a minute! The whole thing's an *act*!" Well, of course it's an act. We knew that when we bought our tickets.

Turn it another way. Suppose we granted the premise that Taylor admits he cannot quite prove but for which he amasses an impressive array of circumstantial evidence: that Shakespeare was a moderate Catholic, just as Middleton was (more demonstrably) a moderate Puritan. What would it mean to be a moderate Catholic or a moderate Puritan in early modern England? It might mean any number of things. To the degree that one felt inclined to assert the doctrinal differences between one's position and that of a rival confession, one might engage in all sorts of polemics. This is only another way of saying that religious (or dramatic) language inclines to polemics when the myths informing the speaker's (or the playwright's) beliefs break down into the constituent contraries that the myths have traditionally held in suspension. At such times religious language finds its cultural counterpart in the satirical comedies and polemical tragedies of the popular stage. To the degree that a believer felt inclined to occupy the vast territory of doctrinal overlap between and among the various shades of Christianity, the tensional myths informing that believer's faith would remain in suspension. At such times religion's theatrical complement finds its most resonant voice in Shakespeare.

An act? To be sure—and a hard act to follow.

Notes

Chapter 1

1. "Ex formis antiquissimorum templorum atq; scriptis S. Patrum satis cognoscitur, fuisse stationem Cleri apud veteres in mediis templis, quae ferè rotunda erant . . . ," Martin Bucer, *Martini Buceri Scripta Anglicana* . . . (Basel, 1577), p. 457. In keeping with standard practice in modern editions of Renaissance plays, I have modernized spelling, capitalization, and, occasionally, punctuation in all citations (except titles) of Renaissance theological works.

2. For treatments of the mage in Renaissance culture, see Keith Thomas, *Religion and the Decline of Magic* (New York: Scribner, 1971); and Ioan Couliano, *Eros and Magic in the Renaissance* (Chicago: University of Chicago Press, 1987). Louis Montrose provides some suggestive speculations about the relations among "the theatrical playing space, the ecclesiastical sacred space, and the charmed circle" in "The Purpose of Playing: Reflections on a Shakespearean Anthropology," *Helios* 7 (1980): 51–74, p. 62.

3. On antitheatricalism in Western culture, see Jonas Barish, *The Antitheatrical Prejudice* (Berkeley: University of California Press, 1981). Invectives against playgoing, especially on Sunday, can be found in numerous Paul's Cross sermons, including those by Thomas White, John Stockwood, John Walsall, Robert Sparke, Francis Marbury, William Holbrooke, and Robert Milles. See John Stockwood, *A Sermon Preached at Paules Crosse on Barthelmew day, being the 24. of August, 1578* (London, 1578), pp. 23–24; Francis Marbury, *A Sermon Preached at Paules Crosse the 13. of June, 1602* (London, 1602), Millar MacLure, *Register of Sermons Preached at Paul's Cross 1534–1642*, rev. Peter Pauls and Jackson Campbell Boswell (Ottawa: Dovehouse Editions, 1989), pp. 58–59, 94, 97. See also John Field, *A Godly Exhortation, by occasion of the late judgment of God, shewed at Paris-garden, the thirteenth day of January: where were assembled by estimation; above a thousand persons, whereof some were slain; and of that number, at the least, as is credibly reported, the third person maimed and hurt* (London, 1583), pp. 17–18, 32; and Philip Stubbes, *Anatomy of Abuses . . .* , ed. F. J. Furnivall, New Shakespeare Society, vols. 4, 6, 12 (1877–82). (Rpt. Millwood, N.Y.: Kraus, 1965), pp. 143–44.

4. See Annabel Patterson, *Censorship and Interpretation* (Madison: University of Wisconsin Press, 1984), p. 45, and Jonathan Dollimore, *Radical Tragedy: Religious Ideology and Power in the Drama of Shakespeare and his Contemporaries* (Brighton: Harvester Press, 1984), p. 25. Even Margot Heinemann, who has done a great deal to illuminate the relations between drama and theology, occasionally slips into the assumption that since drama after 1606 is "compulsorily secular," playwrights indeed avoid religious issues, *Puritanism and Theatre* (Cambridge: Cam-

bridge University Press, 1980), p. 10. Cf. Martin Butler, "Ecclesiastical Censorship of Early Stuart Drama: The Case of Jonson's *The Magnetic Lady*," *Modern Philology* 89 (1992): 469–81.

5. *Henry V*, Prologue, 13. All quotations from Shakespeare's plays are from *The Riverside Shakespeare*, gen. ed. G. Blakemore Evans (Boston: Houghton Mifflin, 1974).

6. The tracing of the circle before the speech is assumed by the First Folio's stage direction at 5.1.57: "Here enters Ariel before; then Alonso, with a frantic gesture, attended by Gonzalo; Sebastian and Antonio in like manner, attended by Adrian and Francisco. They all enter the circle which Prospero had made, and there stand charm'd; which Prospero observing, speaks."

7. While a good deal of work has been done to establish the indebtedness of Renaissance literary forms to the principle of contrariety in the Platonic tradition, no study to date has sufficiently addressed the rhetorical relations between this literature and the paradoxical mentality of Reformation theology. A number of commentators have argued that paradox becomes unusually pervasive in early modern England. See especially Rosalie L. Colie, *Paradoxia Epidemica* (Princeton, N.J.: Princeton University Press, 1966), p. 22. While Colie's study focuses on lyric poetry rather than drama or theology, it is still the most thoroughgoing treatment of literary handlings of Renaissance paradox. Useful supplements include Robert Grudin's *Mighty Opposites: Shakespeare and Renaissance Contrariety* (Berkeley: University of California Press, 1980); Norman Rabkin's work on complementarity, especially in the first chapter of *Shakespeare and the Common Understanding* (New York: Macmillan, 1967); and Joel B. Altman's insights on ambivalence in *The Tudor Play of Mind* (Berkeley: University of California Press, 1978). See also Thomas S. Kuhn, *The Structure of Scientific Revolutions* (Chicago: University of Chicago Press, 1962).

8. A fair number of Norman round churches may have survived into Bucer's day (remains of several still exist), but only four in England have survived into the twentieth century. In addition to the Church of the Holy Sepulchre in Cambridge are the Temple Church in London and churches in Northampton and Little Maplestead, Essex.

9. "Quando vedi uno archo mezzo tondo, l'occhio tuo non è impedito niente quando tu lo risguardi. . . ." Quoted in Rudolf Wittkower, *Architectural Principles in the Age of Humanism* (New York: Random House, 1971), p. 10n.

10. Wittkower, p. 10.

11. Nikolaus Pevsner, *An Outline of European Architecture* (London: John Murray, 1951), p. 83; Wittkower, pp. 10–12.

12. Wittkower, p. 10.

13. "hoc Antichristianum est. Chori tanta à reliquo templo seiunctio, eò seruit, ut ministri, qualescunq; fide sint & vita, ipso tamen ordine & loco habeantur quasi Deo propinquiores quàm laici: & qui possint his placare Deum vi externorum operum, quae faciunt sibi propria . . .," Bucer, p. 457. My translation.

14. Walter Ong, *The Presence of the Word: Some Prolegomena for Cultural and Religious History* (New Haven, Conn.: Yale University Press, 1967), p. 200; Elizabeth L. Eisenstein, *The Printing Press as an Agent of Change* (Cambridge: Cambridge University Press, 1980), pp. 303–78.

15. The term "social drama" is Victor Turner's. He calls social dramas "pub-

lic episodes of tensional irruption" in *Dramas, Fields, and Metaphors* (Ithaca, N.Y.: Cornell University Press, 1974), p. 33. Turner develops the concept more fully in "Social Dramas and Stories about Them," in *On Narrative*, ed. W. J. T. Mitchell (Chicago: University of Chicago Press, 1981), pp. 137–64, and *The Anthropology of Performance* (New York: PAJ Publications, 1987), pp. 94ff. For an application of the term to the Protestant Reformation, see Huston Diehl, *Staging Reform, Reforming the Stage: The Protestant Aesthetics of English Renaissance Tragedy* (Ithaca, N.Y.: Cornell University Press, forthcoming 1996).

16. Rosalie Colie, *The Resources of Kind* (Berkeley: University of California Press, 1973).

17. Martha Tuck Rozett, *The Doctrine of Election and the Emergence of Elizabethan Tragedy* (Princeton, N.J.: Princeton University Press, 1984), pp. 15–25. J. W. Blench remarked more than thirty years ago that the influence of preaching on the dramatists of sixteenth-century England "is more pervasive and powerful than has generally been recognized," *Preaching in England in the Late Fifteenth and Sixteenth Centuries* (Oxford: Basil Blackwell, 1964), p. 349. Despite the valuable work done in the last twenty years on the interdependence of Renaissance literature and theology, the mutual influence of preachers and playwrights is still not widely acknowledged. Barbara Lewalski's *Protestant Poetics and the Seventeenth-Century Religious Lyric* (Princeton, N.J.: Princeton University Press, 1979) is an invaluable study of the relations between Reformation theology and Renaissance poetry, but it has little to say about drama. Nor does Debora Kuller Shuger's illuminating *Habits of Thought in the English Renaissance: Religion, Politics, and the Dominant Culture* (Berkeley: University of California Press, 1990). The important work on Renaissance drama and theology by Margot Heinemann, Martha Tuck Rozett, and Ritchie Kendall does not address in much detail the rhetorical relations between sermons and stage plays. See Heinemann, *Puritanism and Theatre*, Rozett, and Kendall, *The Drama of Dissent: The Radical Poetics of Nonconformity, 1380–1590* (Chapel Hill: University of North Carolina Press, 1986).

18. "Silver tongu'd Smith, whose well tun'd style hath made thy death the general tears of the Muses, quaintly couldst thou devise heavenly ditties to Apollo's lute, and teach stately verse to trip it as smoothly as if Ovid and thou had but one soul," Thomas Nashe, *Pierce Penilesse his Supplication to the Divell*, 1:137–245 in *Works of Thomas Nashe*, ed. R. B. McKerrow, 5 vols. (London: Sidgwick and Jackson, 1910), pp. 192–93; Henry Smith, *The Trumpet of the Soule, Sounding to Judgement* (London, 1592), sigs. A8^v–B1^r.

19. Martin Butler, *Theatre and Crisis 1632–1642* (Cambridge: Cambridge University Press, 1984), p. 91.

20. Other occasional playwrights include popular preachers as varied in sensibility as Thomas Goffe, John Hacket, William Cartwright, and Jasper Mayne.

21. John Foxe, preface to the 1571 edition of *The Reformation of Ecclesiastical Laws of England, 1552*, ed. and trans. James Spalding (Kirksville, Mo.: Sixteenth Century Essays and Studies, 1992), Appendix I, p. 306.

22. Heinemann, p. 21.

23. See John Calvin, *Institution of the Christian Religion*, trans. Thomas Norton (London, 1561), 1.6.2, 1.14.20, 2.6.1, 3.20.23, and Heinemann, p. 26.

24. G. N. Clark remarks that Restoration sermons differed from those of the

Renaissance, which were considered divinely inspired and therefore authoritative in a way that later ones were not, and which were rhetorically more innovative and effective than later ones. As such, Clark claims, late Tudor and early Stuart sermons compose a significant branch of literature, *The Later Stuarts: 1660–1714* (Oxford: Clarendon Press, 1949), pp. 347–48.

25. Andreas Hyperius, *The Practise of preaching, otherwise Called the Pathway to the Pulpet*, trans. John Ludham (London, 1577), p. 41^r.

26. Quoted in Gale H. Carrithers, Jr., *Donne at Sermons: A Christian Existential World* (Albany: State University of New York Press, 1972), p. 3.

27. Samuel Hieron, *The Preachers Plea; or, A Treatise in forme of a plaine dialogue, making known the worth and necessity of that which we call preaching* . . . (London, 1605), p. 2.

28. W. Fraser Mitchell, *English Pulpit Oratory from Andrewes to Tillotson: A Study of its Literary Aspects* (New York: Macmillan, 1932).

29. See Shuger's discussion of role in Lorenzo Valla, Lancelot Andrewes, and George Herbert, *Habits of Thought*, pp. 95–97.

30. Stephen Gosson, *The Trumpet of Warre. A Sermon preached at Paules Crosse the seventh of Maie 1598* (London, 1598), sigs. C4^v–5^r.

31. Hieron, *The Dignity of Preaching: In a Sermon upon I. Thessal. 5:20* (London, 1616), p. 3. Archbishop Edmund Grindal makes the same distinction in his 1576 letter to Queen Elizabeth. *The Remains of Archbishop Grindal* (Cambridge: Parker Society, 1843), p. 385.

32. Calvin, *Institutes*, 4.17.39; 4.14.4; Thomas Cartwright, *Reply to an Answer to M. Doc. Whitgift* (London, 1573), p. 163.

33. William Sclater, *A Threefold Perservative . . . Prescribed in a Sermon at S. Pauls Crosse in London, September 17, 1609* (London, 1610), sig. E4^r. See also Thomas Becon, *The Displaying of the Popish Masse . . . Written by Thomas Becon; in the dayes of Queene Mary* (London, 1637), pp. 28–29.

34. Geneva Bible, 1560 ed. (Madison: University of Wisconsin Press, 1969). As the Geneva was by far the most popular translation of the Bible in Reformation England, I use it for all biblical citations. Between 1578 and 1583, for example, a period that saw no new printing of the Bishops' Bible, the Geneva Bible went through sixteen printings.

35. Henry Smith, *The True Triall of the Spirits*, 1:127–44 in *The Works of Henry Smith*, 2 vols. (Edinburgh: James Nichol, 1866), p. 135. See also Smith's *The Art of Hearing*, in *Works*, 1:324.

36. Hieron, *Dignity*, p. 20. See also William Perkins, *A Case of Conscience, the greatest that ever was; How a man may know whether he be the childe of God, or no* (London, 1592), sig. A3.

37. John Marbecke, *A Book of Notes and Commonplaces with their Expositions* (London, 1581), quoted in Heinemann, p. 51. Marbecke was grandfather to Mary Marbecke, who married the playwright Thomas Middleton.

38. Gosson, sig. E7^r.

39. William Perkins, *The Art of Prophecying*, in *The Workes of that Famous and Worthie Minister of Christ, in the University of Cambridge, M. William Perkins*, 3 vols. (London, 1609), 2:731.

40. George Gifford, *A Briefe discourse of certaine points of the religion, which is among the common sort of Christians, which may bee termed the Countrie Divinitie* (London, 1581), p. 53ᵛ; John Donne, *The Sermons of John Donne*, ed. George R. Potter and Evelyn M. Simpson (Berkeley: University of California Press, 1953–62), 8: 6.505, 513. See also Shuger, *Habits of Thought*, p. 208.

41. Richard Baxter, *The Reformed Pastor*, quoted in Horton Davies, *The Worship of the English Puritans* (Westminster: Dacre Press, 1948), p. 183.

42. George Herbert, *The Country Parson, The Temple*, ed. John N. Wall, Jr. (New York: Paulist Press, 1981), p. 62.

43. John Eachard, supposed author. *A Free and Impartial Inquiry into the Causes of that very great Esteem and Honour that the Nonconforming Preachers are generally in with their Followers* (London, 1673), pp. 118–119.

44. Robert South, *Sermons Preached upon Several Occasions*, 7 vols. (Oxford: Clarendon Press, 1823), 3:37.

45. John King, *Lectures upon Jonas* (London: 1584), p. 3.

46. Thomas Playfere, *The sick-mans Couch. A Sermon Preached before the most noble Prince Henrie at Greenwich, Mar. 12. Ann. 1604.* (London, 1611), ded. epistle.

47. Henry Smith, *The Sermons of Maister Henrie Smith* (London, 1597), sig. A3ᵛ.

48. Richard Hooker, *The Folger Library Edition of the Works of Richard Hooker*, 6 vols., ed. W. Speed Hill (Cambridge, Mass.: Harvard University Press, 1977–93), 5.21.2.

49. See, e.g., Hieron, *Preachers Plea*, pp. 172, 212–13; Thomas Gibson, *A Fruitful Sermon, preached at Occham in the County of Rutland, the Second of November. 1583* (London, 1583), sigs. A3–4.

50. See Ronald B. Bond's introduction to *Certain Sermons or Homilies (1547) and A Homily against Disobedience and Rebellion* (Toronto: University of Toronto Press, 1987), p. 9.

51. Horton Davies, *Like Angels from a Cloud: The English Metaphysical Preachers, 1588–1645* (San Marino, Calif.: Huntington Library, 1986), p. 175.

52. Barish, pp. 101–6 et passim. For an account of the political motivations underlying the fear of Proteus, see Jean E. Howard, "Renaissance Antitheatricality and the Politics of Gender and Rank in *Much Ado about Nothing*," in *Shakespeare Reproduced: The Text in History and Ideology*, ed. Jean E. Howard and Marion F. O'Connor (London: Methuen, 1987), pp. 163–87.

53. Richard James, *A Sermon Delivered in Oxford. Concerning the Apostles Preaching and ours* (London, 1630), sig. D1ʳ.

54. Patrick Collinson, *The Elizabethan Puritan Movement* (Berkeley: University of California Press, 1967), pp. 280–81.

55. Richard Bancroft, *A sermon preached at Paules Crosse the 9. of Februarie . . . 1588* [i.e., 1589] (London, 1589), pp. 25–26.

56. John Chamberlain, *The Letters of John Chamberlain*, 2 vols., ed. Norman Egbert McClure (Philadelphia: American Philosophical Society, 1939), 2:451.

57. Shuger, *Habits of Thought*, p. 11. See also Robert S. Knapp, *Shakespeare— The Theater and the Book* (Princeton, N.J.: Princeton University Press, 1989), p. 86.

58. Shuger, *passim*; Colie, *Paradoxia*, p. 22.

59. Stephen Greenblatt, *Marvelous Possessions: The Wonder of the New World* (Chicago: University of Chicago Press, 1991), p. 72.

60. John Donne, *John Donne's Poetry*, ed. A. L. Clements (New York: Norton, 1966), p. 90.

61. George Puttenham, *The Arte of English Poesie*, ed. Gladys D. Willcock and Alice Walker (Cambridge: Cambridge University Press, 1936), pp. 225–26; John Lyly, *Euphues: The Anatomy of Wit, Euphues & His England*, ed. Morris W. Croll and Harry Clemens (London: Routledge, 1916), p. 39; Joseph Hall, "The Christian's Crucifixion with Christ," *The Works of the Right Reverend Joseph Hall, D. D.*, 10 vols. (Oxford: Oxford University Press, 1863), 5:380–93, p. 380; Thomas Playfere, *The Meane in Mourning, A Sermon preached at Saint Maryes Spittle in London on Tuesday in Easter weeke, 1595* (London, 1596), p. 21.

62. Ralph Venning, *Orthodox Paradoxes. Or, a Beleever Clearing Truth by Seeming Contradictions* (London, 1647). Venning's collection of 234 theological paradoxes went through five new editions in the five years after its first publication.

63. Herbert Palmer, *The Character of a Christian in Paradoxes and Seeming Contradictions* (London, 1656).

64. William O. Scott, "The Paradox of Timon's Self-Cursing," *Shakespeare Quarterly* 35 (1984): 290–304, p. 291.

65. Munday's translation is actually of Charles Estienne's 1583 *Paradoxes, ce sont propos Contre la Commune Opinion*, a translation of Lando's 1534 *Cicero Relegatus et Cicero Revocatus*. Donne wrote the *Paradoxes* in the 1590s while a student at Thavies and Lincoln's Inn. See John Donne, *Paradoxes and Problems*, ed. Helen Peters (Oxford: Clarendon Press, 1980), p. xv.

66. P. J. Finkelpearl, *John Marston of the Middle Temple* (Cambridge, Mass.: Harvard University Press, 1969), p. 228.

67. See, e.g., Sidney's sixth sonnet, in which he lampoons poets who speak "Of living deaths, dear wounds, fair storms, and freezing fires," *Sir Philip Sidney: Selected Poems*, ed. Katharine Duncan-Jones (Oxford: Clarendon Press, 1973), p. 119.

68. Grudin, *Mighty Opposites*, pp. 16–17. See also Colie, *Paradoxia*, p. 111.

69. Colie finds it "odd—or paradoxical—that paradoxes are so often designed to assert some fundamental and absolute truth" only because she is mistaken in assuming that the paradox relies on "the concept of relativity," that it is "an oblique criticism of absolute judgment," *Paradoxia*, p. 10.

70. See Giordano Bruno, *The Heroic Frenzies*, trans. Paul E. Memmo (Chapel Hill: University of North Carolina Press, 1965), pp. 121–22, 134–37, 226–27, and Memmo's introduction, pp. 39–43; Edgar Wind, *Pagan Mysteries in the Renaissance* (New York: Norton, 1968), p. 11; Davies, *Like Angels*, pp. 107–8; Colie, *Paradoxia*, pp. 25–29, 169; Grudin, *Mighty Opposites*, pp. 15, 25, 34–35; and Mitchell, *English Pulpit Oratory*, p. 141.

71. See, e.g., Hans Blumenberg, *The Legitimacy of the Modern Age*, trans. Robert M. Wallace (Cambridge, Mass.: MIT Press, 1983), p. 130: "Gnosticism's systematic intention forced the Church, in the interest of consolidation, to define itself in terms of dogma. . . . The formation of the Middle Ages can only be understood as an attempt at the definitive exclusion of the Gnostic syndrome." See also Adolf von Harnack, *Marcion: The Gospel of the Alien God*, trans. John E. Steely and Lyle D. Bierma (Durham: Labyrinth Press, 1990), esp. ch. 7.

72. See, e.g., Martin Luther, *Lectures on Genesis*, ed. Jaroslav Pelikan (1966), 8:134; *Psalms II*, ed. Jaroslav Pelikan (1956), 13:236–37, 413; and *Lectures on Romans*, ed. Hilton C. Oswald (1972), 25:376, in Luther's *Works*, 55 vols. (St. Louis: Concordia, 1952ff.).

73. Martin Luther, *Selected Psalms III*, *Works*, 14:31.

74. Steven Ozment, *The Age of Reform, 1250–1550* (New Haven, Conn.: Yale University Press, 1980), pp. 434–37.

75. William J. Bouwsma, paper read at the Folger Library Conference on Hooker, September 1993; Shuger, *Habits of Thought*, p. 10; Bouwsma, *John Calvin: A Sixteenth-Century Portrait* (Oxford: Oxford University Press, 1988), p. 34. See also Sampson Price, *London's Warning By Laodicea's Luke-warmnesse. Or A Sermon Preached at Paules-Crosse, the 10. of October, 1613* (London, 1613), p. 24.

76. Martin Luther and Desiderius Erasmus, *Luther and Erasmus: Free Will and Salvation*, ed. E. Gordon Rupp and Philip S. Watson, Library of Christian Classics, vol. 17 (Philadelphia: Westminster Press, 1969).

77. Calvin says of the doctrine of predestination, "Neither yet is there any otherwhere the upholding stay of sound affiance" (*Institutes* 3.32.1). "This predestination, if it be rightly thought upon, bringeth not a shaking of faith, but rather the best strengthening of it" (3.24.8; printer's error; should be 3.24.9). See also Luther's *Lectures on Galatians, Chapters 1–4*, *Works*, vol. 26.

78. Arthur Dent, *The plaine mans path-way to heaven; wherein every man may clearly see, whether he shall be saved or damned* (London: 1601), sig. A4. See also Dent's *The Opening of Heaven Gates, or The ready way to everlasting life* (London, 1611), pp. 86–87. Dent's emphasis on assurance of salvation is anything but unusual in the late Tudor and early Stuart periods. William Perkins, another enormously popular preacher, brings the matter of certainty of salvation to something like an exact science. See especially Perkins, *A Golden Chaine, or the description of theologie, containing the order of the causes of salvation and damnation according to Gods word* (London, 1591), in its eighth printing by 1612, especially p. 290; and *A Case of Conscience*, in its seventh printing by 1611, especially pp. 25–26. Cf. Shuger's qualification of Perkins's position, p. 7. See also Thomas Sparke, *A Short Treatise, very comfortable for all those Christians that be troubled and disquieted in their consciences* (London, 1580), sigs. Aii-Aiii; Field, *Godly Exhortation*, pp. 1, 18; and Jean Taffin, *Of the Markes of the Children of God, and of their comforts in afflictions*, trans. Anne Prowse (London, 1597).

79. Michael MacDonald and Terence R. Murphy, *Sleepless Souls: Suicide in Early Modern England* (Oxford: Clarendon Press, 1990), pp. 28–41; Emile Durkheim, *Suicide: A Study in Sociology*, trans. John A. Spaulding (New York: Free Press, 1966), pp. 152–70.

80. As Lewalski points out, *Protestant Poetics*, pp. 24–27, Protestant poets of the early seventeenth century express varying degrees of doubt about their election. Herbert, for example, seems to assume his election but has excruciating doubts about his spiritual progress. Donne doubts both his election and his progress. His second "Holy Sonnet," for example, ends with the lines, "Oh I shall soon despair, when I do see / That Thou lov'st mankind well, yet wilt not choose me, / And Satan hates me, yet is loath to lose me," *John Donne's Poetry*, p. 83. See also Robert Burton, *Anatomy of Melancholy* (Oxford, 1621), which is sympathetic to those who get increasingly tangled in doubts about their election. Certainly the intensity of

such doubts, whether about election or the process of sanctification, can be seen as both reflecting the pervasive Renaissance concern with paradox and adding to the pressure for its further explication.

81. This doctrine is a mainstay among the second generation of Calvinists. See, e.g., Theodore Beza, *An evident Display of Popish Practices, or Patched Pelagianisme*, trans. W. H. (London, 1578), Stubbes, p. 144, Perkins' *Golden Chain*, p. 278, and Chapter 2 below.

82. Desiderius Erasmus and Martin Luther, *Discourse on Free Will*, ed. Ernst F. Winter (New York: Ungar, 1961), p. 1.

83. Luther, *The Bondage of the Will, Works*, ed. Philip S. Watson, 33:59.

84. Eisenstein, *Printing Press*, pp. 701–4; A. G. Dickens, *The English Reformation* (New York: Schocken Books, 1964), pp. 131–35.

85. Gary Taylor points out that "the Church of England establishment was from the beginning, and remains, subject to criticism from the unreconciled partisans of the two factions it sought to incorporate and appease," "Forms of Opposition: Shakespeare and Middleton," *English Literary Renaissance* 24 (1994): 283–314, p. 288. According to Patrick Collinson, even the Puritan element in the church was composed of contrary impulses held uneasily together, p. 262.

86. Ong says, "probably no culture has been more riotously polemic in its verbal production than Europe in the two centuries after Gutenberg," p. 238. Cf. Eisenstein, *Printing Press*, pp. 303–78.

87. The seminal work here is Greenblatt's *Renaissance Self-Fashioning from More to Shakespeare* (Chicago: University of Chicago Press, 1980).

88. William Symonds, *A Sermon Preached at White-chappel, in the presence of many, honourable and worshipfull, the adventurers and planters for Virginia* (London, 1609), pp. 12–13.

89. Jean E. Howard, "The New Historicism in Renaissance Studies," *ELR* 16 (1986): 13–43, p. 16; Dollimore, *Radical Tragedy*, pp. 153ff.; Couliano, *Eros and Magic*, pp. xix–xx.

Chapter 2

1. James Pilkington, *The Works of James Pilkington, D. D.*, ed. James Scholefield (Cambridge: Parker Society, 1842), pp. 647–48.

2. James Pilkington, *A Confutation* (London, 1563).

3. Heinemann, *Puritanism and Theatre*, p. 20, and Brian Morris, *English Drama to 1710*, vol. 3 in *The Sphere History of Literature in the English Language*, ed. Christopher Ricks (London: Sphere, 1971), pp. 65–66. While Morris erroneously sees Puritans as united in their opposition to the stage, he is quite right about the ground of Puritan objections: the theater seemed too similar to religious ritual.

4. Victor Turner develops the concept of the "cultural performance" in *The Anthropology of Performance*.

5. Steven Mullaney, *The Place of the Stage: License, Play, and Power in Renaissance England* (Chicago: University of Chicago Press, 1988), and Louis A. Mon-

trose, "The Purpose of Playing: Reflections on a Shakespearean Anthropology" *Helios* 7 (1980): 51–74, p. 64. Timothy J. Reiss argues that dramatic tragedy in particular arises at moments of "seemingly abrupt epistemic change," *Tragedy and Truth: Studies in the Development of a Renaissance and Neoclassical Discourse* (New Haven: Yale University Press, 1980), p. 2. See also Robert S. Knapp, *Shakespeare— The Theater and the Book*, p. 3. As Davies says of the late sixteenth century, "this was a period of great turbulence and transition in England: from Catholicism to Protestantism; from an international to a national Church; from the Petrine pope to the paper pope of the Bible; from a geocentric to a heliocentric universe, in which the heavens had grown very far off; from a position where religion had once been a widely accepted tradition, and was now a matter of acute controversy," *Like Angels from a Cloud*, p. 123.

6. Keith Thomas, *Religion and the Decline of Magic* (New York: Scribner, 1971), p. 76.

7. Michael O'Connell, "The Idolatrous Eye: Iconoclasm, Anti-Theatricalism, and the Image of the Elizabethan Theater," *ELH* 52 (1985): 279–310, p. 307.

8. Huston Diehl makes a similar point, drawing somewhat different conclusions, in "Observing the Lord's Supper and the Lord Chamberlain's Men: The Visual Rhetoric of Ritual and Play in Early Modern England," *Renaissance Drama* 22 (1991): 147–74.

9. Clifford Geertz, *Interpretation of Cultures: Selected Essays* (New York: Basic Books, 1973), p. 143, and "Art as a Cultural System," *MLN* 91 (1976): 1473–99.

10. Turner, *Dramas, Fields, and Metaphors*, pp. 46–47. In *The Ritual Process* (Chicago: Aldine Publishing Company, 1969), Turner defines communitas as "an unstructured and relatively undifferentiated *comitatus*, community, or even communion of equal individuals," p. 96.

11. Homi K. Bhabha, "The Commitment to Theory," *New Formations* 5 (1988): 5–23.

12. See David Bevington's observations on Turner and the liminality of drama in *Action Is Eloquence: Shakespeare's Language of Gesture* (Cambridge, Mass.: Harvard University Press, 1984), pp. 3–5, 50.

13. *Dramas, Fields, and Metaphors*, pp. 88–89. See also Turner's treatment of ritual and paradox in *Revelation and Divination in Ndembu Ritual* (Ithaca, N.Y.: Cornell University Press, 1975), pp. 182–85.

14. Turner, *The Anthropology of Performance*, esp. pp. 33, 104.

15. Norman Rabkin, "Either/Or: Responding to *Henry V*," in his *Shakespeare and the Problem of Meaning* (Chicago: University of Chicago Press, 1981), pp. 33–34. The essay is an expanded version of "Rabbits, Ducks, and *Henry V*," *Shakespeare Quarterly* 28 (1977): 279–96.

16. Marjorie O'Rourke Boyle, *Rhetoric and Reform: Erasmus' Civil Dispute with Luther* (Cambridge, Mass.: Harvard University Press, 1983), pp. 6, 35.

17. Quoted in Boyle, p. 160.

18. For a full account of the process, see Hans Blumenberg, *The Legitimacy of the Modern Age*, trans. Robert M. Wallace (Cambridge, Mass.: MIT Press, 1983), esp. pp. 130ff.

19. *Sermons*, 4:192.

20. Gosson, *The Trumpet of Warre*, sig. F1ʳ.

21. Sampson Price, *London's Warning By Laodicea's Luke-warmnesse*, p. 31. For an account of "holy violence," see John R. Knott, *The Sword of the Spirit: Puritan Responses to the Bible* (Chicago: University of Chicago Press, 1980), p. 44.

22. John Foxe, quoted in E. K. Chambers, *The Elizabethan Stage*, 4 vols. (Oxford: Clarendon Press, 1923), 1:242n.

23. For treatments of self-definition in reaction to a demonized "other," see Stephen Greenblatt's *Renaissance Self-Fashioning from More to Shakespeare* (Chicago: University of Chicago Press, 1980), p. 9; and Martha Tuck Rozett, *The Doctrine of Election and the Emergence of Elizabethan Tragedy* (Princeton, N.J.: Princeton University Press, 1984), pp. 70–73 et passim. Although accusations of atheism were frequent in Elizabethan England, Greenblatt claims that actual atheism was extremely rare. See his *Shakespearean Negotiations* (Berkeley: University of California Press, 1988), pp. 21–23.

24. See Alan F. Herr, *The Elizabethan Sermon: A Survey and Bibliography* (Philadelphia: University of Pennsylvania Press, 1940), pp. 11–24.

25. *The Reformation of the Ecclesiastical Laws of England, 1552*, ed. and trans. James C. Spalding. Vol. XIX, Sixteenth Century Essays and Studies (Kirksville, Mo.: Sixteenth Century Journal, 1992), p. 90. See also Millar MacLure, *The Paul's Cross Sermons* (University of Toronto Press, 1958), pp. 3–17, and Rozett, pp. 41–42.

26. Francis Marbury, *A Sermon Preached at Paules Crosse the 13. of June, 1602* (London, 1602), sig. E3ʳ.

27. Millar MacLure, *Register of Sermons Preached at Paul's Cross, 1534–1642*, rev. Peter Pauls and Jackson Campbell Boswell (Ottawa: Dovehouse Editions, 1989), pp. 19, 21, 26–27, 30, 31, 36, 43, 52.

28. In a 1554 sermon, for example, Nicholas Harpsfield used the "rod of correction" to beat five penitents. See Rozett, p. 41; MacLure, Pauls, and Boswell, *Register*, p. 37. Ordinarily it was the penitent who held the rod of correction. See MacLure, *The Paul's Cross Sermons*, p. 16, and A. F. Scott Pearson, *Thomas Cartwright and Elizabethan Puritanism* (Cambridge: Cambridge University Press, 1925), p. 154.

29. See Rozett's account of this process, pp. 41–42.

30. A fray erupted, for example, at the April 11, 1540 Paul's Cross sermon.

31. MacLure, Pauls, and Boswell, *Register*, pp. 34–35.

32. Quoted in MacLure, Pauls, and Boswell, *Register*, p. 50.

33. Edwin Sandys, *The Sermons of Edwin Sandys, D.D.* (Cambridge: Parker Society, 1841), p. 333.

34. William Laud, *The Works of the Most Reverend Father in God, William Laud, D. D. . . . ,* 9 vols. (Oxford: Parker, 1847–1860), 7:47.

35. Cf. the description of the Son of Man in Revelation 1:16: "And he had in his right hand seven stars: and out of his mouth went a sharp two-edged sword: and his face shone as the Sun shineth in his strength" (Geneva Bible).

36. George Gifford, *A Briefe Discourse*, p. 56ᵛ.

37. *Works*, 25:376.

38. Henry Smith, *The Art of Hearing, Works*, 1:328.

39. Richard Bancroft, *A sermon preached at Paules Crosse*, pp. 38–39.

40. George Abbot, *Exposition upon the Prophet Jonah*, 2 vols. (London, 1600), 2:44–45. The same *topos* appears in Shakespeare's *Measure for Measure* during Angelo's self-scrutiny: "it is I / That, lying by the violet in the sun, / Do as the carrion does, not as the flow'r, / Corrupt with virtuous season" (2.2.165–68).

41. William Perkins, *The Art of Prophecying*, p. 730^v.

42. John Taylor, prefatory verses to Thomas Heywood, *An Apology for Actors* (London, 1612; rpr. New York: Scholars' Facsimiles, 1941), sig. A3^v. See also Robert S. Knapp, *Shakespeare—The Theater and the Book*, p. 27.

43. Heywood, sigs. G1^v–2^v. See also Christy Desmet's analysis in *Reading Shakespeare's Characters: Rhetoric, Ethics, and Identity* (Amherst: University of Massachusetts Press, 1992), p. 21.

44. I. G., *A Refutation of the Apologie for Actors* (London, 1615; rpr. New York: Scholars' Facsimiles, 1941), pp. 43–44.

45. See Knapp, pp. 32–33.

46. *Articles . . . for the stablyshing of consent touchyng true religion* (London, 1564), unpaginated. The biblical basis for the idea of God's taking pleasure in the fruits of sanctification is 1 Thess. 4:1–4. The fruits of sanctification are described in Galatians 5:22–23 as "love, joy, peace, longsuffering, gentleness, goodness, faith, meekness, temperancy" (Geneva Bible).

47. Jean Taffin, *Of the Markes of the Children of God.*

48. Arthur Dent, *The Plaine Mans Path-way to Heaven*, p. 31.

49. See *Institutes*, 3.24.4.

50. Richard Helgerson, *Forms of Nationhood: The Elizabethan Writing of England* (Chicago: University of Chicago Press, 1992), p. 266; Benedict Anderson, *Imagined Communities: Reflections on the Origins and Spread of Nationalism* (London: Verso, 1983).

51. John Knewstub, *A Confutation of monstrous and horrible heresies, taught by H. N. and embraced of a number, who call themselves the Familie of Love* (London, 1579), p. 3^v.

52. John Denison, *The Heavenly Banquet* (London, 1619), p. 2. See also Smith, *The Art of Hearing*, *Works*, 1:328.

53. Richard Rogers, *Seven Treatises containing such directions as is gathered out of Holie Scriptures* (London, 1605), p. 57.

54. Peter Lake, *Anglicans and Puritans?* (London: Unwin Hyman, 1988), pp. 227ff.

55. Theodore Beza, *An evident Display of Popish Practises, or Patched Pelagianisme* (London, 1578), p. 8.

56. See Steven Ozment, *The Age of Reform, 1250–1550* (New Haven, Conn.: Yale University Press, 1980), pp. 437–38.

57. A comment in Luther's *Lectures on the Psalms* is also instructive: "[The Psalmist] wants to teach us that none are to be condemned and made to despair of Christ's salvation. Nor ought anyone regard himself as the only one saved and judge others," *Works*, 10:457.

58. 1 Timothy 2:1–4 reads, "I exhort therefore, that first of all supplications,

prayers, intercessions, and giving of thanks be made for all men. . . . For this is good and acceptable in the sight of God our Savior, Who will that all men shall be saved, and come unto the acknowledging of the truth" (Geneva Bible).

59. John Dove, *A Sermon Preached at Paules Crosse, the Sixt of February* (London, 1597).

60. See Champlin Burrage, *The Early English Dissenters*, 2 vols. (Cambridge: Cambridge University Press, 1912), 2:9, 140.

61. William Holbrooke, *Loves Complaint, for Want of Entertainment* (London, 1609).

62. Thomas Adams, *The Gallant's Burden*, in *The Workes of Tho: Adams* (London, 1629), pp. 1–31, p. 13.

63. Thomas Hobbes, *Leviathan*, ed. C. B. Macpherson (New York: Penguin, 1985), p. 179.

Chapter 3

1. Jasper Mayne, prefatory encomiastic poem to William Cartwright, *Comedies, Tragi-Comedies, with other Poems* (London, 1651). An earlier version of this chapter appeared as Bryan Crockett, "'Holy Cozenage' and the Renaissance Cult of the Ear," *Sixteenth Century Journal* 24 (1993): 47–65.

2. Playfere, *The Meane in Mourning*. Looking out at the weeping audience, Playfere says, "you shall never repent you of this repentance: you shall never be sorry for this sorrow," p. 117.

3. In the sermon's dedicatory epistle (to Lady Elizabeth Carey) Playfere says of the pirated editions, "I had rather have had my head broken than to have my sermon so mangled" (sig. A2^r).

4. See Knott, *The Sword of the Spirit*, p. 42.

5. See Joan Webber, "Celebration of Word and World in Lancelot Andrewes' Style," in *Seventeenth-Century Prose*, ed. Stanley E. Fish (Oxford: Oxford University Press, 1971), pp. 336–52, p. 337.

6. John Stockwood, *A Sermon preached at Paules Crosse on Barthelmew day, being the 24. of August, 1578* (London, 1578), p. 4. For theories of the opposition between "plain" and "metaphysical" styles, see Fish, *Self-Consuming Artifacts* (Berkeley: University of California Press, 1972), pp. 374–82; Robert M. Adolph, *The Rise of Modern Prose Style* (Cambridge, Mass.: MIT Press, 1968); and Harold Fisch, "The Puritans and the Reform of Prose Style," *ELH* 19 (1952): 229–48.

7. Abbot, *An Exposition upon the Prophet Jonah*, 2:331.

8. Hooker, *Of the Lawes of Ecclesiastical Polity, Folger Library Edition*, 5.35.2.

9. Hyperius, *The Practise of preaching*, pp. 12^r, 177^{r-v}, 37^v.

10. Mayne, prefatory poem to Cartwright, *Comedies*.

11. Mitchell, *English Pulpit Oratory*, p. 194.

12. Lancelot Andrewes, *Lancelot Andrewes and His Private Devotions: A Biography, a Transcript, and an Interpretation*, ed. Alexander Whyte, 2nd ed. (London: Oliphant Anderson and Ferrier, 1896), pp. 16, 19.

13. Samuel Hieron, *The Preachers Plea*, pp. 195–96.

14. George Gifford, *A Sermon on the Parable of the Sower* (London, 1582), sig. B2^r.

15. Gosson, *The Trumpet of Warre*, sig. E6^r.

16. See Jonas Barish, *The Antitheatrical Prejudice* (Berkeley: University of California Press, 1981).

17. Mayne, prefatory poem to Cartwright, *Comedies*.

18. Cf. the anonymous author of *A Second and Third Blast of Retrait from Plaies and Theaters* (London, 1590), who distrusts all sensory perception but who considers idolatry primarily a matter of sight: "There cometh much evil in at the ears, but more at the eyes; by these two open windows death breaketh into the soul" (pp. 95–96). See Michael O'Connell, "The Idolatrous Eye," p. 282. Cf. Gosson, section V in the present chapter.

19. Ralph Brownrig, fifth Transfiguration sermon, *Sixty Five Sermons by the Right Reverend Father in God, Ralph Brownrig, Late Bishop of Exceter* (London, 1674), p. 83.

20. Henry Smith, *Seven Godly and Learned Sermons upon Seven divers Textes of Scripture* (London, 1591), p. 174.

21. William Rankins, *A mirrour of monsters: Wherein is plainely described the manifold vices, & spotted enormities, that are caused by the infectious sight of playes, with the description of the subtile sights of Sathan, making them his instruments . . .* (London, 1587).

22. *Sermons*, 6:10.459–68. Cf. Donne's statement, "The organ that God hath given the natural man is the eye; he sees God in the creature. The organ that God hath given the Christian is the ear; he hears God in his Word" (2:3:114).

23. Huston Diehl, "Oberving the Lord's Supper and the Lord Chamberlain's Men," p. 158.

24. Thomas Becon, *The Displaying of the Popish Masse*, pp. 178–79.

25. Becon, pp. 182–83. For accounts of the widespread currency of the belief in the efficacy of viewing the Host, see Margaret R. Miles, *Image as Insight: Visual Understanding in Western Christianity and Secular Culture* (Boston: Beacon Press, 1985), p. 97, and Horton Davies, *The Worship of the English Puritans*, pp. 139–40.

26. John Calvin, *The Psalmes of David and Others, with J. Calvins Commentaries*, trans. Arthur Golding (London, 1571), p. 24^r.

27. See Peter Lake, *Anglicans and Puritans?* p. 227.

28. Henry Hammond, *A View of the New Directorie, and a Vindication of the Ancient Liturgie of the Church of England*, 3rd ed. (Oxford: 1646), p. 69.

29. For an account of the metaphysical preachers' characteristic rhetorical techniques see Davies, *Like Angels*, pp. 45–88.

30. Quoted in Davies, *Like Angels*, p. 5.

31. The first four books were published in 1594 and the fifth in 1597—all to meager sales. The sixth, seventh, and eighth books were were not published until 1648, 1662, and 1651 respectively. See H. C. Porter, ed., *Puritanism in Tudor England* (Columbia: University of South Carolina Press, 1971), p. 244.

32. Even the sermons of John Donne contain their share of anti-Roman invectives, despite evidence in Donne's private correspondence that he favored a less

divisive theological rhetoric. In a letter to a friend, Donne writes, "You know, I never fettered nor imprisoned the word 'religion,' not . . . immuring it in a Rome, or a Wittenberg, or a Geneva; they are all virtual beams of one sun. . . . They are not so contrary as the North and South poles," quoted in Owen Chadwick, *The Reformation* (New York: Penguin, rev. 1972), p. 371. Jasper Mayne's plea for tolerance has a similar sound, but it came a bit late—in a sermon in August 1646, near the end of the Civil War: "They of the more free and open carriage and behaviour, who call a severe regularity and strictness of life 'preciseness' and 'an abridgement of Christian liberty,' have called those of a more reserved and locked up and demure conversation 'Puritans' and 'Round-heads,' and I know not what other names of contumely and reproach. And they of the more strict behaviour have equally as faultly called those of a freer and less composed conversation 'Libertines' and 'Papists': the usual words of infamy made to signify a Cavalier. These two words, my brethren, have almost destroyed a flourishing kingdom between them," *A Sermon Concerning Unity and Agreement Preached in Carfax Church in Oxford, August 9, 1646* (London, 1646), p. 29.

33. Richard Bancroft, *A Sermon preached at Paules Crosse*, p. 105.

34. Jeremiah Burroughs, *Irenicum to the Lovers of Truth and Peace* (London, 1646), quoted in J. Sears McGee, *The Godly Man in Stuart England: Anglicans, Puritans, and the Two Tables, 1620–1670* (New Haven, Conn.: Yale University Press, 1976), p. 1.

35. See Lake, pp. 163, 172.

36. See Davies, p. 191.

37. Turner, *Dramas, Fields, and Metaphors*, p. 64.

38. See Chapters 5 and 7 below for treatments of a few of Shakespeare's plays in which this sort of rhetoric operates.

39. See Earl Miner, *The Metaphysical Mode from Donne to Cowley* (Princeton, N.J.: Princeton University Press, 1969), p. 47.

40. George Puttenham, *The Arte of English Poesie*, ed. Baxter Hathaway (Kent, Ohio: Kent State University Press, 1970), p. 233.

41. This is not to deny that some paradoxical conceits are more stylistic than doctrinal, as when Andrewes plays on the meaning of *"crucifige,"* "fasten": "but that fastening was but his loosing; of it lost him and cost him his life," or when Playfere comments on the woman's washing Christ's feet with her tears: "A strange sight. I have oftentimes seen the heaven wash the earth. But I never before saw the earth wash the heaven: yet here I see it. An earthly and sinful woman washeth the heavenly feet of Christ." See Lancelot Andrewes, *XCVI Sermons* (London, 1629), p. 59, and Playfere, p. 12.

42. Stephen Greenblatt, *Marvelous Possessions*, pp. 148–51.

43. Playfere, p. 49. A fairly common *topos*, but a source, perhaps, for *Hamlet* 4.3.19–25?

44. John Cosin, *The Works of the Right Reverend Father in God, John Cosin, Lord Bishop of Durham*, 5 vols. (Oxford: Parker, 1843), 1:18.

45. Joseph Hall, "The Christian's Crucifixion with Christ," *Works*, 5:380.

46. Not all metaphysical preachers favor text-crumbling. George Herbert, "metaphysical" in his poetry and perhaps in his preaching (none of his sermons

survive), is far from alone in his condemnation of the practice: "Crumbling a text into small parts, as the person speaking or spoken to, the subject and object, and the like, hath neither in it sweetness, nor gravity, nor variety, since the words apart are not Scripture, but a dictionary," *A Priest in the Temple* (London, 1652), in *The Works of George Herbert*, ed. F. E. Hutchinson, 4th ed. (Oxford: Clarendon Press, 1959), pp. 234–35.

47. Davies, *Like Angels*, p. 107. Cf. Winifried Schleiner, *The Imagery of John Donne's Sermons* (Providence, R.I.: Brown University Press, 1970), p. 183: Donne "draws his analogies from the natural world less in order to explain the divine than to infer by his carefully worked out paradoxes the supernatural quality of the event."

48. Daniel Featley, *Ancilla Pietatis, or the Handmaid to Private Devotion* (London, 1626), pp. 208–9.

49. Thomas Adams, *The Lost are Found*, in *Workes of Tho: Adams*, pp. 877–87, p. 879.

50. See Fish, *Self-Consuming Artifacts*.

51. Thomas Goffe, *Deliverance from the Grave. A Sermon Preached at Saint Maries Spittle in London on Wednesday in Easter Weeke last, March 28, 1627* (London, 1627), p. 33.

52. Andrewes, *XCVI Sermons*, p. 395.

53. Andrewes, *A sermon preached before the king in Whitehall, Christmas Day, 1612*, ibid., p. 59.

54. William Cartwright, *An Off-Spring of Mercy, Issuing out of the Womb of Cruelty. Or, a Passion Sermon Preached at Christs Church in Oxford* (London, 1652), p. 30.

55. Thomas Jackson, *Diverse Sermons, with a short Treatise befitting these present times* (Oxford, 1637), p. 14.

56. William Fisher, *A Godly Sermon preached at Paules Crosse the 31. day of October 1591* (London, 1592), unpaginated.

57. Brownrig, The second sermon for Christmas Day, *Sixty Five Sermons*, p. 94.

58. Stephen Gosson, *The Schoole of Abuse*, ed. Edward Arber, in *English Reprints*, vol. 1 (London: Bloomsburg, 1869, rpt. New York: AMS Press, 1966), p. 32.

59. Ben Jonson, *The Staple of News*, vol. 6, *Ben Jonson*, 11 vols., ed. C. H. Herford, Percy Simpson, and Evelyn Simpson (Oxford: Clarendon Press, 1925–52), Prologue for the Stage, 1–6.

Chapter 4

1. Ben Jonson, *Discoveries*, p. 801. All quotations from Jonson's works are from *Ben Jonson*, ed. C. H. Herford, Percy Simpson, and Evelyn Simpson, 11 vols. (Oxford: Clarendon Press, 1925–52). Spelling modernized.

2. William Perkins, "To All Ignorant People that Desire to be Instructed," quoted in *Puritanism in Tudor England*, ed. H. C. Porter (Columbia: University of South Carolina Press, 1971), p. 279.

3. John Chamberlain, *The Letters of John Chamberlain*, 2 vols., ed. N. E. McClure (Philadelphia: American Philosophical Society, 1939), 1:334.

4. Millar MacLure, *The Paul's Cross Sermons*, p. 233.

5. I can locate no historical source for the claim.

6. Quoted in Thomas Middleton and Thomas Dekker, *The Roaring Girl*, New Mermaids, ed. Andor Gomme (New York: Norton, 1976), Gomme's introduction, p. xiii. All citations of *The Roaring Girl* are from Gomme's edition.

7. Address to the Reader, 20–21; cf. Prologue, 16–26.

8. On Moll Cutpurse's lack of disguise, see Mary Beth Rose, "Women in Men's Clothing: Apparel and Social Stability in *The Roaring Girl*," *ELR* 14 (1984): 367–91, p. 389; Jean E. Howard, "Crossdressing, the Theatre, and Gender Struggle in Early Modern England," *Shakespeare Quarterly* 39 (1988): 418–40, p. 436; Marjorie Garber, "The Logic of the Transvestite: The Roaring Girl," in *Staging the Renaissance: Reinterpretations of Elizabethan and Jacobean Drama*, ed. David Scott Kastan and Peter Stallybrass (New York: Routledge, 1991), pp. 221–34, p. 232.

9. It should be noted that three of these scholars acknowledge the play's tendency to contain its potentially subversive impulses. See Rose, pp. 385–86; Linda Woodbridge, *Women and the English Renaissance: Literature and the Nature of Humankind* (Urbana: University of Illinois Press, 1984), p. 145; Jonathan Dollimore, "Subjectivity, Sexuality, and Transgression: The Jacobean Connection," *Renaissance Drama* 17 (1986): 53–81, pp. 65–72. Howard sees *The Roaring Girl* as an exception to the general rule of containment.

10. I use the term "Puritan" in full awareness of Christopher Hill's warning that the word provides "an admirable refuge from clarity of thought" and Patrick Collinson's statement that it is impossible "to distinguish absolutely between Puritanism and, so to speak, mere Protestantism." See Hill's *Society and Puritanism in Pre-Revolutionary England* (New York: Schocken Books, 1964), p. 13; and Collinson's "Towards a Broader Understanding of the Early Dissenting Tradition," in *The Dissenting Tradition*, ed. C. Robert Cole and Michael E. Moody, (Athens: Ohio University Press, 1975)," pp. 3–38, p. 11. Collinson's demotion of the "P" in "Puritan" to lower case hardly solves the problem; nor does his substitution of the term "the godly." As the word "Puritan" was in widespread use in early seventeenth-century England, I adopt it here for lack of a better term to denote the large body of believers who insisted on further reformation of the church. It should be noted, though, that Puritanism encompasses a great variety of theological perspectives. Certainly Puritans were not unanimously opposed to the theater. See David Norbrook, "The Reformation of the Court Masque" in *The Court Masque*, ed. David Lindley (Manchester: Manchester University Press, 1984), pp. 94–111, and Margot Heinemann, *Puritanism and Theatre*.

11. MacLure, *The Paul's Cross Sermons*, p. 30.

12. Quoted in MacLure, p. 30.

13. Edward Lord Herbert of Cherbury, "The History of Henry VIII," in *A Complete History of England*, ed. White Kennett, 3 vols. (London, 1706), 2:213.

14. Ibid. Cf. MacLure, p. 31.

15. Huston Diehl, "Observing the Lord's Supper and the Lord Chamberlain's Men."

16. John Howson, *A Second Sermon, preached at Paules Crosse, the 21. of May, 1598* (London, 1598), p. 44.

17. George Gifford, *A Briefe discourse, . . . which may bee termed the Countrie Divinitie*, p. 54ʳ.

18. Patrick Collinson, *The Elizabethan Puritan Movement* (Berkeley: University of California Press, 1967), p. 348.

19. The *Admonition*, drafted by John Field and Thomas Wilcox in 1572, demanded immediate and sweeping reformation of the Church of England along presbyterian lines. Whitgift, soon to be Bishop of London and then Archbishop of Canterbury, attacked the dissenters, while Cartwright defended the presbyterian position.

20. Peter Lake, *Anglicans and Puritans?*, pp. 28–30, 37.

21. Quoted in Lake, p. 38.

22. Stephen Gosson, *Playes Confuted in Five Actions*, sig. C6, in *Markets of Bawdrie: The Dramatic Criticism of Stephen Gosson* ed. Arthur F. Kinney (Salzburg: Institut fur Englische Sprache, 1974), p. 161.

23. Alfred Harbage, *Shakespeare and the Rival Traditions* (New York: Macmillan, 1952), p. 71.

24. See, e.g., Richard N. Watson, *Ben Jonson's Parodic Strategy* (Cambridge, Mass.: Harvard University Press, 1987), p. 49; Anne Barton, *Ben Jonson, Dramatist* (Cambridge: Cambridge University Press, 1984), p. 113; "Shakespeare's Comedies" in *The Complete Signet Classic Shakespeare*, gen. ed. Sylvan Barnet (New York: Harcourt, 1972), p. 33; and Ray L. Heffner, Jr., "Unifying Symbols in the Comedy of Ben Jonson," in *Ben Jonson: A Collection of Critical Essays*, ed. Jonas A. Barish (Englewood Cliffs, N.J.: Prentice-Hall, 1963), pp. 133–146, p. 146.

25. Robert Milles, *Abrahams Suite for Sodome. A Sermon Preached at Pauls Crosse the 25. of August. 1611.* (London, 1612), sig. D6ʳ.

26. The derogatory reference to Jonson has been noted by MacLure, *The Paul's Cross Sermons*, pp. 139–140, and David Riggs, *Ben Jonson: A Life* (Cambridge, Mass.: Harvard University Press, 1989), p. 195. See also Bryan Crockett, "Cicero, Ben Jonson, and the Puritans," *Classical and Modern Literature* 15 (1995): 000–00.

27. Cicero, *In Catilinam* 1.1.2, *Cicero in Twenty-Eight Volumes*, vol. 10, ed. C. MacDonald (Cambridge, Mass.: Harvard University Press, 1977).

28. H. C. Porter, *Reformation and Reaction in Tudor Cambridge* (Cambridge: Cambridge University Press, 1958), p. 140.

29. Quoted in Collinson, p. 393.

30. See Stephen Greenblatt's discussion of the demonized "other" in *Renaissance Self-Fashioning from More to Shakespeare*, pp. 8ff.

31. This is not to say that all of Middleton's or Beaumont's or Jonson's plays always display an exclusivist rhetoric. One might point to Jonson's later plays, his "dotages," as exceptions. But if *The New Inn* and *The Sad Shepherd* tend toward a more inclusive rhetoric, it is also true that these plays have been viewed traditionally as less effective dramatically than the earlier comedies. See Watson, p. 13.

32. Thomas Middleton, *A Chaste Maid in Cheapside*, ed. Alan Brissenden, New Mermaids (London: Ernest Benn, 1968), 1.1.89–90.

33. Francis Beaumont, *The Knight of the Burning Pestle*, ed. Sheldon P. Zitner (Manchester: Manchester University Press, 1984), 4.92–94.

34. As Calvin puts the matter, "no goodness could ever be wrought out of our heart unless it be made throughly new" (*Institutes*, 2.3.6).

35. Alan C. Dessen, *Jonson's Moral Comedy* (Evanston, Ill.: Northwestern University Press, 1971), p. 250.

36. Jonathan Swift, Preface to *The Battle of the Books*, in *A Tale of a Tub, to which is added The Battle of the Books . . .* , ed. A. C. Guthkelch and D. N. Smith, 2nd ed. (Oxford: Clarendon Press, 1958), p. 215.

37. See Heinemann, *Puritanism and Theatre*, p. 97.

38. Katharine Eisaman Maus, "Satiric and Ideal Economies in the Jonsonian Imagination," *ELR* 19 (1989): 42–64.

39. Thomas Middleton, *Michaelmas Term*, ed. Richard Levin, Regents Renaissance Drama (Lincoln: University of Nebraska Press, 1966), 5.3.90–91.

40. Watson points out that *Bartholomew Fair* has traditionally been viewed as more "generous" than Jonson's earlier comedies, and then concludes, "For all its generosity, *Bartholomew Fair* continues the practice of Jonson's earlier comedies, deploying the parodic strategy against the indulgences of romantic melodrama" (p. 170).

41. Jonas Barish, *The Antitheatrical Prejudice*, pp. 132–33. See also Michael O'Connell, "The Idolatrous Eye"; and Una Ellis-Fermor, *The Jacobean Drama: An Interpretation*, 2nd ed. (London: Methuen, 1947), pp. 99–100.

42. Richard Helgerson, *Self-Crowned Laureates: Spenser, Jonson, Milton, and the Literary System* (Berkeley: University of California Press, 1983), pp. 101ff.

43. Margo Todd, *Christian Humanism and the Puritan Social Order* (Cambridge: Cambridge University Press, 1987).

44. Walter Ong, *The Presence of the Word: Some Prolegomena for Cultural and Religious History* (New Haven, Conn.: Yale University Press, 1967), p. 269. See also Barish, pp. 138–40, and O'Connell, pp. 298–99.

45. See Barish, pp. 135, 167.

Chapter 5

1. Porter, ed., *Puritanism in Tudor England*, p. 7. Porter also mentions James I's remark that a Puritan is a protestant strayed out of his wits, and one more generalization that I can't resist repeating here: H. L. Mencken's that Puritanism is the haunting fear that someone, somewhere, may be happy.

2. John Field, *A Godly Exhortation*, (London, 1583).

3. I use the word "comedy" in the broad sense of a play that ends in a happy resolution of the conflict—a characteristic shared by Shakespeare's romances and his "dark" as well as "festive" comedies.

4. See the treatments in Chapter 3 above of sermons by Thomas Playfere, George Abbot, Ralph Brownrig, John Donne, Jasper Mayne, Lancelot Andrewes, Joseph Hall, William Fisher, John Cosin, Henry Smith, Daniel Featley, Thomas Adams, and Thomas Jackson. Other Reformation preachers who frequently explore paradoxes include William Fisher, Thomas White, James Blisse, Mark Frank,

Robert Wakeman, Nathaniel Cannon, Thomas Walkington, John Hacket, and Arthur Lake.

5. Sampson Price, *London's Warning By Laodicea's Luke-warmnesse*, p. 51.

6. Examples could easily be multiplied; the word *mishpat* appears in the Hebrew Bible more than 250 times, and *krisis* appears in the New Testament more than fifty times.

7. The marginal gloss in the 1560 Geneva Bible makes it plain that David cannot be referring to his relationship with God; "my righteousness" is glossed "As touching my behavior toward Saul and mine enemies."

8. A rare exception is Psalms 143:2: "And enter not into judgment with thy servant: for in thy sight shall none that liveth be justified." See also Psalms 51:5. Of course, Calvinist theologians would see such passages as well as Genesis 3:21, 4:7, and Leviticus 7:5, to list only a few, as implying original sin.

9. See Steven Ozment's account of Luther's paradoxical sensibility, *The Age of Reform*, pp. 437–38.

10. Often such reformers see the immediate establishment of the presbyterian system as the definitive act of obedience to God's will. See Peter Lake, *Anglicans and Puritans?*, p. 77.

11. Sig. B1^r. The unsettling imagery is derived from the third Psalm.

12. G. Wilson Knight, "*Measure for Measure* and the Gospels," in *Shakespeare: Measure for Measure*, Casebook Series (London: Macmillan, 1971). Cf. the treatments in Jonathan Dollimore, "Transgression and Surveillance in *Measure for Measure*," in Jonathan Dollimore and Alan Sinfield, *Political Shakespeare: New Essays in Cultural Materialism* (Ithaca, N.Y.: Cornell University Press, 1985), pp. 72–87; Robert S. Knapp, *Shakespeare—The Theater and the Book*, p. 218; and Christy Desmet, *Reading Shakespeare's Characters*, pp. 152–54.

13. Prospero's speech contains echoes of a prayer by Ovid's Medea (*Met.* 7.192ff.), but Prospero also departs from Medea in some significant ways. For example, Medea's speech contains no mention of lightning, and Prospero does not merely provide an exit for ghosts (*manesque exire sepulcris, Met.* 7.206) but actually awakens the dead, bodies and all. The whole passage has biblical overtones. See Rev. 6:12: "And I beheld when [the Lamb] had opened the sixth seal, and, lo, there was a great earthquake, and the sun was as black as sackcloth of hair, and the moon was like blood." Cf. Rev. 4:5: "And out of the throne proceeded lightnings, and thunderings, and voices," and John 5:28–29: "Marvel not at this: for the hour shall come, in the which all that are in the graves, shall hear his voice. And they shall come forth, that have done good unto the resurrection of life: but they that have done evil, unto the resurrection of condemnation."

14. For treatments of Prospero's acceptance of his limitations see Ralph Berry, "The Tempest," in Berry, *The Shakespearean Metaphor* (Totowa, N.J.: Rowman and Littlefield, 1978), pp. 101–17, esp. p. 111; and Robert Grudin, "Prospero's Magic and the Structure of *The Tempest*," *South Atlantic Quarterly* 71 (1972): 401–09.

15. Good treatments of *The Winter's Tale* in light of the demands of tragicomedy are Theresa M. Krier, "The Triumph of Time: Paradox in *The Winter's Tale*," *Centennial Review* 26 (1982): 341–53, esp. pp. 341–43, and C. D. Hardman,

"Theory, Form, and Meaning in Shakespeare's *The Winter's Tale*," *Review of English Studies* 36 (1985): 228–35, esp. p. 231.

16. An interesting rhetorical analysis of the whole play is John Taylor, "The Patience of *The Winter's Tale*," *Essays in Criticism* 23 (1973): 333–56. William H. Matchett provides thoughtful analyses of Leontes's jealousy, Antigonus's death, and the statue scene in "Some Dramatic Techniques in *The Winter's Tale*," *Shakespeare Survey* 22 (1969): 93–107. A good rhetorical treatment of the last scene is Adrien Bonjour, "The Final Scene of *The Winter's Tale*," *English Studies* 33 (1952): 193–201, esp. pp. 199–201.

17. Inga-Stina Ewbank says that these lines reveal the "unnatural haste of Leontes' thoughts and acts; and this frenzied hurry is all the more marked for being set against the references to naturally progressing time with which the play opened," "The Triumph of Time," in *Shakespeare: The Winter's Tale*, ed. Kenneth Muir, Casebook Series (London: Macmillan, 1968), pp. 98–115, p. 101.

18. Arthur Quiller-Couch, Introduction to *The Winter's Tale* (Cambridge: Cambridge University Press, 1959), p. xx.

19. Nevill Coghill, "Six Points of Stage-craft," in *Shakespeare: The Winter's Tale*, ed. Muir, pp. 198–213, p. 203.

20. See, e.g., 2 Kings 2:23–24: "And [Elisha] went up from thence unto Bethel: and as he was going up by the way, there came forth little children out of the city, and mocked him, and said unto him, Go up, thou bald head; go up, thou bald head. And he turned back, and looked on them, and cursed them in the name of the Lord. And there came forth two she bears out of the wood, and tare forty and two of them." Cf. Jeremiah in Lam. 3:10: "[The Lord] was unto me as a bear lying in wait, and as a lion in secret places." See also God's warning to his people in Hos. 13:8: "I will meet them as a bear that is bereaved of her whelps." Bears are associated with apocalyptic destruction in Dan. 7:5 and Rev. 13:2.

21. Ewbank says of these lines, "Time is in a firm Elizabethan tradition when he insists on the multiplicity of his powers—and rather more successful than most pageant Father Times in reconciling his opposed attributes . . . he is a concrete image of the multiplicity which the play as a whole dramatizes and which is a leading theme of the second half of the play" (107).

22. Ernest Schanzer, "The Structural Pattern of *The Winter's Tale*," *Review of English Literature* 5 (1964): 72–82, p. 79.

23. William Blissett, "This Wide Gap of Time: *The Winter's Tale*," *ELR* 1 (1971): 52–70, p. 56.

24. See Robert C. Ketterer, "Machines for the Suppression of Time: Statues in *Suor Angelica*, *The Winter's Tale*, and *Alcestis*," *Comparative Drama* 24 (1990): 3–23. See also A. Leigh Deneef's treatment of artistic ritual in *"This Poetick Liturgie": Herrick's Ceremonial Mode* (Durham: Duke University Press, 1974), pp. 4ff., 176ff.

25. See Martin Mueller, "Hermione's Wrinkles," *Comparative Drama* (1971): 226–39. Mueller sees these lines as evidence of a profound but modest triumph over time in the play: "The wrinkles of Hermione symbolize the acceptance of temporality, and in the spirit of resigned acceptance, embodied also in the touching marriage of Camillo and Paulina, time is both conquering and conquered," p. 236.

26. Bertrand Evans, *Shakespeare's Comedies* (Oxford: Clarendon Press, 1960),

pp. 314–15. See also John K. Hall, "The Maturing of Romance in *The Winter's Tale*," *Parergon* 3 (1985): 147–62, p. 159.

27. Northrop Frye, "Recognition in *The Winter's Tale*," in *Shakespeare: The Winter's Tale*, ed. Muir, pp. 184–97, p. 197.

28. Louis A. Montrose, "The Purpose of Playing," p. 62.

29. Howard Felperin, *Shakespearean Romance* (Princeton, N.J.: Princeton University Press, 1972), p. 243.

Chapter 6

1. John Foxe, *Acts and Monuments*, ed. Stephen Reed Cattley, 8 vols. (London: Seeley and Burnside, 1837), 4:694.

2. Hans Blumenberg, *The Legitimacy of the Modern Age*, p. 151.

3. See Steven Ozment, *The Age of Reform*, pp. 61–62; Blumenberg, pp. 149–54; and Robert Ornstein, *The Moral Vision of Jacobean Tragedy* (Madison: University of Wisconsin Press, 1960).

4. Gifford, *A Briefe discourse . . . which may bee termed the Countrie Divinitie* (London, 1581).

5. Polemical dialogues are common enough in sixteenth-century England, and they run the whole range of dramatic tension from George Gifford's highly charged confrontation between well-developed characters to Arthur Dent's dramatically slack interview between an ignorant straw man and the author's spokesman. In Dent's *The Opening of Heaven Gates* (London, 1611), p. 2, for example, a dialogue between Reason and Religion, Reason is given such lead-in lines as, "I pray you, what are we to think of God, that wonderful workmaster?" Needless to say, Religion is happy to reply, and at great length.

6. See Chapter 2 above.

7. See Chapter 4 above.

8. Other Tudor/Stuart plays that might be analyzed along the same lines include Marlowe's *Doctor Faustus* and Greville's *Mustapha*.

9. William Empson, arguing against those who would impugn the Duchess's Christian integrity, says that "a play can give the pleasure of debate without leaving any doubt which side the author is on. The moral of this play, driven home as with the sledge-hammer of Dickens I should have thought, is not that the Duchess was wanton but that her brothers were sinfully proud." See Empson, "Mine Eyes Dazzle," in *Twentieth Century Interpretations of The Duchess of Malfi*, ed. Norman Rabkin (Englewood Cliffs, N.J.: Prentice-Hall, 1968), pp. 90–95, p. 91. Peter B. Murray, *A Study of John Webster* (The Hague: Mouton, 1969), pp. 118, 259, argues that the Duchess's religious integrity indicates that Webster's vision greatly transcends Bosola's. D. C. Gunby, "*The Duchess of Malfi*: A Theological Approach," in *John Webster*, ed. Brian Morris (London: Ernest Benn, 1970), sees the world of the play as "essentially a world of theodicy," p. 181. Dominic Baker-Smith, while emphasizing the hiddenness of Webster's God, sees the play as essentially Christian in its portrayal of the Duchess's suffering. See "Religion and John Webster" in *John*

Webster, ed. Morris, esp. p. 226. While John L. Selzer expresses the Duchess's virtue in terms of "integrity of life" rather than specifically Christian sanctity, he clearly feels that the moral order the Duchess represents is vindicated by the play, "Merit and Degree in Webster's *The Duchess of Malfi*," in *John Webster's The Duchess of Malfi*, ed. Harold Bloom (New York: Chelsea House, 1987), pp. 87–96, p. 96.

10. For Ian Jack, Webster is "a decadent . . . incapable of realizing the whole of life in the form in which it revealed itself to the Elizabethans," "The Case of John Webster," *Scrutiny* 16 (1949): 38–43, p. 43. Alvin Kernan calls *The Duchess of Malfi* "the most pessimistic Jacobean play," *The Cankered Muse: Satire in the English Renaissance* (New Haven, Conn.: Yale University Press, 1959), p. 242. Gunnar Boklund, *The Duchess of Malfi* (Cambridge, Mass.: Harvard University Press, 1962), p. 135, sees Webster's attempt to enrich his gloomy vision with pearls of wisdom as shoddy craftsmanship. Ornstein says that in Webster's tragedies "the Elizabethan faith in didacticism—in the moral power of words—is blown away by the first gust of violence," p. 134. Alan Sinfield, *Literature in Protestant England, 1560–1660* (Totowa, N.J.: Barnes & Noble, 1983), p. 121, maintains that the main theme of *The Duchess of Malfi*, as well as Webster's other tragedies, is that the universe is without purpose.

11. Charles Forker, *Skull Beneath the Skin: The Achievement of John Webster* (Carbondale: Southern Illinois University Press, 1986), p. 366.

12. As Jonathan Dollimore and Alan Sinfield remark, *The Selected Plays of John Webster*, p. 137, in staging *The Duchess of Malfi* one feels constrained into an either/ or mentality. Lois Potter bears out the accuracy of the remark in her study of the problems of staging the play, "Realism Versus Nightmare: Problems of Staging *The Duchess of Malfi*," in *The Triple Bond* ed. Joseph G. Price (University Park: Penn State University Press, 1975), pp. 170–89. See esp. pp. 188–89.

13. John Webster, *The Duchess of Malfi*, ed. Elizabeth Brennan, New Mermaids (New York: Norton, 1983), 1.2.419. All citations of *The Duchess of Malfi* are from Brennan's edition.

14. Also instructive are biblical usages of a mist as a figure for spiritual blindness. In Acts 13:11 the sorcerer Barjesus's spiritual perversity leads to his literal blindness; a "mist" (Geneva Bible; Gr., "*achlus*"; Vulg., "*caligo*") descends upon him. 2 Pet. 2:17 concerns false prophets "to whom the mist (KJV; Gr., '*zophos*'; Vulg., '*caligo*') of darkness is reserved forever." Cf. Francis Marbury, who claims that those who are taken in by the sales of indulgences are "sophisticated with the devil's mists," *A Sermon Preached at Paules Crosse the 13. of June, 1602* (London, 1602), sig. D1[r].

15. See Deut. 8:2 and Matt. 4:1. The wilderness is also the locus of divine favor in Is. 35:6, 41:19; Jer. 31:2; Ezek. 19:12–13, 34:25; Hos. 9:10; Matt. 3:1, 15: 33–37. Particularly instructive is Rev. 12:6, where the woman clothed with the sun, who is about to give birth to a ruler, takes refuge in the wilderness, "where she hath a place prepared of God" (Geneva Bible).

16. Huston Diehl, "Into the Maze of Self," esp. pp. 284–89, points out the tendency in Protestant emblem books to transform the medieval image of the labyrinth, which may be long but which can be negotiated by anyone who perseveres. In Protestant iconography, the outcome is much less certain; the mazes are more

complicated, and the pilgrim who relies on his own efforts fails to extricate himself. Only the one to whom God has given faith is successful.

17. Sinfield makes the questionable assertion that the Duchess's final word, "Mercy" (spoken on hearing that her husband and children are alive and reconciled to her brothers), "locates her final consolation in the marriage which has provoked her suffering" (p. 104). It can also, of course, be maintained that she perceives mercy in the workings of the Christian God. On the same page, Sinfield says, "If we could feel confident that the Duchess dies in a manner pleasing to God, Webster would have reconciled human assertion and the protestant sense of human worthlessness. He would have dissolved the dichotomy which, I have argued, characterizes other tragedies of the period. But the Duchess does not invoke God's strength." It might be objected to Sinfield that she invokes "heaven" twice as she is strangled (4.2.227–28), and that Webster could hardly have had her call on the Christian God since the use on the stage of the words "God," "Christ Jesus," "Holy Ghost," and "Trinity" was forbidden after 1606, some seven years before the play was written. See G. P. V. Akrigg's comments in "The Name of God and *The Duchess of Malfi,*" *Notes and Queries* 195 (1950): 231–33.

18. She does, after all, make arrangements for Cariola to look after the children, who are, as far as she knows, dead (4.2.200–202).

19. See Bettie Anne Doebler's treatment of the Duchess's death in the cultural context of the *ars moriendi* tradition, "Continuity in the Art of Dying: *The Duchess of Malfi,*" in *John Webster's The Duchess of Malfi,* ed. Harold Bloom (New York: Chelsea House, 1987), pp. 65–74.

20. See Jacqueline Pearson's treatment of the play's structure, "'To Behold My Tragedy': Tragedy and Anti-tragedy in *The Duchess of Malfi,* in *John Webster's The Duchess of Malfi,* ed. Harold Bloom (New York: Chelsea House, 1987), pp. 75–96, esp. pp. 78ff. It is Pearson's thesis that the fifth act is deliberately separated from the rest of the play as an ironic, tragicomic qualification of the Duchess's tragedy.

21. See Sinfield, p. 122.

22. Sir Philip Sidney, *The Countess of Pembroke's Arcadia,* 3rd ed. (London, 1598), repr. Scholars' Facsimiles and Reprints, 2 vols. (Delmar, N.Y., 1984), 2:453. Webster's plays rely heavily on Sidney's works. Robert W. Dent catalogues no fewer than 57 instances of Webster's citations of Sidney in *The Duchess of Malfi* alone. See Dent, *John Webster's Borrowing* (Berkeley: University of California Press, 1960).

23. R. W. Dent's comment on the change is instructive, if only in its resort to a merely metrical explanation of a passage that would seem to be either misogynous or ironic: "In this play, where the Duchess displays more courage than any of the male characters, one wonders if Webster changed 'wormish' to 'womanish' for any reason other than metre" (*John Webster's Borrowing,* p. 265).

24. The choice has been made, that is, apart from a revolutionary overturning of the audience member's prejudiced structure of interpretation—in Heideggerian terms, the audience member's *Vorurteile.* Yet even such a revolutionary experience would fit the Protestant paradigm of conversion.

25. An excellent treatment of this mentality and its historical development is Joel B. Altman's *The Tudor Play of Mind.*

26. Gunby, pp. 181ff., finds evidence of Webster's Anglicanism, but it should

be remembered that "Anglicanism" in the early seventeenth century is a broad category indeed, and it may be anachronistic to apply it with much precision. As Patrick Collinson reminds us, the Jacobean Church of England contains all sorts, and yet it is impossible "to distinguish absolutely between Puritanism and, so to speak, mere Protestantism," "Towards a Broader Understanding of the Early Dissenting Tradition," pp. 305–06. Charles Forker, p. 315, mentions the portrait of the Cardinal as evidence of Webster's anti-Catholicism, but there are elements that make it difficult to view the play as any sort of direct polemic against Rome. For one thing, although Duke Ferdinand's court is decidedly corrupt, Webster contrasts it to the French court, not that of a nation that has become Protestant by Webster's day (1.1.4). Moreover, no criticism seems to be implied when characters who have the audience's sympathy perform Catholic devotions, as when the Duchess, Antonio, and their children are at the shrine (3.4.1ff.). And Bosola disguised as bellman (he may or may not have the audience's sympathy at this point) assumes that an icon such as a crucifix can effectively confer a blessing on the Duchess (4.2.190).

27. Stephen Greenblatt remarks in "Invisible Bullets," pp. 21–65 in Greenblatt, *Shakespearean Negotiations* (Berkeley: University of California Press, 1988), that while there is a great deal of accusation of atheism in the late Tudor period, there are almost no professed atheists at the time (p. 22).

28. Christopher Ricks says of Bosola's "We are merely the stars' tennis-balls," "about the whole episode there hangs the unexalted suspicion that the characters (and the audience) are not the stars' tennis-balls but Webster's—struck and banded which way please him," *English Drama to 1710* (London: Barrie & Jenkins, 1971), p. 323.

29. It has been suggested that Ferdinand and the madmen are Webster's primary spokesmen since they are better emblems of absurdity than is Bosola. See Boklund, pp. 129–30. It is worth noting, though, that Ferdinand's madness is precipitated by his perception of meaning in the Duchess's life (4.2.251ff). And the catalogue of madmen includes, for example, a tailor "craz'd i' th' brain / With the study of new fashion" and "a gentleman usher / Quite beside himself with care to keep in mind / The number of his lady's salutations" (4.2.51–54). It might be argued that these madmen appear to have been driven crazy by a world obsessed with appearances, not a world devoid of meaning.

Chapter 7

1. Jasper Mayne, lines 57–64 of commendatory poem published with the 1633 edition of Donne's *Poems* (London, 1633).

2. Izaak Walton, *Lives of Donne and Herbert*, ed. S. C. Roberts (Cambridge: Cambridge University Press, 1957), p. 52.

3. John Donne, *Letters to Severall Persons of Honour*, ed. Charles E. Merrill, Jr. (New York: Sturgis & Walton, 1910), p. 210.

4. John Donne, *Sermons*, 8:6.506–9.

5. Jeremiah 27:1–11 and Acts 21:10–11.

6. Victor Turner develops the idea of liminality in several anthropological contexts. See, e.g., *The Anthropology of Performance*, pp. 26–26; *From Ritual to Theatre*, pp. 25–27, 41–42; and *Dramas, Fields, and Metaphors*, pp. 231–70.

7. For a discussion of literary and artistic treatments of the "seven ages" topos, see Samuel C. Chew, "'This Strange Eventful History,'" in *Joseph Quincy Adam Memorial Studies*, ed. James G. MacManaway, et al., (Washington, D.C.: Folger Shakespeare Library, 1948), pp. 157–82.

8. See Kenneth Burke, *A Rhetoric of Motives* (Berkeley: University of California Press, 1969), esp. pp. xiii, 61ff. See also Christine Oravec, "Kenneth Burke's Concept of Association and the Complexity of Identity," in *The Legacy of Kenneth Burke*, ed. Herbert W. Simons and Trevor Melia (Madison: University of Wisconsin Press, 1989) pp. 174–95.

9. Paul R. Sellin argues this point effectively in *John Donne and "Calvinist" Views of Grace* (Amsterdam: Boekhandel/Uitgeverij, 1983). An index of the difficulty of accepting Donne's Calvinism is that even Potter and Simpson think it necessary to mitigate Donne's position when in *Deaths Duell* the preacher mentions in passing that as human beings, "we may be damned, though we be never born" (10:232, 279).

10. See Turner, *Dramas, Fields, and Metaphors*, pp. 67–69, 87–88.

11. Robert S. Knapp, *Shakespeare—The Theatre and the Book*, p. 41; Norman Rabkin, *Shakespeare and the Problem of Meaning* (Chicago: University of Chicago Press, 1981), pp. 109–10.

12. Alan Sinfield, *Literature in Protestant England*, p. 110. Cf. G. I. Duthie, *Shakespeare* (London: Hutchinson University Press, 1959), p. 118: "There is no doubt that Shakespeare saw history in the same light as Halle saw it," and A. P. Rossiter's comment on Duthie, *Angel with Horns*, p. 21.

13. See, e.g., R. Chris Hassel, Jr., *Songs of Death: Performance, Interpretation, and the Text of Richard III* (Lincoln: University of Nebraska Press), 1987, pp. 89–121; William Shakespeare, *King Richard III*, ed. Anthony Hammond (London: Methuen, 1981), p. 72; Emrys Jones, *The Origins of Shakespeare* (Oxford: Clarendon Press, 1977), pp. 204–5; Robert Grams Hunter, *Shakespeare and the Mystery of God's Judgments* (Athens: University of Georgia Press, 1976), pp. 94–96; and Moody E. Prior, *The Drama of Power: Studies in Shakespeare's History Plays* (Evanston: Northwestern University Press, 1973), p. 56.

14. For treatments of the audience's dual response to Richard, see, e.g., Martha Tuck Rozett, *The Doctrine of Election and the Emergence of Elizabethan Tragedy*, p. 251; Alexander Leggatt, *Shakespeare's Political Drama* (London: Routledge, 1988), pp. 32–33; Ralph Berry, "*Richard III*: Bonding the Audience," in *Mirror up to Shakespeare*, ed. J. C. Gray (Toronto: University of Toronto Press, 1984), p. 121; Rossiter, p. 78; and Norman Rabkin, *Shakespeare and the Common Understanding*, p. 251.

15. Rabkin, *Meaning*, pp. 94–95. Rabkin points out, p. 154, n. 41, that one must go to *3 Henry VI* for evidence that Richard is politically ambitious; such rational motivation is curiously absent from *Richard III*.

16. The term "reprobate other" is Rozett's, pp. 64, 140, 172.

17. James L. Calderwood, *Shakespeare and the Denial of Death* (Amherst: Uni-

versity of Massachusetts Press, 1987), p. 134. Cf. Rabkin, *Meaning*, p. 97: Richard is "a black comic masterpiece, a surrogate playwright, a saturnalian actor-out of universal human aggressiveness, a vice-presenter whose hideous and joyous triumphs make us their willing accomplices." See also Leggatt, p. 34.

18. By my count, there are 59 references to these words and their derivatives in *Richard III* and 65 in *Othello*.

19. For a review of recent treatments of the Pauline allusions in *Richard III*, see R. Chris Hassel, Jr., "Last Words and Last Things: St. John, Apocalypse, and Eschatology in *Richard III*," *Shakespeare Studies* 18 (1986): 25–40, p. 25.

20. 1.2.57. Cf. *2 Henry VI*, in which Young Clifford says to Richard, "Hence, heap of wrath, foul indigested lump, / As crooked in thy manners as thy shape!" (5.1.157–58). See also Hunter, p. 93.

21. I owe this observation to Robert Smallwood, via Miriam Gilbert.

22. Jean E. Howard, *Shakespeare's Art of Orchestration* (Urbana: University of Illinois Press, 1984), p. 58.

23. Rabkin, *Meaning*, p. 97.

24. Stephen Greenblatt, *Marvelous Possessions*, pp. 14, 148–51.

25. Of course, to some degree histories and tragedies set up different generic expectations. Both *Richard III* and *Othello* function rhetorically as tragedies, however, and so it makes sense to compare them in terms of Shakespeare's tragic vision. It is noteworthy that both plays were listed as tragedies in the Stationers' Register. Moreover, we have seen that in *Richard III* Shakespeare takes substantial liberties with his chronicle sources—sources that themselves can by no means be called history in the modern sense. While Shakespeare could not very well have, say, made Richard defeat Richmond at Bosworth, it is clear that the playwright shaped his materials with the tragic form in mind.

26. Rosalie Colie, *Paradoxia Epidemica*, p. 248.

27. Robert Grudin, *Mighty Opposites*, pp. 134–35.

28. Knapp, *Shakespeare—The Theatre and the Book*, p. 228.

29. An example of one such attempt to define *Othello's* ideological import in non-paradoxical terms is Alan Sinfield's claim that the audience's experience of contrariety leads to the exposure and the dismantling of the paradox of divine justice and mercy. In Sinfield's reading, Desdemona's willingness to forgive her husband is "a standing rebuke to the retributive God assumed by Othello and the contemporary church," p. 126. It might be objected to Sinfield that his analysis mistakes Othello's actions for God's, that the play indicts not God's retributive nature but Othello's. Moreover, it could be argued that a play that leaves Iago, *this* Iago, alive at the end makes Desdemona's compassion, taken by itself, as incomplete a response as Othello's vengeance.

Bibliography

Primary Sources

Abbot, George. *An Exposition upon the Prophet Jonah*. 2 vols. London, 1600.
Adams, Thomas. *The Workes of Tho: Adams*. London, 1629.
Andrewes, Lancelot. *Lancelot Andrewes and His Private Devotions: A Biography, a Transcript, and an Interpretation*. Ed. Alexander Whyte, 2nd ed. London: Oliphant Anderson and Ferrier, 1896.
———. *XCVI Sermons*. London, 1629.
Articles . . . for the stablyshing of consent touchyng true religion. London, 1564.
Augustine of Hippo. *On Christian Doctrine*. Ed. D. W. Robertson, Jr. Indianapolis: Bobbs-Merrill, 1958.
Bancroft, Richard. *A sermon preached at Paules Crosse the 9. of Februarie . . . 1588* [i.e., 1589]. London, 1589.
Barlow, William. *The Sermon Preached at Paules Crosse the tenth day of November, being the next Sunday after the Discoverie of this late Horrible Treason*. London, 1606.
Baxter, Richard. *The Saints Everlasting Rest*. London, 1650.
Beaumont, Francis. *The Knight of the Burning Pestle*. Ed. Sheldon P. Zitner. Manchester: Manchester University Press, 1984.
Becon, Thomas. *The Displaying of the Popish Masse . . . Written by Thomas Becon; in the dayes of Queene Mary*. [Basel, 1559]. London, 1637.
Beza, Theodore. *An evident Display of Popish Practises, or Patched Pelagianisme*. Trans. W. H. London, 1578.
Brownrig, Ralph. *Sixty Five Sermons by the Right Reverend Father in God, Ralph Brownrig, Late Bishop of Exceter*. London, 1674.
Bruno, Giordano. *The Heroic Frenzies*. Trans. Paul E. Memmo. Chapel Hill: University of North Carolina Press, 1965.
Bucer, Martin. *Martini Buceri Scripta Anglicana . . . .* Basel, 1577.
Burroughs, Jeremiah. *Irenicum to the Lovers of Truth and Peace*. London, 1646.
Burton, Robert. *The Anatomy of Melancholy*. Oxford, 1621.
Calvin, John. *Institution of the Christian Religion*. Trans. Thomas Norton. London, 1561.
———. *The Psalmes of David and Others, with J. Calvins Commentaries*. Trans. Arthur Golding. London, 1571.
Cartwright, Thomas. *Reply to an Answer to M. Doc. Whitgift*. London, 1573.
Cartwright, William. *Comedies, Tragi-Comedies, with other Poems*. London, 1651.

————. *An Off-Spring of Mercy, Issuing out of the Womb of Cruelty. Or, a Passion Sermon Preached at Christs Church in Oxford.* London, 1652.

Certain Sermons or Homilies 1547 and A Homily against Disobedience and Rebellion. Ed. Ronald B. Bond. Toronto: University of Toronto Press, 1987.

Chamberlain, John. *The Letters of John Chamberlain,* 2 vols. Ed. Norman Egbert McClure. Philadelphia: American Philosophical Society, 1939.

Cicero. *In Catilinam.* In *Cicero in Twenty-Eight Volumes,* vol. 10. Ed. C. MacDonald. Cambridge, Mass.: Harvard University Press, 1977.

Cosin, John. *The Works of the Right Reverend Father in God, John Cosin, Lord Bishop of Durham.* 5 vols. Oxford: Parker, 1843.

Denison, John. *The Heavenly Banquet.* London, 1619.

Dent, Arthur. *The Opening of Heaven Gates, or The ready way to everlasting life.* London, 1611.

————. *The plaine mans path-way to heaven; wherein every man may clearly see, whether he shall be saved or damned.* London, 1601.

Donne, John. *John Donne's Poetry.* Ed. A. L. Clements. New York: Norton, 1966.

————. *Letters to Severall Persons of Honour.* Ed. Charles E. Merrill, Jr. New York: Sturgis & Walton, 1910.

————. *Paradoxes and Problems.* Ed. Helen Peters. Oxford: Clarendon Press, 1980.

————. *The Sermons of John Donne.* 10 vols. Ed. George R. Potter and Evelyn M. Simpson. Berkeley: University of California Press, 1953–1962.

Dove, John. *A Sermon Preached at Paules Crosse, the Sixt of February.* London, 1597.

Eachard, John, supposed author. *A Free and Impartial Inquiry into the Causes of that very great Esteem and Honour that the Nonconforming Preachers are generally in with their Followers.* London, 1673.

Erasmus, Desiderius and Martin Luther. *Discourse on Free Will.* Ed. Ernst F. Winter. New York: Ungar, 1961.

Featley, Daniel. *Ancilla Pietatis, or the Handmaid to Private Devotion.* London, 1626.

Field, John. *A Godly Exhortation, by occasion of the late judgment of God, shewed at Paris-garden, the thirteenth day of January: where were assembled by estimation; above a thousand persons, whereof some were slain; and of that number, at the least, as is credibly reported, the third person maimed and hurt.* London, 1583.

Field, John and Thomas Wilcox. *An Admonition to Parliament.* London, 1572.

Fisher, William. *A Godly Sermon preached at Paules Crosse the 31. day of October 1591.* London, 1592.

Foxe, John. *Acts and Monuments.* 8 vols. Ed. Stephen Reed Cattley. London: Seeley and Burnside, 1837.

————. Preface to the 1571 edition of *The Reformation of Ecclesiastical Laws of England, 1552.* Ed. and trans. James Spalding. Kirksville, Mo.: Sixteenth Century Essays and Studies, 1992. Appendix I.

G., I. *A Refutation of the Apologie for Actors.* London, 1615; rpt. New York: Garland, 1973.

Geneva Bible. 1560. Madison: University of Wisconsin Pr., 1969.

Gibson, Thomas. *A Fruitful Sermon, preached at Occham in the County of Rutland, the Second of November. 1583.* London, 1583.

Gifford, George. *A Briefe discourse of certaine points of the religion, which is among the common sort of Christians, which may bee termed the Countrie Divinitie*. London, 1581.

―――. *Fifteene Sermons upon the Song of Salomon*. London, 1598.

―――. *A Sermon on the Parable of the Sower*. London, 1582.

Goffe, Thomas. *Deliverance from the Grave. A Sermon Preached at Saint Maries Spittle in London on Wednesday in Easter Weeke last, March 28, 1627*. London, 1627.

Gosson, Stephen. *Playes Confuted in Five Actions*. In *Markets of Bawdrie: The Dramatic Criticism of Stephen Gosson*. Ed. Arthur F. Kinney. Salzburg: Institut fur Englische Sprache, 1974.

―――. *The Schoole of Abuse. English Reprints*, vol. 1. Ed. Edward Arber. London: Bloomsburg, 1869. Reprint New York: AMS Press, 1966.

―――. *The Trumpet of Warre. A Sermon preached at Paules Crosse the seventh of Maie 1598*. London, 1598.

Grindal, Edmund. *The Remains of Archbishop Grindal*. Cambridge: Parker Society, 1843.

Hall, Joseph. *The Works of the Right Reverend Joseph Hall, D. D.* 10 vols. Oxford: Oxford University Press, 1863.

Hammond, Henry. *A View of the New Directorie, and a Vindication of the Ancient Liturgie of the Church of England*, 3rd ed. Oxford, 1646.

Herbert, Edward. "The History of Henry VIII." *A Complete History of England*. Ed. White Kennett. 3 vols. London, 1706.

Herbert, George. *The Country Parson, The Temple*. Ed. John N. Wall, Jr. New York: Paulist Pr., 1981.

―――. *The Works of George Herbert*. Ed. F. E. Hutchinson. 4th ed. Oxford: Clarendon Press, 1959.

Heywood, Thomas. *An Apology for Actors*. London, 1612. Reprint Delmar, N.Y.: Scholars' Facsimiles and Reprints, 1941.

Hieron, Samuel. *The Dignity of Preaching: In a Sermon upon I. Thessal. 5.20*. London, 1616.

―――. *The Preachers Plea; or, A Treatise in forme of a plaine dialogue, making known the worth and necessity of that which we call preaching . . . .* London, 1605.

Hobbes, Thomas. *Leviathan*. Ed. C. B. Macpherson. New York: Penguin, 1985.

Holbrooke, William. *Loves Complaint, for Want of Entertainment*. London, 1609.

Hooker, Richard. *The Folger Library Edition of The Works of Richard Hooker*. 6 vols. Ed. W. Speed Hill. Cambridge, Mass.: Harvard University Press, 1977–93.

Howson, John. *A Second Sermon, preached at Paules Crosse, the 21. of May, 1598*. London, 1598.

Hyperius, Andreas. *The Practise of preaching, otherwise Called the Pathway to the Pulpet*. Trans. John Ludham. London, 1577.

Jackson, Thomas. *Diverse Sermons, with a short Treatise befitting these present times*. Oxford, 1637.

James, Richard. *A Sermon Delivered in Oxford. Concerning the Apostles Preaching and ours*. London, 1630.

Jonson, Ben. *Ben Jonson*. 11 vols. Ed. C. H. Herford, Percy Simpson, and Evelyn Simpson. Oxford: Clarendon Press, 1925–52.

King, John. *Lectures upon Jonas*. London, 1584.

——. *The Staple of News*. Ed. Devra Roland Kifer. Lincoln: University of Nebraska Press, 1975.

Knewstub, John. *A Confutation of monstrous and horrible heresies, taught by H. N. and embraced of a number, who call themselves the Familie of Love*. London, 1579.

——. *A Sermon preached at Paules Crosse the Fryday before Easter, commonly called good Fryday, in the yeere of our Lorde. 1576*. London, 1576.

Laud, William. *The Works of the Most Reverend Father in God, William Laud, D. D.* . . . . 9 vols. Oxford: Parker, 1847–60.

Luther, Martin. *Works*. 55 vols. Gen. ed. Jaroslav Pelikan. St. Louis: Concordia, 1952ff.

Luther, Martin and Desiderius Erasmus. *Luther and Erasmus: Free Will and Salvation*. Ed. E. Gordon Rupp and Philip S. Watson. Library of Christian Classics, vol. 17. Philadelphia: Westminster Press, 1969.

Lyly, John. *Euphues: The Anatomy of Wit, Euphues & His England*. Ed. Morris W. Croll and Harry Clemens. London: Routledge, 1916.

Manningham, John. *Diary of John Manningham, of the Middle Temple* . . . . Ed. John Bruce. London: Camden Society, 1868.

Marbecke, John. *A Book of Notes and Commonplaces with their Expositions*. London, 1581.

Marbury, Francis. *A Sermon Preached at Paules Crosse the 13. of June, 1602*. London, 1602.

Mayne, Jasper. *A Sermon Concerning Unity and Agreement Preached in Carfax Church in Oxford, August 9, 1646*. London, 1646.

Middleton, Thomas. *A Chaste Maid in Cheapside*. Ed. Alan Brissenden. New Mermaids. London: Ernest Benn, 1968.

——. *A Mad World, My Masters*. Ed. Standish Henning. Regents. London: Edward Arnold, 1965.

——. *Michaelmas Term*. Ed. Richad Levin. Regents Renaissance Drama. Lincoln: University of Nebraska Press, 1966.

Middleton, Thomas and Thomas Dekker. *The Roaring Girl*. Ed. Andor Gomme. New Mermaids. New York: Norton, 1976.

Milles, Robert. *Abrahams Suite for Sodome. A Sermon Preached at Pauls Crosse the 25. of August. 1611*. London, 1612.

Myriell, Thomas. *The Devout Soules Search* . . . . *In a Sermon Preached at Paules Crosse*. London, 1610.

Nashe, Thomas. *Works of Thomas Nashe*. 5 vols. Ed. R. B. McKerrow. London: Sidgwick and Jackson, 1910.

Northbrooke, John. *A Treatise Against Dicing, Dancing, Plays, and Interludes*. Ed. John P. Collier. London: The Shakespeare Society, 1843.

Ovid. *Metamorphoses*. Ed. William S. Anderson. Leipzig: Teubner, 1982.

Palmer, Herbert. *The Character of a Christian in Paradoxes and Seeming Contradictions*. London, 1656.

Perkins, William. *A Case of Conscience, the greatest that ever was; How a man may know whether he be the childe of God, or no*. London, 1592.

——. *A Golden Chaine, or the description of theologie, containing the order of the causes of salvation and damnation according to Gods word*. London, 1591.

————. *The Workes of that Famous and Worthie Minister of Christ, in the Universitie of Cambridge, M. William Perkins.* 3 vols. London, 1609.

Pilkington, James. *A Confutation.* London, 1563.

————. *The Works of James Pilkington, D. D.* Ed. James Scholefield. Cambridge: Parker Society, 1842.

Playfere, Thomas. *The Meane in Mourning, A Sermon preached at Saint Maryes Spittle in London on Tuesday in Easter weeke, 1595.* London, 1596.

————. *The sick-mans Couch. A Sermon Preached before the most noble Prince Henrie at Greenwich, Mar. 12. Ann. 1604.* London, 1611.

Price, Sampson. *London's Warning By Laodicea's Luke-warmnesse. Or A Sermon Preached at Paules-Crosse, the 10. of October, 1613.* London, 1613.

Procter, William. *The Watchman Warning. A Sermon preached at Pauls Crosse the 26. of September, 1624.* London, 1625.

Prynne, William. *Histriomastix, The Players Scourge or Actors Tragedie.* London, 1633.

Puttenham, George. *The Arte of English Poesie.* Ed. Baxter Hathaway. Kent, Ohio: Kent State University Press, 1970.

Rankins, William. *A mirrour of monsters: Wherein is plainely described the manifold vices, & spotted enormities, that are caused by the infectious sight of playes, with the description of the subtile slights of Sathan, making them his instruments . . . .* London, 1587.

The Reformation of Ecclesiastical Laws of England, 1552. Ed. and trans. James C. Spalding. Sixteenth Century Essays and Studies, vol. 19. Kirksville, Mo.: Sixteenth Century Journal, 1992.

Rogers, Richard. *Seven Treatises containing such directions as is gathered out of Holie Scriptures.* London, 1605.

Sandys, Edwin. *The Sermons of Edwin Sandys, D.D.* Cambridge: Parker Society, 1841.

Sclater, William. *A Threefold Perservative . . . Prescribed in a Sermon at S. Pauls Crosse in London, September 17, 1609.* London, 1610.

A Second and Third Blast of Retrait from Plaies and Theaters. London, 1590.

Serlio, Sebastiano. *The fift Booke of Architecture, made by Sebastian Serly, wherein there are set downe certayne formes of Temples, according to the Ancient manner . . . .* London, 1611.

Shakespeare, William. *The Complete Signet Classic Shakespeare.* Gen. ed. Sylvan Barnet. New York: Harcourt, 1972.

————. *King Richard III.* Ed. Anthony Hammond. London: Methuen, 1981.

————. *The Riverside Shakespeare.* Ed. G. Blakemore Evans. Boston: Houghton Mifflin, 1974.

Sidney, Sir Philip. *The Countess of Pembroke's Arcadia.* 3rd ed. London, 1598. 2 vols. Reprint Delmar, N.Y.: Scholars' Facsimiles and Reprints, 1984.

————. *Sir Philip Sidney: Selected Poems.* Ed. Katharine Duncan-Jones. Oxford: Clarendon Press, 1973.

Smith, Henry. *The Sermons of Maister Henrie Smith.* London, 1597.

————. *Seven Godly and Learned Sermons upon Seven divers Textes of Scripture . . . .* London, 1591.

———. *The Trumpet of the Soule, Sounding to Judgement*. London, 1592.

———. *The Works of Henry Smith*. 2 vols. Edinburgh: James Nichol, 1866.

South, Robert. *Sermons Preached upon Several Occasions*. 7 vols. Oxford: Clarendon Press, 1823.

Sparke, Thomas. *A Short Treatise, very comfortable for all those Christians that be troubled and disquieted in their consciences*. London, 1580.

Stockwood, John. *A Sermon Preached at Paules Crosse on Barthelmew day, being the 24. of August, 1578*. London, 1578.

Stubbes, Phillip. *The Anatomy of Abuses*. Ed. Frederick J. Furnivall. New Shakespeare Society, vols. 4, 6, 12 (1877–82). Reprint Millwood, N.Y.: Kraus, 1965.

Swift, Jonathan. *A Tale of a Tub, to which is added The Battle of the Books . . . .* Ed. A. C. Guthkelch and D. N. Smith. 2nd ed. Oxford: Clarendon Press, 1958.

Symonds, William. *A Sermon Preached at White-chappel, in the presence of many, honourable and worshipfull, the adventurers and planters for Virginia*. London, 1609.

Taffin, Jean. *Of the Markes of the Children of God, and of their comforts in afflictions*. Trans. Anne Prowse. London, 1597.

Venning, Ralph. *Orthodox Paradoxes. Or, a Beleever Clearing Truth by Seeming Contradictions*. London, 1647.

Walton, Izaak. *Lives of Donne and Herbert*. Ed. S. C. Roberts. Cambridge: Cambridge University Press, 1957.

Webster, John. *The Duchess of Malfi*. Ed. Elizabeth M. Brennan. New Mermaids. New York: Norton, 1983.

———. *The Selected Plays of John Webster*. Ed. Jonathan Dollimore and Alan Sinfield. Cambridge: Cambridge University Press, 1983.

Secondary Sources

Addleshaw, G. W. O. and Frederick Etchells. *The Architectural Setting of Anglican Worship*. London: Faber and Faber, 1948.

Adolph, Robert M. *The Rise of Modern Prose Style*. Cambridge, Mass.: MIT Press, 1968.

Akrigg, G. P. V. "The Name of God and *The Duchess of Malfi*." *Notes and Queries* 195 (1950): 231–33.

Altman, Joel B. *The Tudor Play of Mind: Rhetorical Inquiry and the Development of Elizabethan Drama*. Berkeley: University of California Press, 1978.

Anderson, Benedict. *Imagined Communities: Reflections on the Origins and Spread of Nationalism*. London: Verso, 1983.

Baker-Smith, Dominic. "Religion and John Webster." *John Webster*. Ed. Brian Robert Morris. London: Ernest Benn, 1970.

Barish, Jonas. *The Antitheatrical Prejudice*. Berkeley: University of California Press, 1981.

Barton, Anne. *Ben Jonson, Dramatist*. Cambridge: Cambridge University Press, 1984.

Berry, Ralph. "*Richard III*: Bonding the Audience." *Mirror up to Shakespeare: Essays in Honour of G. R. Hibbard*. Ed. J. C. Gray. Toronto: University of Toronto Press, 1984.

——. *The Shakespearean Metaphor: Studies in Language and Form*. Totowa, N.J.: Rowman and Littlefield, 1978.

Bevington, David. *Action Is Eloquence: Shakespeare's Language of Gesture*. Cambridge, Mass.: Harvard University Press, 1984.

Bhabha, Homi K. "The Commitment to Theory." *New Formations* 5 (1988): 5–23.

Blench, J. W. *Preaching in England in the Late Fifteenth and Sixteenth Centuries*. Oxford: Basil Blackwell, 1964.

Blissett, William. "This Wide Gap of Time: *The Winter's Tale*." *ELR* 1 (1971): 52–70.

Blumenberg, Hans. *The Legitimacy of the Modern Age*. Trans. Robert M. Wallace. Cambridge, Mass.: MIT Press, 1983.

Boklund, Gunnar. *The Duchess of Malfi*. Cambridge, Mass.: Harvard University Press, 1962.

Bonjour, Adrien. "The Final Scene of *The Winter's Tale*." *English Studies* 33 (1952): 193–201.

Bouwsma, William J. *John Calvin: A Sixteenth-Century Portrait*. Oxford: Oxford University Press, 1988.

Boyle, Marjorie O'Rourke. *Rhetoric and Reform: Erasmus' Civil Dispute with Luther*. Cambridge, Mass.: Harvard University Press, 1983.

Breen, Quirinus. *Christianity and Humanism: Studies in the History of Ideas*. Grand Rapids, Mich.: Eerdmans, 1968.

Burke, Kenneth. *A Rhetoric of Motives*. Berkeley: University of California Press, 1969.

Burrage, Champlin. *The Early English Dissenters*. 2 vols. Cambridge: Cambridge University Press, 1912.

Butler, Martin. "Ecclesiastical Censorship of Early Stuart Drama: The Case of Jonson's *The Magnetic Lady*." *Modern Philology* 89 (1992): 469–81.

——. *Theatre and Crisis 1632–1642*. Cambridge: Cambridge University Press, 1984.

Calderwood, James L. *Shakespeare and the Denial of Death*. Amherst: University of Mass. Press, 1987.

Carrithers, Gale H., Jr. *Donne at Sermons: A Christian Existential World*. Albany: State University of New York Press, 1972.

Chadwick, Owen. *The Reformation*. New York: Penguin, 1972.

Chambers, E. K. *The Elizabethan Stage*. 4 vols. Oxford: Clarendon Press, 1923. Reprint 1974.

Clark, G. N. *The Later Stuarts: 1660–1714*. Oxford: Clarendon Press, 1949.

Coghill, Nevill. "Six Points of Stage-craft." *Shakespeare: The Winter's Tale: A Casebook*. Ed. Kenneth Muir. Casebook Series. London: Macmillan, 1968. 198–213.

Colie, Rosalie L. *Paradoxia Epidemica: The Renaissance Tradition of Paradox*. Princeton, N.J.: Princeton University Press, 1966.

——. *The Resources of Kind: Genre-Theory in the Renaissance*. Berkeley: University of California Press, 1973.

Collinson, Patrick. *The Elizabethan Puritan Movement*. Berkeley: University of California Press, 1967.

——. "Towards a Broader Understanding of the Early Dissenting Tradition." *The Dissenting Tradition: Essays for Leland H. Carlson.* Ed. C. Robert Cole and Michael E. Moody. Athens: Ohio University Press, 1975. 3–38.

Couliano, Ioan. *Eros and Magic in the Renaissance.* Trans. Margaret Cook. Chicago: University of Chicago Press, 1987.

Crockett, Bryan. "Cicero, Ben Jonson, and the Puritans." *Classical and Modern Literature* 15 (1995): 000–00.

——. "'Holy Cozenage' and the Renaissance Cult of the Ear." *Sixteenth Century Journal* 24 (1993): 47–65.

Davies, Horton. *Like Angels from a Cloud: The English Metaphysical Preachers, 1588–1645.* San Marino, Calif.: Huntington Library, 1986.

——. *Worship and Theology in England, Volume I: 1534–1603.* Princeton, N.J.: Princeton University Press, 1970.

——. *The Worship of the English Puritans.* Westminster: Dacre Press, 1948.

Deneef, A. Leigh. *"This Poetick Liturgie": Herrick's Ceremonial Mode.* Durham, N.C.: Duke University Press, 1974.

Dent, Robert W. *John Webster's Borrowing.* Berkeley: University of California Press, 1960.

Desmet, Christy. *Reading Shakespeare's Characters: Rhetoric, Ethics, and Identity.* Amherst: University of Massachusetts Press, 1992.

Dessen, Alan C. *Jonson's Moral Comedy.* Evanston, Ill.: Northwestern University Press, 1971.

Dickens, A. G. *The English Reformation.* New York: Schocken Books, 1964.

Diehl, Huston. "Into the Maze of Self: The Protestant Transformation of the Image of the Labyrinth." *Journal of Medieval and Renaissance Studies* 16 (1986): 281–301.

——. "Observing the Lord's Supper and the Lord Chamberlain's Men: The Visual Rhetoric of Ritual and Play in Early Modern England." *Renaissance Drama* 22 (1991): 147–74.

——. *Staging Reform, Reforming the Stage: The Protestant Aesthetics of English Renaissance Tragedy.* Ithaca, N.Y.: Cornell University Press, forthcoming 1996.

Doebler, Bettie Anne. "Continuity in the Art of Dying: *The Duchess of Malfi.*" *John Webster's The Duchess of Malfi.* Ed. Harold Bloom. New York: Chelsea House, 1987. 65–74.

Dollimore, Jonathan. *Radical Tragedy: Religious Ideology and Power in the Drama of Shakespeare and his Contemporaries.* Brighton: Harvester Press, 1984.

——. "Subjectivity, Sexuality, and Transgression: The Jacobean Connection." *Renaissance Drama* 17 (1986): 53–81.

Dollimore, Jonathan and Alan Sinfield. *Political Shakespeare: New Essays in Cultural Materialism.* Ithaca, N.Y.: Cornell University Press, 1985.

Durkheim, Emile. *Suicide: A Study in Sociology.* Trans. John A. Spaulding. New York: Free Press, 1966.

Duthie, George Ian. *Shakespeare.* London: Hutchinson University Press, 1959.

Eisenstein, Elizabeth L. *The Printing Press as an Agent of Change.* Cambridge: Cambridge University Press, 1980.

Ellis-Fermor, Una. *The Jacobean Drama: An Interpretation.* 2nd edition. London: Methuen, 1947.

Empson, William. "Mine Eyes Dazzle." *Twentieth Century Interpretations of The Duchess of Malfi.* Ed. Norman Rabkin. Englewood Cliffs, N.J.: Prentice-Hall, 1968. 90–95.

Evans, Bertrand. *Shakespeare's Comedies.* Oxford: Clarendon Press, 1960.

Ewbank, Inga-Stina. "The Triumph of Time." *Shakespeare: The Winter's Tale.* Ed. Kenneth Muir. Casebook Series. London: Macmillan, 1968. 98–115.

Felperin, Howard. *Shakespearean Romance.* Princeton, N.J.: Princeton University Press, 1972.

Finkelpearl, P. J. *John Marston of the Middle Temple.* Cambridge, Mass.: Harvard University Press, 1969.

Fisch, Harold. "The Puritans and the Reform of Prose Style." *ELH* 19 (1952): 229–48.

Fish, Stanley E. *Self-Consuming Artifacts: The Experience of Seventeenth-Century Literature.* Berkeley: University of California Press, 1972.

Forker, Charles. *Skull Beneath the Skin: The Achievement of John Webster.* Carbondale: Southern Illinois University Press, 1986.

Frye, Northrop. "Recognition in *The Winter's Tale.*" *Shakespeare: The Winter's Tale: A Casebook.* Ed. Kenneth Muir. Casebook Series. London: Macmillan, 1968. 184–97.

Frye, Roland Mushat. *Shakespeare and Christian Doctrine.* Princeton, N.J.: Princeton University Press, 1963.

Garber, Marjorie. "The Logic of the Transvestite: *The Roaring Girl.*" *Staging the Renaissance: Reinterpretations of Elizabethan and Jacobean Drama.* Ed. David Scott Kasdan and Peter Stallybrass. New York: Routledge, 1991. 221–34.

Geertz, Clifford. "Art as a Cultural System." *MLN* 91 (1976): 1473–1499.

———. *Interpretation of Cultures: Selected Essays.* New York: Basic Books, 1973.

Greenblatt, Stephen. *Marvelous Possessions: The Wonder of the New World.* Chicago: University of Chicago Press, 1991.

———. *Renaissance Self-Fashioning from More to Shakespeare.* Chicago: University of Chicago Press, 1980.

———. *Shakespearean Negotiations: The Circulation of Social Energy in Renaissance England.* Berkeley: University of California Press, 1988.

Grudin, Robert. *Mighty Opposites: Shakespeare and Renaissance Contrariety.* Berkeley: University of California Press, 1980.

———. "Prospero's Magic and the Structure of *The Tempest.*" *South Atlantic Quarterly* 71 (1972): 401–09.

Gunby, D. C. "*The Duchess of Malfi*: A Theological Approach." *John Webster.* Ed. Brian Robert Morris. London: Ernest Benn, 1970.

Hall, John K. "The Maturing of Romance in *The Winter's Tale.*" *Parergon* 3 (1985): 147–62.

Harbage, Alfred. *Shakespeare and the Rival Traditions.* New York: Macmillan, 1952.

Hardman, C. D. "Theory, Form, and Meaning in Shakespeare's *The Winter's Tale.*" *Review of English Studies* 36 (1985): 228–35.

Harnack, Adolf von. *Marcion: The Gospel of the Alien God.* Trans. John E. Steely and Lyle D. Bierma. Durham: Labyrinth Press, 1990.

Hassel, R. Chris, Jr. "Last Words and Last Things: St. John, Apocalypse, and Eschatology in *Richard III.*" *Shakespeare Studies* 18 (1986): 25–40.

――. *Songs of Death: Performance, Interpretation, and the Text of Richard III*. Lincoln: University of Nebraska Press, 1987.

Heffner, Ray L., Jr. "Unifying Symbols in the Comedy of Ben Jonson." *Ben Jonson: A Collection of Critical Essays*. Ed. Jonas A. Barish. Englewood Cliffs, N.J.: Prentice-Hall, 1963. 133–146.

Heinemann, Margot. *Puritanism and Theatre: Thomas Middleton and Oppositional Drama under the Early Stuarts*. Cambridge: Cambridge University Press, 1980.

Helgerson, Richard. *Forms of Nationhood: The Elizabethan Writing of England*. Chicago: University of Chicago Press, 1992.

――. *Self-Crowned Laureates: Spenser, Jonson, Milton, and the Literary System*. Berkeley: University of California Press, 1983.

Herr, Alan F. *The Elizabethan Sermon: A Survey and Bibliography*. Dissertation, University of Pennsylvania, 1940.

Hill, John Edward Christopher. *Society and Puritanism in Pre-Revolutionary England*. New York: Schocken Books, 1964.

Howard, Jean E. "Crossdressing, the Theatre, and Gender Struggle in Early Modern England." *Shakespeare Quarterly* 39 (1988): 418–40.

――. "The New Historicism in Renaissance Studies." *ELR* 16 (1986): 13–43.

――. "Renaissance Antitheatricality and the Politics of Gender and Rank in *Much Ado about Nothing*." *Shakespeare Reproduced: The Text in History and Ideology*. Ed. Jean E. Howard and Marion F. O'Connor. London: Methuen, 1987. 163–87.

――. *Shakespeare's Art of Orchestration*. Urbana: University of Illinois Press, 1984.

Hunter, Robert Grams. *Shakespeare and the Mystery of God's Judgments*. Athens: University of Georgia Press, 1976.

Jack, Ian. "The Case of John Webster." *Scrutiny* 16 (1949): 38–43.

Jameson, Fredric. "Religion and Ideology: A Political Reading of *Paradise Lost*." *Literature, Politics, and Theory: Papers from the Essex Conference, 1976–84*. Ed. Francis Barker, et al. New York: Methuen, 1986.

Jones, Emrys. *The Origins of Shakespeare*. Oxford: Clarendon Press, 1977.

Kendall, Ritchie. *The Drama of Dissent: The Radical Poetics of Nonconformity, 1380–1590*. Chapel Hill: University of North Carolina Press, 1986.

Kernan, Alvin. *The Cankered Muse: Satire in the English Renaissance*. New Haven, Conn.: Yale University Press, 1959.

Ketterer, Robert C. "Machines for the Suppression of Time: Statues in *Suor Angelica, The Winter's Tale*, and *Alcestis*." *Comparative Drama* 24 (1990): 3–23.

Kinney, Arthur F. *Continental Humanist Poetics: Studies in Erasmus, Castiglione, Marguerite de Navarre, Rabelais, and Cervantes*. Amherst: University of Massachusetts Press, 1989.

――. *Humanist Poetics: Thought, Rhetoric, and Fiction in Sixteenth-Century England*. Amherst: University of Massachusetts Press, 1986.

――. *Markets of Bawdrie: The Dramatic Criticism of Stephen Gosson*. Salzburg: Institut fur Englische Sprache, 1974.

Knapp, Robert S. *Shakespeare—The Theater and the Book* Princeton, N.J.: Princeton University Press, 1989.

Knight, G. Wilson. "*Measure for Measure* and the Gospels." *Shakespeare: Measure for Measure*. Casebook Series. London: Macmillan, 1971.

Knott, John R. *The Sword of the Spirit: Puritan Responses to the Bible*. Chicago: University of Chicago Press, 1980.

Krier, Theresa M. "The Triumph of Time: Paradox in *The Winter's Tale*." *Centennial Review* 26 (1982): 341–53.

Kuhn, Thomas S. *The Structure of Scientific Revolutions*. Chicago: University of Chicago Press, 1962.

LaCapra, Dominick. "Bakhtin, Marxism, and the Carnivalesque." LaCapra, *Rethinking Intellectual History: Texts, Contexts, Language*. Ithaca, N.Y.: Cornell University Press, 1983.

Lake, Peter. *Anglicans and Puritans?* London: Unwin Hyman, 1988.

Leggatt, Alexander. *Shakespeare's Political Drama: The History Plays and the Roman Plays*. London: Routledge, 1988.

Levin, Harry. *Shakespeare and the Revolution of the Times*. Oxford: Oxford University Press, 1976.

Lewalski, Barbara K. *Protestant Poetics and the Seventeenth-Century Religious Lyric*. Princeton, N.J.: Princeton University Press, 1979.

MacDonald, Michael and Terence R. Murphy. *Sleepless Souls: Suicide in Early Modern England*. Oxford: Clarendon Press, 1990.

MacLure, Millar. *The Paul's Cross Sermons, 1534–1642*. Toronto: University of Toronto Press, 1958.

———. *Register of Sermons Preached at Paul's Cross 1534–1642*. Rev. Peter Pauls and Jackson Campbell Boswell. Ottawa: Dovehouse Editions, 1989.

Matchett, William H. "Some Dramatic Techniques in *The Winter's Tale*." *Shakespeare Survey* 22 (1969): 93–107.

Maus, Katharine Eisaman. "Satire and Ideal Economies in the Jonsonian Imagination." *ELR* 19 (1989): 42–64.

McGee, J. Sears. *The Godly Man in Stuart England: Anglicans, Puritans, and the Two Tables, 1620–1670*. New Haven, Conn.: Yale University Press, 1976.

Miles, Margaret R. *Image as Insight: Visual Understanding in Western Christianity and Secular Culture*. Boston: Beacon Press, 1985.

Milward, Peter. *Shakespeare's Religious Background*. Bloomington: Indiana University Press, 1973.

Miner, Earl. *The Metaphysical Mode from Donne to Cowley*. Princeton, N.J.: Princeton University Press, 1969.

Mitchell, W. Fraser. *English Pulpit Oratory from Andrewes to Tillotson: A Study of Its Literary Aspects*. New York: Macmillan, 1932.

Montrose, Louis A. "The Purpose of Playing: Reflections on a Shakespearean Anthropology." *Helios* 7 (1980): 51–74.

Morris, Brian. *English Drama to 1710*. *The Sphere History of Literature in the English Language*, gen. ed. Christopher Ricks. Vol. 3. London: Sphere, 1971.

Mueller, Martin. "Hermione's Wrinkles." *Comparative Drama* (1971): 226–39.

Mulholland, P. A. "The Date of *The Roaring Girl*." *Review of English Studies* 28 (1977): 18–31.

Mullaney, Steven. *The Place of the Stage: License, Play, and Power in Renaissance England*. Chicago: University of Chicago Press, 1988.

Murray, Peter B. *A Study of John Webster*. The Hague: Mouton, 1969.

Norbrook, David. "The Reformation of the Court Masque." *The Court Masque*. Ed. David Lindley. Manchester: Manchester University Press, 1984. 94–111.

O'Connell, Michael. "The Idolatrous Eye: Iconoclasm, Anti-Theatricalism, and the Image of the Elizabethan Theater." *ELH* 52 (1985): 279–310.

Ong, Walter. *The Presence of the Word: Some Prolegomena for Cultural and Religious History*. New Haven, Conn.: Yale University Press, 1967.

Oravec, Christine. "Kenneth Burke's Concept of Association and the Complexity of Identity." *The Legacy of Kenneth Burke*. Ed. Herbert W. Simons and Trevor Melia. Madison: University of Wisconsin Press, 1989. 174–95.

Orgel, Stephen, ed. Introduction. *The Tempest*. Oxford: Clarendon Press, 1987.

Ornstein, Robert. *The Moral Vision of Jacobean Tragedy*. Madison: University of Wisconsin Press, 1960.

Ozment, Steven. *The Age of Reform, 1250–1550: An Intellectual and Religious History of Late Medieval and Reformation Europe*. New Haven, Conn.: Yale University Press, 1980.

Patterson, Annabel. *Censorship and Interpretation*. Madison: University of Wisconsin Press, 1984.

Pearson, A. F. Scott. *Thomas Cartwright and Elizabethan Puritanism*. Cambridge: Cambridge University Press, 1925.

Pearson, Jacqueline. " 'To Behold My Tragedy': Tragedy and Anti-tragedy in *The Duchess of Malfi*." *John Webster's The Duchess of Malfi*. Ed. Harold Bloom. New York: Chelsea House, 1987. 75–96.

Pevsner, Nikolaus. *An Outline of European Architecture*. London: John Murray, 1951.

Porter, Harry Culverwell, ed. *Puritanism in Tudor England*. Columbia: University of South Carolina Press, 1971.

———. *Reformation and Reaction in Tudor Cambridge*. Cambridge: Cambridge University Press, 1958.

Potter, Lois. "Realism Versus Nightmare: Problems of Staging *The Duchess of Malfi*." *The Triple Bond: Plays, Mainly Shakespearian, in Performance*. Ed. Joseph G. Price. University Park: Pennsylvania State University Press, 1975. 170–89.

Prior, Moody E. *The Drama of Power: Studies in Shakespeare's History Plays*. Evanston, Ill.: Northwestern University Press, 1973.

Quiller-Couch, Arthur, ed. Introduction. *The Winter's Tale*. Cambridge: Cambridge University Press, 1959.

Rabkin, Norman. "Rabbits, Ducks, and *Henry V*." *Shakespeare Quarterly* 28 (1977): 279–96.

———. *Shakespeare and the Common Understanding*. New York: Macmillan, 1967.

———. *Shakespeare and the Problem of Meaning*. Chicago: University of Chicago Press, 1981.

Reiss, Timothy J. *Tragedy and Truth: Studies in the Development of a Renaissance and Neoclassical Discourse*. New Haven, Conn.: Yale University Press, 1980.

Ricks, Christopher. *English Drama to 1710*. London: Barrie & Jenkins, 1971.

Ricoeur, Paul. *Interpretation Theory: Discourse and the Surplus of Meaning*. Fort Worth: Texas Christian University Press, 1976.

Riggs, David. *Ben Jonson: A Life*. Cambridge, Mass.: Harvard University Press, 1989.

Rose, Mary Beth. "Women in Men's Clothing: Apparel and Social Stability in *The Roaring Girl*." *ELR* 14 (1984): 367–91.

Rossiter, A. P. *Angel with Horns: And Other Shakespeare Lectures*. Ed. Graham Storey. New York: Theatre Arts Books, 1961.

———. "*Measure for Measure*." *Modern Critical Interpretations: Measure for Measure*. Ed. Harold Bloom. New York: Chelsea House, 1987. 45–60.

Rozett, Martha Tuck. *The Doctrine of Election and the Emergence of Elizabethan Tragedy*. Princeton, N.J.: Princeton University Press, 1984.

Schanzer, Ernest. "The Structural Pattern of *The Winter's Tale*." *Review of English Literature* 5 (1964): 72–82.

Schleiner, Winifried. *The Imagery of John Donne's Sermons*. Providence, R.I.: Brown University Press, 1970.

Scott, William O. "The Paradox of Timon's Self-Cursing." *Shakespeare Quarterly* 35 (1984): 290–304.

Sellin, Paul R. *John Donne and "Calvinist" Views of Grace*. Amsterdam: Boekhandel/ Uitgeverij, 1983.

Selzer, John L. "Merit and Degree in Webster's *The Duchess of Malfi*." *John Webster's The Duchess of Malfi*. Ed. Harold Bloom. New York: Chelsea House, 1987. 87–96.

Shuger, Debora Kuller. *Habits of Thought in the English Renaissance: Religion, Politics, and the Dominant Culture*. Berkeley: University of California Press, 1990.

———. *The Renaissance Bible: Scholarship, Sacrifice, and Subjectivity*. Berkeley: University of California Press, 1994.

———. *Sacred Rhetoric: The Christian Grand Style in the English Renaissance*. Princeton, N.J.: Princeton University Press, 1988.

Sinfield, Alan. *Literature in Protestant England, 1560–1660*. Totowa, N.J.: Barnes & Noble, 1983.

Taylor, Gary. "Forms of Opposition: Shakespeare and Middleton." *English Literary Renaissance* 24 (1994): 283–314.

Taylor, John. "The Patience of *The Winter's Tale*." *Essays in Criticism* 23 (1973): 333–56.

Thomas, Keith. *Religion and the Decline of Magic: Studies in Popular Beliefs in Sixteenth and Seventeenth Century England*. New York: Scribner, 1971.

Todd, Margo. *Christian Humanism and the Puritan Social Order*. Cambridge: Cambridge University Press, 1987.

Turner, Victor. *The Anthropology of Performance*. New York: PAJ Publications, 1987.

———. *Dramas, Fields, and Metaphors*. Ithaca, N.Y.: Cornell University Press, 1974.

———. *From Ritual to Theatre*. New York: PAJ Publications, 1982.

———. *Revelation and Divination in Ndembu Ritual*. Ithaca, N.Y.: Cornell University Press, 1975.

———. *The Ritual Process*. Chicago: Aldine Publishing Co., 1969.

———. "Social Dramas and Stories About Them." *On Narrative*. Ed. W. J. T. Mitchell. Chicago: University of Chicago Press, 1981. 137–164.

Watson, Richard N. *Ben Jonson's Parodic Strategy*. Cambridge, Mass.: Harvard University Press, 1987.

Webber, Joan. "Celebration of Word and World in Lancelot Andrewes' Style." *Seventeenth-Century Prose: Modern Essays in Criticism*. Ed. Stanley E. Fish. Oxford: Oxford University Press, 1971. 336–52.

Whyte, Alexander, ed. *Lancelot Andrewes and His Private Devotions: A Biography, a Transcript, and an Interpretation*. 2nd edition. London: Oliphant Anderson and Ferrier, 1896.

Wilson, John Dover. *The Essential Shakespeare*. Cambridge: Cambridge University Press, 1932.

Wind, Edgar. *Pagan Mysteries in the Renaissance*. Revised edition. New York: Norton, 1968.

Wittkower, Rudolf. *Architectural Principles in the Age of Humanism*. New York: Random House, 1971.

Woodbridge, Linda. *Women and the English Renaissance: Literature and the Nature of Humankind*. Urbana: University of Illinois Press, 1984.

Index

This book has been set in Carter & Cone Galliard. Galliard was designed for Mergenthaler in 1978 by Matthew Carter. Galliard retains many of the features of a sixteenth-century typeface cut by Robert Granjon but has some modifications that give it a more contemporary look.

Printed on acid-free paper.